Plagiarism, Copyright Violation
and Other Thefts of Intellectual Property

Plagiarism, Copyright Violation and Other Thefts of Intellectual Property

*An Annotated Bibliography
with a Lengthy Introduction*

by

JUDY ANDERSON

McFarland & Company, Inc., Publishers
Jefferson, North Carolina and London

British Library Cataloguing-in-Publication data are available

Library of Congress Cataloguing-in-Publication Data

Anderson, Judy, 1946–
    Plagiarism, copyright violation and other thefts of intellectual
property : an annotated bibliography with a lengthy introduction /
by Judy Anderson.
        p.   cm.
    Includes indexes.
    ISBN 0-7864-0463-9 (sewn softcover : 50# alkaline paper) ∞
    1. Copyright infringement—Bibliography.   2. Copyright infringement—
United States—Bibliography.   3. Intellectual property—Bibliography.
4. Intellectual property—United States—Bibliography.   I. Title.
Z551.A68   1998
016.3467304'82—DC21   97-44084
                                                                       CIP

Manufactured in the United States of America

*McFarland & Company, Inc., Publishers
  Box 611, Jefferson, North Carolina 28640*

to Helen and Rudy Jacobson,
who raised me to believe
that honesty does matter

Contents

Preface

Ideas. How has our society come to think we can put a price tag on them and when does using the idea of another become theft?

This work permits the exploration of many facets of plagiarism and the theft of intellectual property. The four-part Introduction summarizes and dissects the many currents of the present situation (late 1997). It includes definitions, cases, the underlying sense of "follow the money" that seems to permeate this ethereal realm, and the means used to prove or disprove the accusations of misconduct.

Defining terms seems to be an appropriate prelude to this bibliography. Briefly stated, intellectual property is the product of one's ideas. It is intangible, but the right of the individual to exclusive control over the ideas as represented in their concrete expression—writings, inventions, trademarks, trade secrets, music—is protected by law in many countries. The creator, and in some cases the beneficiary of the creator, has the right to benefit from the idea to the exclusion of all others. This exclusion continues for a specific period of years and then becomes available for anyone's use as part of the body of knowledge in *public domain*. If the person feels this proprietary right has been violated—stolen, repackaged, misrepresented—they may challenge the perceived misuse in the courts.

Definitions play an integral part in deciding fault or innocence when people accuse others of infringement. This work embraces many interpretations of the definitions. The information presented has been found indexed under the main heading or subheading "plagiarism" or "intellectual property," under such categories as literary ethics, misconduct in science, and journalism, movies, education, music, politics, publishing, copyright laws, trade agreements, trade negotiations, trademarks and trade secrets.

The topics of plagiarism and intellectual property rights have many facets and potential tangents. This bibliography cites sources indexed in common electronic and paper sources (Reader's Guide, Expanded Academic Index, ERIC, etc.) appearing from 1900 through 1995. Books were selected using various books in print publications. Because the expression of valid ideas takes many forms, popular and humorous, as well as scholarly articles and books, are included. The bibliography is limited to works written in English.

The topics forgery, imitation of literature, and instructional effectiveness are not included, nor are patent searching, self help on filing trademarks and patents. Changes in patent systems, copyright and tax laws are not addressed. Some of the articles and books reviewed may include these issues, but they are not a primary focus of this bibliography. All formats and types of property are covered. The work is organized chronologically to indicate trends. Subject, author (and coauthor) and title indexes are provided.

Considering the emotional, and in many cases financial, impact that plagiarism and other thefts of intellectual property have had on the literary, academic and commercial worlds, I was surprised to find limited compiled research on the subject. There have been a few well-documented texts working with portions of the subject. *Plagiarism and Originality* by Alexander Lindey, 1952 (**#34** in the Annotated Bibliography) includes a 10 page bibliography. *An Intellectual Property Law Primer*, 1975 (**#55**), by Earl W. Kintner and Jack L. Lahr, offers extensive case notes. Sections of larger bibliographies, such as "Recent Literature on Government Information" by Patrick Ragains, *Government Publications Review* 20(1993):183-205, also have some information. None of these predecessor texts constituted an organized, annotated reference tool, a starting point, for those needing a wide range of information on plagiarism and intellectual property rights.

The introductory matter is not intended as a legal discourse on the subject, but aspects of the law will be covered as points of discussion or outcomes of specific cases.

It is my goal with both the Introduction and the Annotated Bibliography sections to provide a reliable resource for writers, business persons, paralegals, librarians, students, scholars, journalists, and others wanting to educate themselves in one or many facets of plagiarism and intellectual property. This is a starting point for information gathering and organizing.

I wish I could say my interest in the topic came from the inner reaches of an ethical self. In truth, it was Ellen Altman's interest in *Fraud in Science* and Robert Hauptman's interest and subsequent publication of two issues of *Journal of Information Ethics* devoted to plagiarism that began this work. I am most grateful for his insight and encouragement. A special thanks also to McFarland for allowing me to include abstracts originally printed in my bibliography, "Fraud in Research: An Annotated Bibliography" which appeared in *Journal of Information Ethics,* fall 1994. As a librarian, I find annotated resources to be most helpful when researching a topic, and, much to my surprise, I enjoy the delving, reading, compiling and synthesizing needed to create such works. My gratitude also extends to my husband, Curt, for his amazing organizational skills and willingness to tackle the "tote 'n' carry" which of necessity goes with this type of adventure.

Judy Anderson
February 1998

Introduction

1. Trends in Definition

Most articles, books or stories on plagiarism start with some type of definition. The most common is the dictionary's derivative view. It seems so simple. Plagiarism is the act of using the words of another without giving the originator credit. But just like trying to define *race* as it refers to groups of people, defining plagiarism becomes murky and foggy if one tries to put exact boundaries on it. Instead, it seems to fall under the same category as defining art. "I don't know what it is, but I know it when I see it."

Intellectual property protection is about money and the freedom to develop ideas into works and products for the benefit of society. To promote discovery and creative development, the law gives an originator a prescribed amount of time to control the content and disbursement of any products which result from their idea. This control of property may vary from a few years to indefinitely depending on the type of product and current laws governing intellectual property rights. Infringement, i.e., theft of intellectual property, occurs when someone uses the written word, pictures, inventions, marketing strategies, formulas, anything that is a concrete example of a person's ideas, without their consent. Infringements are classified under copyright, patents, trademarks and trade secrets, depending on the type of property being protected. Each area carries its own set of definitions, regulation and law. The rules may vary from state to state and country to country.

Plagiarism has its roots in Western civilization's concept of property and ownership. During the Greco-Roman era, authors and orators borrowed from one another. The discovery of such theft was met with sarcasm and sometimes public ridicule. There was no financial recovery for such behavior. The reputation of the plagiarist was the only issue at stake.

In British and European feudal states, any invention, any concrete representation of an idea, belonged to the landowner, be he king, lord or bishop. Charles I in Milton's *Eikonoklastes* exemplified this practice. In it, the king was portrayed as stealing the ideas and thoughts of his subjects and using those ideas to claim authority and power [Magnus, 1991; **#269**]. In exchange for food, shelter and security, the subject gave all rights of ownership to the landowner.

1

The breakdown in the feudal system brought the need for many to earn an income to support their families. The arrival of moveable type in the mid-1400s made publishing, i.e., making duplicates of written works at a less costly price, a viable way to secure that income. Publishing houses sprang up as the demand for written material blossomed. In this new industry, authors wanting to have works published had to sign all rights of reproduction over to the publisher. To protect their interests and insure profits, publishers' guilds petitioned government to secure a monopoly. In England during the late 15th and early 16th centuries, this resulted in the Stationers' Company, a house of approximately a hundred publishers and booksellers. These hundred controlled the print and distribution of all materials in England during that time.

Calvinism with its stress on thrift, sobriety, responsibility and industry gave a foundation for the emerging capitalist philosophy. In this reasoned doctrine, the originators, not the church, the monarch, or the guilds, had a right to benefit from their labors. Milton and Locke were two who spoke out about this new freedom and responsibility. Milton in his *Areopagitica* supported the ideals rising from the working middle class, stressing personal value based on original thought and the lifelong challenging of one's beliefs [Magnus, 1991; **#269**]. John Locke, although he did not believe it possible for man to have original thought, supported the right of each man to benefit from the products of his labors [Scollon, 1995; **#533**]. The discussions on such freedoms brought about adjustments in the law.

In England in 1709, the Statute of Queen Anne moved the right to duplicate works from the publisher to the author. An author had sole right to duplicate his work for 21 years. Now writing plays and novels could generate personal income. The practice of "borrowing" became especially popular after its passing. It took very little time for writers and poets to realize more efficient ways for making money on writings without actually creating original works. Passing off their translations of works from authors in other countries came into vogue. Charles Reade, a strong supporter of international copyright protection, lined his pockets by using works from numerous European authors [Mallon, 1989; **#149**]. A German political economist, A. von Schwarzkopf, was acclaimed for his analysis of an Italian economist's collection of works. N. G. Pierson had actually done the work and translation. Ironically, the work remains known through the fame of von Schwarzkopf, not the skill of Pierson [Hennipman, 1990; **#205**].

Plagiarism was not limited to Britain and Europe. Copying was an especially popular pastime in the Americas. United States citizens enjoyed protection under the Articles of the Constitution, but were less generous in their protection of works written abroad. Publishers and writers such as Izaac Walton, Captain John Smith, Daniel Defoe and Edgar Allan Poe duplicated works from Britain and Europe without compensating the originators. One possible source for the tale of Pocahontas was traced to a Spanish explorer, "The Gentleman of Elvas." The Elvas story of Juan Ortiz closely parallels that of John Smith's rescue by Pocahontas and would have been available for Smith to read in translation [*The New York Times*, 12 July 1995; **#583**]. Walton copied *The Compleat Angler* from the British work *The Arte of Angling* ["G. E. Bentley," 1994; **#477**]. Defoe used *Britannia* by Camden in describing the countryside in his *A Tour Thro' the Whole Island of Great Britain* [Rogers, 1973; **#52**]. Poe, an avid crusader against plagiarism, may have been "protesting too much." *The Raven,* for example, shares commonality with the raven in Charles Dickens' *Barnaby Rudge* [Stewart, 1958; **#40**]. This type of thievery eventually caused changes in agreements among nations. Agreements made at Paris, Berne, Nice, Strasbourg and Budapest recognized the rights of intellectual property and paved the way for greater cooperation among nations. They protected the works of their residents and extended that protection to members of foreign literary and artistic communities.

In the present day, the numerous cultures, disciplines and professions vary in their acceptance of copying the works of another without acknowledging the source. These differing views are based on how the individual is defined in a society or group and the accepted means by which that society or group transfers information. In the European-American culture, the self is a separate and distinct entity which redefines itself through communication of ideas. Through language we objectify ourselves and our ideas [Scollon, 1995; **#533**]. Its frequent redefinition makes each self unique. Persons expect reward and recognition when giving contributions to the whole. Individual contributions are the measure of a person's worth. When viewed this way, taking the product of another's work diminishes the worth of the originator. When discovered, amends must be made to rectify the loss. Simple acknowledgment of the source, or financial restitution, provides the compensation.

There are exceptions to this concept within the Anglo-European culture. These exceptions derive from an agreement between the author or inventor and the one receiving recognition. Institutions and corporations, for example, may put emphasis on a product rather than the individuals who created it. Committees frequently build on information gathered and compiled by former employees. Managers may give speeches written by a subordinate. A celebrity might hire a ghostwriter to write an "autobiography." Politicians have speechwriters on staff to write persuasive words for various audiences. "Thomas Jefferson penned George Washington's Farewell Address.... Theodore Sorenson wrote John F. Kennedy's Pulitzer Prize–winning book, *Profiles in Courage*" [Posner, 1988; **#134**]. In these situations, the self has relinquished personal identity. Such an agreement between the author and the presenter subordinates the originator's need for recognition to the needs of the requester.

The concept of *self* in many philosophies of the Asian and Indian communities differs from that of the West. In the East, the body is metaphor for *self*. The self is not redefined through communication, but is used to strengthen the pre-existing norms of society [Scollon, 1995; **#533**]. In this setting, copying indicates respect for a member of that society by showing a knowledge of the originator's work. Persons are recognized for their reinforcement of the existing body of knowledge. Their contribution ensures the continuation of that society. For those raised in this culture, the concept of plagiarism may be difficult to grasp. What one society condemns, another praises.

Psychologists have reported that incorporating the ideas and words of another may not be the result of a deliberate act to deceive. The study of cryptomnesia (memory which appears to the conscious mind as an original thought — or, inadvertent plagiarism) shows that the reuse of others' thoughts is a normal function of the mind's processing and storing information. Research in human learning and expression has shown that it is quite normal for persons to confuse ideas they have heard with original thoughts. Persons may, after a relatively short period of time, forget who originated an idea and conclude that it is one of their own. This is particularly common among songwriters. The song *My Sweet Lord* by the former Beatles member George Harrison parroted *He's So Fine* by the Chiffons, yet he claims no recollection of having based his work on the older piece. Like Harrison, many songwriters experience a common occurrence of "waking up with a tune in their head" and working with it. The songwriters have no memory of hearing the tune at a performance they attended and consider their work unique. Yet the same song they consider their original design was played during a session or performance they had attended [Brown and Murphy, 1989; **#154**].

Authors also experience this type of selective memory [Peer, 1980; **#71**]. When psychoanalyst Bruno Bettleheim was accused of taking from the works of Julius E. Heuscher, Heuscher simply assumed that Bettleheim had internalized his work and used it without realizing its origin [*Newsweek*, 18 February 1991; **#224**]. When Auberon Waugh brought up the similarity of Nobel Prize–winner William Golding's *Lord of the Flies* and W. L. George's *Children of the Morning* there was no suggestion of impropriety, only of possible subliminal influence from the earlier novel. Golding reinforced this explanation. He has no memory of reading the work [Trewin, 1984; **#86**].

Studies by Brown and Murphy [1989; **#154**], showed subjects most readily adopt the ideas expressed by the person speaking just before them. Additional studies strengthen the possibility of unconscious plagiarism. Marsh and Bower [1993; **#347**] took the social aspect out of research by using computers for interaction when conducting experiments similar to those done by Brown and Murphy. They found that inadvertent plagiarism might be more prevalent than shown in the Brown and Murphy studies. Their findings indicated that the subject used words plagiarized from another more often than the subject used new words. When questioned, the subjects expressed, with a high degree of certainty, the opinion that the plagiarized words were their own, not those of a fellow participant. A follow-up study by Linna and Gulgöz [1994; **#453**] screened out tension as a possible reason for the unconscious plagiarism.

Those who study language and communication also express doubt about the ability of writers to be truly individual in the concrete expression of their ideas. Social positions and roles taken during normal communications when creating the work influence the final product. The ongoing process of communicating implies that the person presenting the idea initially may not be the same person who puts the reworked idea into the final form. Ideologically, plagiarism cannot exist. Works that may be seen as plagiarism actually result from the normal processes of communicating [Scollon, 1995; **#533**].

Most writers and artists concede they build on the works of those before them. To prove this point, occasionally authors will research the origins of works. By doing so, they show that any work can be reduced to plagiarism if enough research is done. As mentioned in *Steal This Plot* [Noble, 1985; **#94**], all stories derive from only 13 plots and 13 "spices."

> *The Plots*: Vengeance; Persecution; Catastrophe; Self-sacrifice; Love and hate; Survival; The chase; Rivalry; Grief and loss; Discovery (quest); Rebellion; Ambition; Betrayal.
>
> *The "Spices"*: Deception; Mistaken identity; Material well-being (increase or loss of); Unnatural affection; Authority; Criminal action (including murder); Making amends; Suspicion; Conspiracy; Suicide; Rescue; Searching; Honor and dishonor.

Originality, i.e., the value, comes in how the parts are presented and reworked. Tales may parallel the times. In *The Deliverance* by Ellen Glasgow, the news of her soldier husband's death blinds a woman of the Southern aristocracy. To spare her, her family creates the illusion of a South winning the war and her estates remaining intact. Along similar lines, in *The Siege of Berlin* by Allophones Daunted, apoplexy strikes a French aristocrat when he sees Napoleon's name appended to a bulletin announcing defeat in a Franco-Prussian battle. The family shields the invalid, through deception, into believing that France is leading in battle [Maurice, 1916; **#4**]. The plots follow a similar course. The skilled reworking by the writer adds the beauty [Richardson, 1931; **#11**].

In Arno Schmidt's [1990; **#206**] comparison of *The Fall of the House of Usher* by Edgar Allan Poe and an earlier work, *The Robber's Castle*, by Heinrich Clauren, Schmidt praises Poe for his writing skill in taking a mediocre story and turning it into a thriller, instead of condemning him for stealing the story line. Stephen J. Gould [1993; **#373**] is also quite charitable in his acceptance of Poe's plagiarism. He defends Poe's role in thieving *The Conchologist's First Book*, a work Poe and Thomas Wyatt took from writings by the British Captain Thomas Brown and the French anatomist George Cuvier. He states that the final work was an improvement on the original and made the purchase price something a citizen could afford. The artistry, not the source, adds value to the piece.

Children's books and popular novels frequently have similar story lines. The publisher Simon & Schuster dismisses charges that *Budgie at Bendick's Point,* written by the Duchess of York, plagiarized *Hector the Helicopter*, by Arthur W. Baldwin because there are a limited number of plots [*People Weekly*, 11 June 1990; **#199**]. Carolina Nabuco lost her case against Du Maurier because the judges stated that *Rebecca* had simply followed the familiar "second-wife" concept [Smith, 1948; **#30**]. It is the skill of the author that makes them unique.

The movie industry is well aware of the limited number of plots. It frequently uses this reason as a defense when faced with the many lawsuits that are filed against it. Lawsuits such as Edward Sheldon v. MGM (*Letty Lynton* from *The Dishonored Lady)* [*Publishers Weekly*, 15 April 1939; **#20**] and Robert Sheets v. Warner Bros. (*The Road to Glory*) [Tigrett and Dawson, 1943; **#24**] fall into this category. In movies as well, it becomes apparent that the value lies in the ability of the writer, director or cinematographer to rework the storyline.

Journalists are also plagued with accusations of plagiarism. Stating that the plot is not original is a common defense here as well. The battle of the Joe and Mary Christmas Story follows this pattern. When Mike Royko, a columnist on the *Chicago Tribune*, accused his long time rival Mike Barnicle of the *Boston Globe* of lifting his theme from Royko's annual Christmas story, Barnicle responded that putting the travels of Joseph and Mary to Bethlehem into modern times was hardly original with Royko [Fitzgerald, 1992, **#281**].

Academic policies tend toward black and white interpretations of citing resources versus lack of acknowledgment. The emphasis is on the product, not on the reason behind the infraction. Reasons for the plagiarism are rarely considered when punishment is being decided. Yet, in our teaching methods, the young writer learns concepts of flow and style by copying the works of others. Students learn the trade through a series of steps that range from copying "great" works of others, to paraphrasing, to true research and the reflecting of one's own ideas. Young writers learn to plagiarize in our process of educating them. Peter Berek used this progression in his interpretation of Greene's *Upstart Crow*. In it he points out that Shakespeare's plagiarism of Greene was an example of a young writer learning to write by copying [Berek, 1984; **#89**]. Rebecca Moore Howard [1995; **#606**] believes that we place too much emphasis on plagiarism. Our emphasis should be on moving students through the legitimate process of "patchwriting" (copying and paraphrasing) for school work to the more sophisticated stylized writing used in their chosen disciplines. During the initial stages, plagiarism should be seen as part of the normal process. We must pair our realization that stories come from a limited number of plots with the willingness to teach others to move beyond the copying and take pleasure in their own creativity. It is the responsibility of the academic community to prepare students for working in the "real" world, a world in which unethical practices and theft of intellectual property may result in lawsuits [Mawdsley, 1985; **#93**].

Some of the best known writers, researchers and artists in the United States have resorted to copying or stealing the ideas of others. The discovery of such improper conduct has been met with varying degrees of condemnation, explanation and justification. Artists view copying differently from advertisers, and lawyers from doctors. Corporate America's standards differ from academia, disciplines within academia disagree and ethnic groups have different perceptions. These differing views make for a colorful debate in the literature.

Those who accept the occurrence of plagiarism show a willingness to believe the theft as an honest mistake resulting from poor note taking or the unconscious use of a concept. Often the originator is flattered. This is frequently the reaction of academics and journalists [Shepard, 1994; #**485**]. Musicians and artists accept that the creative process is fed by the works of others. Theft of art is a tradition. It is "the first-law of creativity" [Cosgrove, 1989; #**170**]. Copyright does not have a place in the world of fine art; it belongs in the world of commercial artists and illustrators [Feliciano, 1995; #**590**]. Even translators might also be classed as plagiarists, says at least one writer. They manipulate text to make the foreign sound native. Yet others praise their works based on how closely the copy resembles the original [Venuti, 1992; #**311**].

Disciplines have different rules for citation. Colleagues in the field of historical biography may expect only a short list of references. They assume peers will recognize information from commonly used sources; it is unnecessary to cite the obvious. A research paper in English literature may require more complete documentation. It may require notes on every source. In some areas, footnotes are considered laborious. Only the most controversial or recent references require citation. Doctors reading a medical journal for content are more interested in the information; extensive footnotes interrupt the flow of reading. Others unite to support a style of rhetoric. When Carson's team discovered that Martin Luther King, Jr., had "borrowed" extensively for his dissertation and speeches, supporters rallied to explain by showing the ethnic differences. His style, they stated, simply followed the black tradition of southern preachers, an oral tradition that relies on repetition. For that ethnic group, the delivery of the message sets the standards, not the words used. In a similar way, the public tolerates politicians and celebrities who rely on the work of others. Speechwriters are on staff to supply legislators with persuasive words; ghostwriters assemble "autobiographies" and memoirs. In business it is likely that a team produced the project report, not one person. Policies are built on the work of previous employees. Everyone accepts adjustments in procedures as acknowledgments of the desirability of meeting the needs of the group.

Those who voice less tolerance when discussing the borrowing of another's work, point out that the process is not just a little mistake or an oversight. To take the work of another without authorization or acknowledgment robs the originator of recognition. It is the theft of self image [Freedman, 1994; **#467**]. For poet Neal Bowers [1994; **#486**], discovery of another person's publishing his work under the other's name was tantamount to robbing him of his life. He hired a private detective to bring the robber to justice. Using the material of another also robs the reader by limiting their exposure to original ideas, taking up publishing space that could have been assigned to a more creative work, and denying legitimate contributors access to resources.

Beyond the more traditional gamut of acceptance to condemnation of plagiarism, there is a small fringe that sees political possibilities in its use. Plagiarism has on occasion been used to promote a point of view, a cause. Alessa Johns [1994; **#465**] suggests Mary Hamilton's borrowing extensively from Daniel Defoe was a commentary on the role of women in the 18th century. To Lawrence Venuti [1992; **#311**], the plagiarism of Tarchetti may have been an attempt to scoff at the bourgeoisie. In more current times, Jeffery Hart [1990; **#197**] has raised questions about accusations of plagiarism on the Dartmouth campus. Is plagiarism being used to place sanctions against student Andrew Baker for his conservative political views in Dartmouth's efforts to promote "sensitivity"?

Plagiarism is a part of writing and oratory. By some it is viewed as a normal part of the creative process, by others the theft of the very essence of one's being. It may be used for quick profit and political gain, or done inadvertently. Because of these varying degrees of acceptance and condemnation, it remains a topic of discussion without resolve. Each case is handled individually by those most closely involved.

Intellectual property rights seem to come to the forefront when change and economic potential are injected into the system. The current phase involves the Internet. What types of protection can and should be offered the originator whose works appear in electronic format? Should there be controls for the transmissions and display of text and images? Discussions involve balancing the rights of the originator against promoting the interests of society.

As with other formats, views expressed about electronic storage and transmission show support along a continuum. Some find the current system of laws and regulations adequate, others think a new category should be established. Attitudes are influenced by the sheer volume of information and access afforded by computer networks. Data are easily captured and modified. The user is protected by anonymity. Fear of discovery and reprisal are minimal.

Issues along the continuum reflect views from all areas of society. Those in business see the possibility of lost profits from stolen or altered data. Artists and writers fear improper use of their materials and lost royalties in electronic access [*Publisher's Weekly*, 22 May 1995; **#567**]. Publishers want tighter restrictions to protect their investments. Librarians and educators are our watchdogs for open access to information. They fear that higher costs will result in loss of *fair use* with society being the loser. Distance learning through the Internet brings issues of *fair use* versus performance royalties, as transmission of the data falls under broadcasting guidelines. Every group voices concerns important to its members.

As was evident in the past, copyright laws evolve slowly. Informal agreements on standards resolve many issues. The late 1990s are a witness to this process, resolving how electronic media fit current copyright practices. Publishers are working with agencies who agree to collect royalties, writer's groups are negotiating with publishers, librarians and teachers are moving in the bureaucracy to balance the profit concerns of industry. Each believes its way is the best way to preserve an atmosphere free of censorship while promoting creativity and research.

In the past, few considered the possibility of stealing from others on the networks (primarily the Internet). It was a relatively small community of users, mostly academics, who were sharing ideas and information. The participants rarely questioned each other's integrity. Trust in the ethics of the user provided the protection needed. To Arthur Tisi [Sipe, 1995; **#612**] and many others, expanding the networks to allow commercial access does not necessarily mean the ethical standards have been lowered. The honesty we relied on when the Internet was a closed community should prevail in this more open market. We must not let the changes in how business is conducted evolve into a police mentality for this form of communication. It is up to individuals and organizations to find fair and equitable ways of working in the electronic environment.

The question of protection for the computer programs that make access possible is also under discussion. Using copyright laws to protect products which use the new electronic medium is only one side. Should the computer programs which make electronic access possible be put into the same category for protection? Initially, since the programs began as written statements, it seemed reasonable. As the industry grew, conflicts began on whether copyright protection is appropriate in an industry that changes so rapidly and relies on the ability to produce compatible functionality across various product lines. The question of whether certain algorithms should come under patent and copyright protection has been and is still being questioned. Small producers of software rely on being able to "break down" programs created by the larger manufacturers in order to create software that will work smoothly with the products of greater market share. If access to certain information through reverse engineering and use of standard algorithms is considered copyright infringement, the cost of development will become too great. Smaller companies looking for a niche in the market share will not be able to compete and innovation will be stifled. The public's needs might not be served [Weisband, 1992; **#322**].

Some of these discussions are being settled in the courts, but the Internet-users community is becoming a very powerful forum for these problems. The legal process is slow and deliberate; the electronic realm promotes open discussion and swift resolution. The battle between Leland Wilkinson of SYSTAT and Pawel Lewicki of StatSoft is a prime example of the power of Internet users. Wilkinson claimed Lewicki had used his software statistical calculations without permission. Before the issue could be brought to the courts, users of the products began discussions on the Internet listservs. Users pointed out flaws in both programs and both products were improved [Marshall, 1992; **#280**]. All benefited from the on-line discourse.

On a more bureaucratic front, the discussion on electronic format showed enough diversity of opinion to warrant a White House task force (White House Information Infrastructure Task Force's Working Group on Intellectual Property Rights) to evaluate current laws and make recommendations. After two years of study (1993–1995) and countless hearings in which persons from business, law, libraries and other interested groups gave opinions, the task force recommended that the current laws were sufficient as stated. Parties on both sides were skeptical since free access and ownership status were still not addressed.

Views on protection of intellectual property in academia are also undergoing a subtle change. Universities, in search of financial resources, move away from pure research as they sign more agreements with industry for research that has the potential for product development. In the past, these institutions did research without regard for profits and controls. Research built on research [Goodman, 1993; **#393**]. World War II brought with it the request from the U.S. government that universities work closely with industry to provide innovations for the war effort. This request brought government funding. The universities expanded their research departments to accommodate the changes. In the 1950s and 1960s, faculty were free to pursue outside research on their own time without restrictions or obligations to the university. Many worked in cooperative ventures with business and industry. Faculty in the 1970s and 1980s were expected to bring in grant money to support research. Both faculty and institution benefited from these ventures, and faculty were still free to pursue personal contracts with outside sources without oversight by the campus hierarchy. In the 1990s, looking for additional sources of revenue, the universities are finding patents and copyright ownership a potential gold mine. This change does come with some negatives attached. The trend at many universities is away from faculty controlled research. University administrations and industry negotiate contracts. It is becoming more common to see patent rights being retained by the university with copyright going to the inventor. The distinction between researchers in industry and those in academia is becoming blurred.

Academics less enchanted with the trend are raising concerns that the confidentiality frequently needed to protect trade secrets and product development may overshadow the pursuit of pure science. The concept of research spawning new research relies on an open flow of information. Contracts with the government and with industry frequently hamper this flow. For industry, the confidentiality of information is a necessary step in bringing a beneficial product to the public [Palmieri, 1989; **#182**]. Lack of secrecy threatens the possibility of recouping research and development costs. Competitors may bring a product to market for less cost if the information is made public too soon. If funding has come from federal sources, academics may be caught between concerns for national security and the public's "right to know" [Nelkin, 1982; **#75**]. Information is no longer free flowing. Contracts regulate to whom and when information is released for public consumption. Opposers, NIH and Harvard, for example, claim that such constraining contracts hamper the free exchange of information and detract from pursuit of scientific knowledge. Supporters, Martin Kenny being one, see the collaboration as a source of funding for additional research [Grassmuck, 1991; **#229**]. It is not easy to find the balance between funding and freedom.

Nations have seen the advantages in respecting intellectual property rights among their citizens. To this end there have been a number of international agreements drawn by participating nations and agreed to by others. For copyright, piracy and plagiarism, many nations subscribe to decisions proposed by the Berne Convention for the Protection of Literary and Artistic Works of 1886 and revised in 1971. Under this pact, nations agree to give the same protection to foreign works as they give to their own citizens. This agreement includes protection of moral rights as well as financial. That is, the originator may object if the work is used in a manner the originator considers unfitting. The World Intellectual Property Organization (WIPO) administers the conditions of the Berne Convention. Until 1989 and a realization that belonging might be of benefit in upcoming trade negotiations [Stanberry, 1991; **#227**], the United States did not participate in that organization. Along similar lines, the Universal Copyright Convention of 1952, sponsored by United Nations Educational, Scientific and Cultural Organization, also provides protection across national boundaries. Countries who comply grant the same protection to foreigners who want to distribute products in their country as they give their own citizens. Other less quoted agreements followed by many of the former Soviet states include the Nice Agreement, the Strasbourg Agreement and the Budapest Treaty. Under these, the signatories agree to offer a system of patent, copyright, trademark and unfair competition laws [Maggs, 1991; **#263**].

The United States patent system is different from other nations in its filing procedures. It supports a "first to invent" policy. This policy allows originators to publish without fear of having others usurp their invention because they were swifter to the patent office. It also assures potential partners of exclusive rights for any products developed [Burd, 1992; **#320**]. Other nations have the "first to file" rule. The "first to file" has the advantage of less processing time, with greater potential for bringing a product to market more quickly. Investors reap profits on a faster time line. The possibility of the United States' moving to the "first to file" process to be more competitive in the world market is being examined.

Trademarks have a long history of international protection under the 1891 Madrid Agreement Concerning the International Registration of Trademarks. This is also administered under the auspices of WIPO.

Each of the aforementioned agreements has two basic flaws. They rely on the existing laws of each nation and there are no provisions for settling disputes should contentions arise. Enter GATT, the General Agreement on Tariffs and Trade. Piracy of both written word and electronic formats in software, music and video by less technologically developed nations brought the issue of protection of intellectual property to the international scene in the late 1980s. Some observers estimate lost revenue to be over $6 billion annually from United States corporations alone. The GATT with its "most preferred nation" trade status and means for handling disputes began discussion on inclusion of intellectual property protection under its trade policy.

Promoters of the protection recall that trade and research flourish when all parties strictly enforce protection of intellectual property. Denunciation comes from advocates for the less technologically developed nations. In their view, nations must have this information and equipment in order to advance but do not have the resources to pay for licensing fees and royalties. There is fear that protection is just another guise to keep less prosperous cultures from developing the potential to compete effectively in the international marketplace.

Machine and intellectual technology is not the only concern. Biotechnology is another major area of disagreement. How should cultures and countries be compensated for their knowledge of plants and plant life, a knowledge needed to bring new information and material to the agricultural, botanical and medical communities. The problems are being addressed in the establishment of gene pools, in licensing with local peoples and in negotiating with governments. Each way being used to provide compensation to the native population addresses some of the issues but has strong dissenters. For those recommending negotiations with local governments, there are questions about whether the benefit will reach the persons directly involved [Brush, 1993; **#392**]. Those advocating direct reimbursement and royalties must contend with communities who do not recognize individual property or who will demolish precious resources in their zeal for the immediate benefits of dollars. This clear-cut rape of nature may result in destroying species that could be useful for future research. Problems even confront those who want to comply on ethical grounds. Anthropologist Carol Jenkins requested a patent on cells found in the blood of a member of the Hagahai in New Guinea. Properties in his blood held the potential for cures for a number of diseases. Outcry was heard across the Internet from members of the Rural Advancement Foundation International even though all proceeds from the patent would be paid to the contributor's family [Taubes, 1995; **#613**].

Definitions of plagiarism and intellectual property are both simple and complex. The views of various cultures and different countries are projectionist or expansive. The philosophical epistemology is varied; the greatest influential factor is and will continue to be the reputations and financial concerns of the participants.

2. Follow the Money

Ideology and ethical behavior give philosophical bases to reasons for being truthful and giving credit where it is due, but money moves the process. Personal recognition for a work benefits the ego, and community recognition does bring feelings of satisfaction, but both greed and legitimate profit provide strong motivations in the struggle of protecting intellectual property rights.

Moving new products to market can be an expensive, time consuming proposition. Publishers, inventors and promoters realize the importance of making the public aware of the new merchandise. Scandal is an effective, inexpensive way to bring a topic to public attention. For writers, publishers and researchers, an accusation of plagiarism tends to get the media's attention and can be used as an inexpensive marketing tool. Mark Twain, when he needed to draw the public's attention to his next work, *The Connecticut Yankee in King Arthur's Court*, used the accusation that he plagiarized from works by Max Adeler [Kruse, 1990; **#266**]. Publisher Simon & Schuster used the controversy between William Manchester and Joe McGinniss. Manchester accused McGinniss of using research material Manchester gathered for his biography of Ted Kennedy. McGinniss claimed the Kennedy family used plagiarism charges to keep his piece from being published [Taylor, 1993; **#380**]. The publishers moved the merchandise to the bookstores two months ahead of schedule just to take advantage of the media coverage [Podolsky, 1993; **#387**]. Scandal and controversy over property rights sell books.

In a slightly convoluted version of the same theme, academic T. W. Graham Solomons claimed authors Morrison and Boyd brought plagiarism charges against his *Organic Chemistry* to discredit his work so their new edition of a similar text would reap the market share [Stinson, 1979; **#68**].

A prime example of plagiarism for publicity came from the son of the editorial director of Random House and the coeditor of *New York Review of Books* [Peer, 1980; **#71**]. Jacob Epstein (*Wild Oats*) in his discourse with Martin Amis (*The Rachel Papers*) was so skillful in selling his work using the publicity from the articles exposing his, Epstein's, plagiarism, that other writers who try similar tactics are tagged with "epping" [Rosen, 1980; **#72**].

Once the product is out in the marketplace, profits are generated and the flow of money to the originator begins. Writers, artists, composers and inventors are paid royalty fees when a copy of their product is sold. This seems like a very straightforward way of rewarding the creator. Make a product, sell the product, give the person who thought up and put to paper the invention or work a part of the income. But as with any situation involving money, there are many discussions about the role royalties should play. How long, for example, should the public pay royalties? There seems to be agreement that writers, artists, and musicians should benefit for their lifetime, but what about the heirs? Count Keyserling [1926; **#7**] believed that society should pursue and vigorously support excellence. To this end he proposed that there should be no status of *public domain*, i.e., ownership by the public, for great works. Instead the royalties should continue after the artist's death. Part of the monies should be put into a special fund to support persons of exceptional talent. This fund should not be administered through the government, as government aspires to mediocrity, not excellence.

George Beahm [1992; **#303**] revisits the concept of extended longevity to the protection of creative works, keeping them out of public domain as well. For him it is not a matter of providing a standard of excellence, but of respecting the right to inherit. Businesses are passed from one generation to another; why should artists, writers and musicians have to give up their assets when others do not? Publishers who reprint books in the public domain, Beahm states, are being given a license to steal. Those profits should be given to the families of the originators of the works. In cases where the family has kept rights to works, the possibilities for profit can be quite high. The claim by Margaret Mitchell's (*Gone with the Wind*) family against Regine Deforges (*La Bicyclette Bleue)* exceeded $16 million [*Time*, 9 October 1989; **#174**].

Each time a new technology emerges, publishers are quick to lobby for coverage of payment under the new medium. Digitizing images, films, music and text has opened a new, lucrative market. Who owns the rights if publishers convert the material to computer readable format or distribute it electronically? In the past, publishers held copyright, but in the early 1990s, writers and composers are examining their possibilities in this new electronic environment. Organizations representing various artists are examining the issues and making recommendations to members. One example of such issues involved the home video market. This market bypasses royalty fees to songwriters, composers and publishers whose works were in the original rendition. Payments by record companies and the Harry Fox Agency topped $400 million in 1995. The originators did not see any of that profit [Altman, 1995; **#596**]. In another example, if the work is stored on CD or housed in a database, authors and graphic artists may see none of the fees users pay for accessing their work. Payment for such situations requires discussion and negotiations among the various factions.

In addition to covering the products of literary and artistic labors, copyright and trademark are taking on a new and very profitable role in the entertainment industry. Persona is considered intellectual property. The royalties for this market are creating a new Hollywood aristocracy. Money is paid to artists for using their images; i.e., others pay for the privilege of imitating or impersonating them. The personality accepting payment makes a clear profit for being a recognized celebrity [Newcomb, 1988; **#143;** Grant, 1995; **#591**].

Benefits for the originator are certainly considered, but the primary reason for intellectual property protection is not personal gain. Protection is in place to induce the originator to share their discovery with society, not hold it in secret to benefit only a few. The person holding the rights to the piece determines royalties and any restrictions for use. To this end, royalties have put up roadblocks to fellow artists and entrepreneurs who want to use the piece in their ventures. There is no set payment schedule or guideline for what should be considered a fair rate or appropriate use. Open negotiations are not at issue, but, at times, payment requested may be out of line with the requester's need for the material. If that happens, the requester simply omits the overpriced or restricted work [Stowe, 1995; **#610**]. Restrictions caused by inappropriate pricing sometimes border on censorship.

From some artists' standpoint, having to pay royalties or licensing fees infringes on freedom of expression. It surprised Jenness Cortez to find, after twenty years of free access to the Saratoga Race Course for painting scenes of the track, that New York Racing Association's new management was now planning to charge her $5000 per year in licensing fees. The Association brought infringement charges against her stating that the public might confuse her work with the official track merchandise. In her view, the works had not been a confusion in the past and she has the right to paint in any style or subject that seems appropriate to her [*New York Times*, 27 December 1995; **#623**].

To others, the cost of payments violates *fair use*. Cane [1950; **#33**] says the free publicity resulting when one of their publications is quoted in another book should please publishers. They should not charge the writer for using the piece. Barzun [1945; **#29**] suggests that it is not even worth trying to acknowledge sources as that only opens the door to possible infringement cases. Stowe [1995; **#610**] recommends that it is time to push the system and risk accusations of copyright infringement in order to test the validity of publishers and owners' demands for payment versus the doctrine of *fair use*.

For those needing to acquire rights to artistic works for CD-ROM products, Milone [1995; **#550**] proposes another possibility for by-passing difficulties associated with dealing directly with the originator or their heirs. Find materials owned by other organizations and work with them for right to use. They generally already have agreements in place from the owners regarding restrictions and distribution, and costs tend to be equitable and reasonable. They are also more familiar with the process and will be able to accommodate quickly.

Skill in negotiating rights, royalties and licensing are a part of the life of the writer, artist and inventor. There must be a balance between cost and availability for society. The successful find the balance. A successful artist, writer, or inventor must also deal with the possibility of litigation. No work is unique. Each has parts which another may believe is their idea. Some less scrupulous may also claim ownership for personal gain from either money or public exposure. Some claims are, of course, justified, but many are nuisance suits, lawsuits by "wanna-be" writers and publishing houses that see potential financial gain from successful works by others. Gene Schoor's suit against Nigel Hamilton came two years after the success of *JFK: Reckless Youth* [Lyall, 1994; **#462**]. If success has brought fame and fortune, there is always the possibility that others may bring suit to try and profit from that fame.

The courts may also be used to curb competition as former MTV Network employee V. J. Adam Curry discovered when the Network brought suit against him for trademark infringement. Their claim, that Curry's web site *mtv.com* could be thought to have affiliation with their Network. They only raised the issue when it was clear that Curry's site was becoming profitable [Gillen, 1994; **#463**].

The movie industry and the theater seem to have a constant run of lawsuits from persons claiming that the idea in the play or film was originally theirs. This is not a new problem. In the 1920s, nearly one-half of all long-playing shows fell victim to the lawsuits [*Nation,* 23 October 1929; **#9**]. By 1945, there were even law firms whose specialty was matching parts of plays with works of little known writers. They would approach the writers with a suggestion to file copyright infringement cases against hit shows [Pollack, 1945; **#27**]. Settlements out of court became standard practice. Even when the accused could find no plagiarism, they paid. It was much less costly to make payment to the writer directly than to go to court and pay court and legal fees in hope of proving the playwright not guilty of plagiarism.

Going to court is a gamble, one that can lead to costly results. Elie Wiesel had accumulated notes for a work on French President Mitterrand. When he discovered 43 passages of interviews he conducted with the President included in *Verbatim* by Jacques Attali, he brought suit for $2.6 million in damages. The court ruled against him and ordered his publisher to pay the legal expenses for Attali's publishers. It did not award the $2.6 million asked [*The New York Times*, 8 June 1994; **#469**]. Covering court costs may not sound like a very large amount, but plagiarism cases can be in the courts for months and sometimes years. When Margaret Walker Alexander (*Jubilee*) and Harold Courlander (*The African*) successfully brought suit against Alex Haley (*Roots*), court costs mounted to approximately $600,000 [*Newsweek*, 22 Jan 1979; **#66**].

Suing, even when it is justified, is not always as profitable as anticipated. Columnist Art Buchwald found this out when he sued Paramount for rights to *Coming to America* credited to Eddie Murphy. He stated the screenplay he had submitted under contract to Paramount in 1983 was too similar for there not to have been borrowing. The courts agreed. Buchwald won his case and was awarded 19 percent of the net profit from the movie. Journalists express doubt that Buchwald will see much cash from the settlement. Film companies are renowned for their expertise in balancing books in ways that show little or no net profit [McDowell, 1990; **#190**].

Some accusations of plagiarism do result in financial restitution for the victim. Roger Gould settled with Dutton for $10,000 plus 10 percent of the royalties when the courts decided that Gail Sheehy did not give proper credit to the work of others in *Passages* [*Time*, 10 May 1976; **#59**]. Although the primary objective in intellectual property protection is not financial gain, monetary restitution does give tangible evidence for righting a wrong.

Generating income within national boundaries has the benefit of working under one set of laws. Once a person or company moves to an international market, additional financial liabilities must be considered. If the country does not respect and enforce intellectual property rights, marketing in a foreign country or setting up business there means to put a product and the potential for a major share of the market for that item at risk. The foreign investor may see the product pirated and duplicated before meeting the research and development costs. If the product is easily reproduced, the foreign market may quickly produce and resell to the manufacturer's or publisher's home market, undercutting the originator. This climate for potential piracy exists in many of the underdeveloped nations as they move to a more global economy. Cheap copies of textbooks, computer software manuals, music and computer software hit the markets in Mexico, Asia, India, Africa and many of the struggling nations formerly belonging to the Union of Soviet Socialist Republics. In Mexico alone, U.S. companies incurred losses estimated at $43 billion to $61 billion between 1986 and 1991 [Pemberton, 1992; **#324**]. The justification for this theft varies. Those supporting the practice state that the offending nations do not have the economic base to purchase the products but need the items and information in order to advance. The more ideological arguments suggest that powerful countries are denying the less powerful access to keep them subjugated, a source of inexpensive labor. But the base line is that piracy has a negative impact on a business that is trying to sell its products at reasonable profits.

There is always a chance that exposure of the pirated product in the local economy may offset the short losses brought about by the thief. Need for the product stimulates demand; the wealth of the area grows. This results in a new market and a more advanced local economic environment. But this cycle is the exception. Businesses must make decisions on whether the potential of the new market is worth the cost of doing business there. In many cases the business decides it is not [Lepkowski, 1992; **#283**]. There is a negative impact on the economy of the less developed nation when this happens. Because they offer no assurance of protection for intellectual property rights, they lose not only local accessibility of the new product, but also the economic activity generated by the company while the product is being researched, designed and manufactured.

Benefit to the consumer weighs into this economic equation as well. The competition in any country selling the pirated merchandise must reevaluate its pricing structure. Pirate merchandise costs less because there are no R&D costs associated with it. Manufacturers of similar products must lower prices to remain competitive. Prices on all like products as well as the costs on the original go down, making the product more affordable for many. This increases the potential market base. If consumers spend less on one product it makes more funds available to spend on other products [Feinberg and Rousslang, 1990; **#188**]. In a roundabout way, violation of intellectual property laws may actually contribute to the proliferation of the concept or product. Greater exposure leads to modification and new ideas, which in turn spur new invention. Intellectual property protection is achieved by not adhering to the standards. The balance of intellectual property rights versus the benefit for the consumer is not a simple one.

The effectiveness of using patents to promote innovation by allowing inventors a monopoly to develop a product has been in doubt from the beginning. Registering a patent does not decide ownership, it simply gives a detailed record of the invention. The courts determine ownership. It is up to the inventor to make claims if there is a question of stealing. Litigation and the threat of litigation have influenced the success or failure for gaining a market share for a product. Only those most skilled in promotion with strong financial backing survived [Cooper, 1991; **#257**]. Seeing flaws in the system, the railroads of the 19th and early 20th centuries chose another route, a route that disproved the theory behind the patent registry. To promote invention, railroads treated innovation as a company asset. They paid employees for any suggestions or inventions that improved productivity. Patent pools kept the information available for all to use. This resulted in improvements, not only in trains but in freight handling, shipping and machinery used in many different industries. It defied the concept that only monopolies would inspire innovation and investment [Usselman, 1991; **#260**].

Sharing patent pools is unusual. Most patent holders file to keep others from using their inventions without compensating them. They are willing to litigate to decide ownership. In the United States, the National Productivity and Innovation Act of 1983 and the creation of the Court of Appeals for the Federal Circuit attempted to put some consistency in court rulings in patent disputes. Uniformity has added confidence in protection for innovation and a new confidence for moving into the world market [Adler, 1984; **#88**].

In the 1890s railroads spurred discussion of patents. In the 1990s filing for the patents in biotechnology has led to new discussion of patent laws and their applicability in today's marketplace. Organizations such as the International Plant Genetic Resources Institute call for stringent guidelines, with the host country receiving negotiated royalty payments. M.S. Swarminathan proposes to finance a community gene fund through a tax on royalties based on gross sales of commercial products. [Putterman, 1994; **#520**]. Those promoting the current procedures stress that firm intellectual property commitments must ensure that the originator will have control of that discovery. The native resource has no profit-making potential unless the investor is willing to chance substantial profit against the risk that the raw material will not produce expected results. Without some assurance that they will have the right to market any potential product which results from the costly research, there is little incentive to pursue it.

The tug-of-war between profits and progress occurs whenever new industries are evolving. In the software industry, for example, holding patents has become increasingly profitable. In companies such as Texas Instruments, the patent holders for basic computer chip designs, licensing fees are a major corporate asset. In 1991, TI collected over $600 million in fees from over 5000 patents [Weber, 1991; **#223**]. Companies build on the achievements of others. They rely on compatibility among products to build a greater demand for all computer markets. To remain compatible companies must purchase licenses for basic designs.

This reliance on seamless product interfaces opens the door for potential litigation. The courts have shown support recently for upholding patent rights. This support does have its negative side. Litigation is becoming a common way for companies to attempt to establish and defend their property rights. In some cases, larger companies use litigation as a market weapon against smaller competitors who have less capital reserves. Paperback Software International found this to be the case when it was sued because its software product too closely resembled Lotus 1-2-3. Legal fees and loss of sales caused the company to face bankruptcy [Pitta, 1989; **#177**].

If carried to the extreme, infringement and resulting litigation have the potential for negative repercussions for both creators and consumers. If licensing and legal fees are too restrictive, only the most profitable companies are able to afford them. This leads to product stagnation. The computer industry thrives on innovation. Those who do not move forward fall by the wayside. Archnet, a communication networking mechanism, exemplifies this fate. Datapoint shielded information about Archnet. The specifications were not available to other developers. Archnet failed to gain a market share. Metcalf, on the other hand, gave Xerox a license to design for Ethernet, a second networking concept. Ethernet became the basis for communications on the Internet [Dyson, 1987; **#111**]. Choices and innovation fuel the computer world. Fewer choices mean higher costs for the consumer, or less standardization among product lines. Again, the consumer loses by having fewer choices in products and higher costs for those available; businesses lose as innovation dies.

The software industry is not the only area to use legal battles to restrict the competition. The PPG lawsuit against Deetz certainly appears to have profit motivations beyond benefit to society. In this case, Deetz, a former researcher for PPG, left the corporation to pursue an idea they were unwilling to fund. His research resulted in IRMA, a portable medical device used to measure gases in the blood. The device cost $5000. It has the potential for replacing PPG's $30,000 hospital laboratory device, the product that PPG researchers continued to develop after Deetz left the company. Deetz chose to pay PPG $5.2 million to stop the lawsuit. Additional litigation would have caused his company to go bankrupt [Welles, 1994; **517**].

Litigation against former employees is also becoming more frequent in our mobile society. People—i.e., employees—are a part of the struggle to retain a market share in our economy. In most enterprises, employers owned any innovations created by employees. There are some exceptions through contract negotiations, but generally the practice holds. Our society has become much more fluid. When people move easily from one corporation to another, who owns the ideas, work patterns and exposure they bring with them from the former job site? Litigation under trade secrets can be quite costly if the plaintiff proves that the employee is using information considered the property of the former employer. Production in the companies benefiting from the information may be stopped; the new employer may have to make appropriate licensing payments to the employee's former employer [Wickens, 1993; **#389**].

Corporations may also manipulate the competition by using trade and tariff laws. When Texas Instruments chose to impose restrictive licensing fees their competitors circumvented the system. They built components covered by TI patents in countries who did not honor the rights. The smaller companies imported the components from the foreign operation and continued production. TI went to the International Trade Commission and effectively stopped the practice by threatening their preferred tariff and tax benefits if they did not contract for royalty payments with TI [McLeod, 1991; **#222**].

In an effort to prevent such financial casualties, a new form of investment is making its way into the fray. Patent holders are finding backers to cover legal fees for a percentage of the settlement. In the mid–1990s this proved to be a profitable venture for the investors [Himelstein, 1993; **#404**].

Litigation does have risks attached. In both local and foreign markets the results of court procedures may have unexpected results. For companies who pursue litigation in foreign markets and less technologically advanced nations, too much litigation may result in a backlash on trade. In instance, litigation between U.S. concerns and Brazil had successfully resulted in trade sanctions for Brazil. All seemed well until the GATT Conferences. When it came time to discuss terms effecting intellectual property rights, Brazil remembered the court settlement against their interests. They successfully persuaded other nations in similar economical situations to band together and successfully blocked the intellectual property inclusions strongly supported by the United States [Dwyer, 1989; **#163**]. One court decision had a ripple of repercussions internationally.

Conducting research is very expensive. Costs for research and development of new products are major expenditures for investors. Until World War II, the roles between the contributions of university researchers and those of private enterprise were fairly well delimited. Academics contributed to the flow through discoveries in *pure* science; private enterprise worked in the *applied* sciences, i.e., research that had a high degree of potential for product development. During and after World War II, the government requested the aid of universities to research in the applied sciences for the war effort. Government grants became a primary means for financing the ventures. Corporations took note of this expansion. To lower their own research costs, they increased the number of contracts to faculty who were already subsidized with tax dollars. Contracts specified intellectual property considerations and publication rights. As the potential for adding to the campus coffers from patents became apparent, administrations began changing policy governing intellectual property. The trend of the 1990s saw faculty becoming "labor for hire," with control over the property rights frequently held by the university or in partnership with them. Along with this change, the line between a faculty's "own time" and the hours paid them by the institution became less distinct [Slaughter and Rhoades, 1993; **#399**]. This merging of government, university and private enterprise has proved a profitable venture for the universities. The University of Pennsylvania, in an agreement with Albert Kligman, the medical faculty member who holds the patent for Retin-A, and Johnson & Johnson, will share an estimated $600 million to $1 billion [Marshall, 1992; **#298**]. In another case, the University of Florida collected approximately $17 million in royalties and licensing fees from Gatorade, a thirst quenching drink [Grassmuck, 1991; **#237**].

Some question, on both economic and philosophical grounds, whether the trend for universities to intermingle private and government grants is an appropriate use of federal government funds. Under rules set by the U.S. Commerce Department in 1994, those participating in the Advanced Technology Program may not file for patents on anything developed using the program's funds. The funds, it stated, are to be used for the benefit of private industry, not academia [Cordes, 1994; **#422**]. There are and should remain fundamental differences between industry's search for profit and academia's contribution toward advancement of science [Krevans, 1984; **#85**]. Others suggest that stress on results and financing have brought problems not often seen outside academia into the public eye. Researchers who would have settled disputes on intellectual property issues through faculty committee and censure are more frequently filing complaints of misconduct and going to court. Concerns of researchers influencing results and in some cases suppressing conflicting information in order to promote products are surfacing [Millstone, 1994; **#511**]. This tentative marriage between government and academia brings a high price in both profits and integrity.

Increased costs in scholarly publishing are tied with rising costs in research. The costs have increased so dramatically for such works that libraries and universities in the 1980s and 1990s began talking about alternatives. Possibilities included resource sharing through more extensive use of interlibrary loan, expansion of university presses, and signing licensing agreements, similar to patent agreements, with publishers who support lower costs [Byrd, 1994; **#500**]. These variations bring up such issues as royalty payments, *fair use* and censorship by exclusion if cost prohibits making them available.

Those who fashioned laws of copyright and protection of intellectual property stressed the importance of moving artistic and literary works and inventions to benefit society. Still they realized that the mechanism could not be triggered by altruism alone. The ability for persons to make a profit from their labors is a driving force in keeping those concepts of ownership alive.

3. Detection, Proof and Punishment

Definitions of intellectual property fall under two categories, ethics and law. One does not necessarily follow the same guidelines as the other. In the ethical realm, intent may be considered in the resolution of the issue; in the courts, intent is not a consideration.

Protection of intellectual property in the United States is founded in the U.S. Constitution, Article 1, Section 8, Clause 8.* It is in place to promote innovation and provide incentive to develop products from that innovation. The products are to be available to society rather than held secret for the benefit and power of the few. To provide incentive, originators are given protection so they may exclusively benefit from their labors. Frequently, a by-product of this protection is money (royalties, licenses), but personal financial gain is not central to this protection of property. The most recognized areas of intellectual property are protection of the written word and protection of inventions, with trademarks and trade secrets being less in the limelight although still quite powerful in the courts.

The law defines intellectual property in four categories—copyright, patents, trademarks, trade secrets. Copyright deals with the written word and performances of those words; patents, with the invention and discovery of things; and trademarks, with unique associations that bring products or services to mind; trade secrets involve any information that gives one company an advantage over another. As with most legal issues, the categories are not black and white. Creators choose which type of coverage will best protect

*"[The Congress shall have Power] To promote the Progress of Science and useful Arts, by securing for limited Times to Authors and Inventors the exclusive Right to their respective writings and Discoveries"

their interests. Infringement against visual work, for example, might best be covered under trademark, not copyright. Trademark infringement relies on visual similarity and possible confusion for the viewer; copyright judges on the amount reproduced from the original and opportunity for stealing [Grant, 1995; #**591**].

Federal law and state statutes cover the rights in each of these categories. For those involving state law, there are minor differences among the states, but coverage is similar. Federal law deals exclusively with patents and copyright; state law covers trademarks, unfair competition, trade secrets and protection of the persona. States have the right to pass laws covering copyright and patents as long as they do not contradict federal law [Kintner and Lahr, 1975; #**55**]. This dual coverage gives persons seeking restitution two avenues to pursue—state and federal courts. If the ruling is unsatisfactory to one of the parties, that party may petition again in the other system.

Some borrowing of intellectual property is allowed. If the borrowing is extensive, the owner of the intellectual property rights for that work may bring charges of infringement and ask for compensation and damages. To prove that copyright infringement has occurred, it must be proven that (1) the copyright exists and is valid, (2) copying has occurred, (3) there is substantial similarity between the two, and (4) the defendant had access to the original. Proving copying is not as straightforward as it may seem. The copying must occur in the part of the material covered under the copyright, not in the public domain areas covered under the 13 plots. Proof must come in the presentation of the material—the order chosen, the phrasing and development, and the underlying theme.

Patents are agreements between the originator of an invention and the public. They require full disclosure of the parts and process of the invention. In return, the originator has the right for a specific number of years to an exclusive use of that invention. Patents give a monopoly in exchange for making the invention public. To be covered under patent, an invention must be proven to be of use, to be novel, and to be unobvious. The original patent legislation was the Patent Act of 1790. In 1952 a major revision added that processes, not just machines and manufactures (i.e., products), were also allowable. Other categories include composition of matter, improvement on an existing patent, designs, and plants. Plant varieties must be distinctive and new, i.e., cultivated by humans. Exemptions to the Act include written works, inventions whose sole purpose is atomic weaponry and any substance found in nature. Synthetic reproductions of natural substances can be patented. United States Patent & Trademark Office researchers can bar a request for a patent if others know the item or process, a patent is already on file, or it is described in a printed publication. If more than one person contributed to the invention, the filing documents must document the extent of each person's contribution. The documentation must show their involvement in moving the idea through the stages of product development, both design and production phase [Kintner and Lahr; **#55**]. Any accusations of infringement are registered with the U.S. Patent Office. Since the office has no procedures for resolving disputes, the resolution must reside in the courts or under a less formal negotiation between the parties.

Trademark protection serves two purposes. It protects from unfair competition by preventing the goodwill created by the company, organization, or persona to be used by another, and it serves to protect the consumer from being misled by mistaking one product or person for another. In trademark protection as with patents, it is up to the holder to police for infringement. The Lanham Trademark Act of 1946 defines trademark in the United States. Trademarks are words, symbols, names and devices which manufacturers or merchants use to identify their goods and distinguish them from similar products sold by others. The act also defines variations on trademark: the service mark is a mark used in advertising services, the certification mark is used under franchise or licensing, and the collective mark is used by organizations to represent members or services of that group.

To have federal protection, trademarks must be established through interstate commerce or intrastate goods or services that support interstate commerce. State protection involves a simple filing process. Protection is covered under state legislation. Infringement in trademarks occurs if the origin of a product or service may be confused with another that is similar. The courts also require proof that the owner does have exclusive right to the mark for his trading area, that the right has been continuous for a specified period of time (usually five years), and that the mark is a valid registry [Kintner and Lahr, 1975; **#55**]. In any case, the strength of the case depends on the likelihood that one product or persona will be confused with another to the extent that the reputation and entry of the second will damage the market share of the first. When Ford Motor Company hired impersonators of Bette Midler and Tom Waits to appear in Ford commercials, the courts found the similarity and possible confusion for the public was great enough to be considered trademark infringement. Artist Dwight Conley imitated the work of sculptor Paul Wegner so closely that Wegner's reputation might have suffered should Conley's work have fallen below standard. Conley was also cited for infringement [Grant, 1995; **#591**] because confusion between the works was highly likely.

Trade secrets registration offers another way to protect an originator's rights. If a business or manufacturer holds the information, process, or formula in secrecy, that right to secrecy is protected against misappropriation by a competitor. United States protection has its foundation in Roman law and English common law. Protection is given to chemical formulas, industrial processes, knowledge of unique ways of doing things, pricing information, products, customer lists, sources of supply, and business information. To qualify as a secret, the product, formula or process must be original and known by only a limited number of persons. Cases of violation of trade secrets involve proving the secret is not known to others, has not been patented, and has not appeared in written publication such as trade flyers, or marketing brochures. For cases involving former employees, the right to earn a living must be reconciled with the employer's right to restrain a former employee from using technology and information learned at the previous position.

Keeping in the spirit of the Constitution, *public domain* and *fair use* give society special consideration beyond the protection afforded the originator. Items are in the *public domain* if they are not under the protection of intellectual property laws; any who wish may use them without charge. *Fair use* gives permission, again without fee, for specific reasons believed to benefit society. It allows educators, students, libraries and others involved in academic pursuits to use copies of another's work without paying royalties. This exception is made to support dissemination of information and to encourage the analysis of that information.

Facts are in the *public domain*, as are works whose copyright or patent has expired. This may sound straightforward, but if the status is questioned, it may be the courts who wind up deciding whether information is in the *public domain*. Cases involving the news wire services and local news broadcasts are examples of such a debate, as are historical works and enhanced research databases. In *Pottstown Daily News Publishing Co. v. Pottstown Broadcasting Co.*, the radio was using news stories directly from the paper in its news broadcasts. They were in violation of copyright because, even though the information presented was factual, the originator's style was unique [Sullivan, 1977; **#62**]. In historic material use of the "facts" defense is common as the number of possible sources is limited. Here again the deciding factor is how the author used the material. In *Frances Hackett v. United Artists, Alexander Korka and London Film Productions, Ltd.,* it is possible to view the treatment of Henry the Eighth as original impressions and interpretations of the facts. Under this view, similarities in works and performances may indeed be plagiarism [*The Saturday Review of Literature,* 4 January 1936; **#15**]. With the increased use of electronic communications in the 1990s and creation of enhanced research databases, the lines are again being defined as "infopreneurs" package products using factual information [Woodmansee and Jaszi, 1995; **#609**]. Even though the concept seems straightforward, *public domain* is being redefined with decisions by the courts. In some instances, the product may have enough enhancements to be considered a new product. It has enough *value-added* features to warrant protection. In others, the reorganization and type of access has not changed sufficiently to warrant moving the facts housed in the database out of coverage under *public domain*.

It is the right of the originator, the discoverer, to decide whether to retain rights on the product or to give them up immediately to *public domain* (section 107 of the Copyright Act) [Turow, 1991; **#265**]. Traditionally, discoveries made in academia and fundamental biotechnology were moved to public use. This was done in the spirit of the advancement of science. This spirit of sharing is less noticeable today; the cash flow involved with patents has become a major financial factor. But if any one company appears to be gaining too much of an advantage over competitors the *public domain* argument reappears. The identification of various genetic materials has come under this type of controversy. The Institute for Genomic Research (TIGR), its for-profit segment, Human Genome Sciences, Inc., (HGS) and SmithKline Beecham are developing a database of gene information invaluable to fellow researchers. The access to this information is available to all who are willing to sign contracts respecting the proprietary rights of TIGR and HGS. These strings have prompted response from Merck, one of SmithKline Beecham's chief competitors, to finance a project to duplicate the information in the TIGR database and put that information into the *public domain* [Marshall, 1994; **#507**].

Public domain is one means of providing for the free dissemination of information; *fair use* is another. As with most laws, interpretations allow exemption for the "good of the community." The difficulty comes in defining *fair use*. Here again it is the court decisions that give specifics. Their decisions are based on the purpose for which the "lifted" material was used, the nature of the original work, the amount taken from the original, and the financial impact that having a portion of the material copied might have on the sales of the original. These measures of *fair use* allow reviewers to include portions of the work reviewed in their articles, educators to provide copies of works for classroom discussion, and libraries and individuals to photocopy under limited guidelines for personal use.

The legality of *fair use* is an issue which must be readdressed with every revision or creation of legislation on copyright. Since it does have some impact on royalties and sales, those on the publishing and innovation end of the chain see benefit for not allowing use of any material without some compensation to the owner. Those on the receiving side view the need for access as a means for making sure that the freedom to access information does not rely on a bank account. Supporters assume that access will reward society through its ability to stimulate creativity [St. Clair, 1992; **#296**]. Libraries are caught in between in the conflict of proper use of electronically stored materials. With guidelines on *fair use* being discussed and revised with each evolution, libraries are put in a position of using best judgment to protect public access to the information. For example, how is the viewing of a video from their tape collection handled? If the patron takes the video home, it comes under fair use. If the family watches that same video in a library viewing area because they have no video player, is it still *fair* use or is it subject to royalty fees under a public performance [Heller, 1992; **#289**]? Advocates for finding a reasonable balance suggest agreements be made with publishers and those involved in using the material. This may involve arrangements with organizations and businesses who register, collect and distribute funds or contracts made directly between the parties involved. In any case, *fair use* is a topic which resurfaces regularly.

Where the courts define copyright protection versus *public domain* and *fair use*, associations and institutions define plagiarism. This divergence results in a variety of interpretations. At the federal level, the NSF (National Science Foundation) and the ORI (Office of Research Integrity) have each adopted a narrow definition of plagiarism within scientific misconduct. For the NSF and ORI, plagiarism includes the theft of words, ideas, findings or methods without giving the original source. They differ in where they place plagiarism in their definitions. The NSF classifies plagiarism within "a serious deviation from accepted practices." In this way, not all plagiarism is considered a serious deviation and may, therefore, not be included as a reason for censure. The ORI defines plagiarism within the listing of types of scientific misconduct. They question the practicality of trying to define "serious deviation." The ORI also makes the intent to deceive a component of plagiarism; the NSF does not. For those judging by NSF standards, intent does not alter the damage done to the originator. As many as 50 percent of the cases presented for review involve plagiarism, but the narrow parameters prevent most from rising to the level of seriousness needed to meet the requirements for investigation by these organizations [Price, 1994]. Disputes over authorship, especially collaborative works, improper use of information gained by persons on review boards, and suspicious grant applications are frequent themes. Case results may range from unscholarly conduct but not plagiarism to charges of scientific misconduct and censure. The most common censures are being barred from serving on peer committees or from applying for grant money for a specific period of time [Parrish, 1995; **#617**], typically five or ten years.

In academia and among professional organizations, the definition is less rigorous. Plagiarism is a term brought into use when the person reading the material questions the originality of the work and brings it to another's attention. Generally, proof involves finding the original source and comparing it with the newer work. To some, word for word copying is plagiarism; to others paraphrasing without acknowledging the source or using a similar method in conducting a research project may be the touchstone. The percentage of the work used might have bearing, as might intent and extent of personal gain. A student who purchases a complete term paper may fall into a different category from one who copies a paragraph from another source for a report. A faculty member who uses a few paragraphs from another might not be violating any standards among those in his discipline. In joint authorship, plagiarism may be a matter of perception. Each brings accusations to the fore based on the accepted guidelines and policies of their discipline or organization.

When confronted, plagiarists have many excuses and justifications for their actions. Some students experience no regret turning in assignments "for the grade" if they consider the information irrelevant. Among academics, pressure to publish is a frequent excuse. For writers, poor note-taking during research holds a high place in justifying how the theft occurred. In any case, when the offense surfaces, different definitions of plagiarism will be used to judge the parties. These standards will vary within the peer group, organization or institution; the means for settling the matter will vary with each case.

Self-plagiarism sounds like an oxymoron. How can a person be charged with using their own work in another personal creation? Finding out the answer cost John Fogerty, songwriter with the music group Creedence Clearwater Revival, "about $400,000 more than the song earned" in legal fees, even though he won his case. Fogerty had used a style in *The Old Man Down the Road* for the Warner Bros. label similar to that he had used in *Run Through the Jungle* owned by Fantasy, Inc. The courts ruled in Fogerty's favor, specifying that a composer had the right to continue his style and expand it. Any other decision would have had serious repercussions on artists selling their wares [Goldberg, 1989; **#151**].

The concept is not unique to music; writers also run the risk of infringement by reusing their work. Self-plagiarism is possible because the originator, in the tradition of publication in the 17th century, assigns rights for duplication to the publisher. The author, by contract, no longer controls the right to the work. Publishers are generally reasonable about the practice of using the same core material for similar pieces as long as the artist or writer follows some simple rules of courtesy and good business. The first work must have priority in the marketplace. If other works are going to follow, original publishers should be notified. The writer should aim any new work at a new audience [*Writer*, 1953; **#36**].

Laws and their effectiveness are topics for debate. Intellectual property laws have dissenters who would like to see changes and, as rational thinkers, the dissenters have suggestions on revisions for others to consider. For R. C. Dreyfuss [1992; **#275**], refashioning copyright and patent laws to mimic those already used for trademarks would give greater flexibility in product groups if viewed on a continuum. Costs incurred in compiling information are legitimate, for example, and should be given consideration beyond *public domain*. In biotechnology, Lisa Raines [1991; **#270**] suggests that the Patent Trademark Office use the *Mancy* case instead of the *Durden* when reviewing patent applications because much of the research in biotechnology involves using startup materials, not making an end product. Raines' greatest opposition for this change is from the generic drug industry and patent lawyers who state that the change would result in uncertainty in the law. Laurie Stearns [1992; **#287**] questions the use of property law for copyright protection. It seems much more appropriate to use contract law for such arrangements. After reexamining the many possibilities for use of that law, she concludes that there is one area that raises doubts about the effectiveness of this method. Contract law, because of its restrictive nature, might stifle creativity and produce results counter to the spirit of the protections. Charles McCutchen [1994; **#489**] reminds us that repetition is a means for moving ideas from research to reality. Narrow definitions of plagiarism stifle the use of new terminology and keep it from becoming part of mainstream language. Accusations of plagiarism should reflect the stealing of the ideas of another, not just a few words and phrases.

Unlike most signers of the Berne Convention agreement, the United States has not, during the time frame covered in this work, recognized the "moral rights" of an author to protect the work. With greater involvement in the international arena and GATT, the United States is discussing the possibility of adding that protection to their coverage. Moral rights protection is in place in other nations to ensure that an originator has control over use of the work even if they have reassigned the rights to another. This preserves the author's right to contest any use that might damage the originator's honor or reputation. The high profile case in the early 1990s between writers Stephen Spender and David Leavitt brought this principle into question. Spender won his charge that Leavitt had not only borrowed extensively from his work, but had misused the autobiographical content from *World Within Worlds* to write *While England Sleeps*. Spender thought the depictions of homosexuality in Leavitt's novel reflected badly on his reputation. Since the trial was in British courts, even though Leavitt's publication is from a U.S. publisher, it was appropriate to use moral rights to claim restitution. To many, one being Rufus King [1991; **#216**], this Strong Right of Integrity is just as compelling an argument as the Strong Right of Attribution currently covered in U.S. statutes.

Lack of reader awareness coupled with the amount of material published make finding copyright infringers a wonder. In some cases the infringer is first to notice similarities. A writer to the "Notes & Comments" section of the *New Yorker* magazine [1985; **#98**] was not sure which was more disconcerting, that readers did not notice that his description of a scene at the Continental Divide mimicked Steinbeck, or his realization of the difficulty in proving his innocence should someone have accused him of plagiarism.

But more often the reader is the first to report possible infringers. Cynthia Martin Kiss is responsible for discovering that passages in Alexander Theroux's *The Primary Colors* closely resembled lines from *Song of the Sky*, a 1954 work by Guy Murchie. Future editions of *Colors* will include acknowledgment or exclude the passages taken from the earlier work. A fan of Dean Koontz alerted him to copies of *Phantoms* brought to market under the titles of *Crawling Dark* and *Demonic Colors* both published under the pseudonym of Pauline Dunn. Discovery does not prevent the offenders from simply moving to a new pseudonym and stealing again [Reid, 1992; **#307**], but it does prevent them from benefiting from royalties for these works.

In some cases there may be slip ups "on the way to the publisher." Dartmouth professor Noel Perrin [1992; **#289**] and the publisher misunderstood each other. The editor incorporated a clipping from Richard Henry Dana into Perrin's own article instead of making it the sidebar Perrin had intended. In other cases, copies repeat an error in the original. Historic maps of Mexico City, and Cuzco, Peru, created in 1528 were stolen from an Italian mapmaker. In reproducing the originals, the map was inverted, swapping north and south. The error remained in reproductions for over 200 years [Tennant, 1988; **#138**].

Chance plays a big part in finding the copy. Peers and colleagues may recognize the efforts of another in the published work. Librarians and reviewers may catch similarities. Readers, as did Cynthia Martin Kiss and Dean Koontz's avid fan, may report the resemblance to the originator or the publisher. Editors and publishers may see the problem. Writers, sensing that another used their work, may bring the similarity to the attention of the offending author. Publishers or educators may notice a work that is "just too well written" [Harris, 1991; **#262**]. The volume of work produced is also a clue. In academia, Alsabti proved to be an excellent con artist. For three years he fooled the scientific community. With false credentials he moved among various research labs, stealing papers and publishing them under his own name. He stole no fewer than 60 articles and reviews from colleagues before he disappeared [Broad, 1980; **#70**].

Occasionally, such as in the controversy over the works of historian Steven Oates, the works come under examination because someone is testing or researching. In these instances, the integrity of those who discover the similarities effects how the information comes to light. Oates' work came into question when two researchers in the NIH decided to test a "plagiarism machine," a software program set up to compare words and phrases between two works. Although such a program might benefit software manufacturers and instructors [Berghel and Sallach, 1985; **#92**], some in the social sciences and humanities did not appreciate it. The outcome of this episode was particularly far reaching. When the comparison of Oates' work with that of another highly regarded historian showed a high percentage of matches, the scientists felt obligated to report their findings to the American Historical Association for possible censure. The resulting discourse led to a lively discussion both for and against the works of the Amherst historian, caused the American Historical Association to re-evaluate their definition of plagiarism and led to the reassignment of Stewart and Feder, the NIH researchers who pointed out the similarities.

When Clayborne Carson, director of a research project assembling the history of Martin Luther King, Jr., discovered that King had been a plagiarist in many of his writings, including his doctoral dissertation, the research team chose to keep silent. The public did not learn of his plagiarism until a year later when members of the academic community outside the core research group learned of the copying and brought it to light. Carson's answer when questioned about the delay in exposing such a high profile case was that the project members were concerned that the information be presented in its proper historical context before making it public [Raymond, 1991; **#218**]. Perhaps because of his charisma, or possibly because of the contributions King made in the civil rights movement, many rose to his defense. No one questioned that he borrowed extensively from the work of scholars, but there was disagreement in intention. Those supporting his honor brought the history of oratory found in the "Bible-belt" preachers and the Southern black culture as a defense. The source of the words was of little importance; presentation separated the average from the great [Miller, 1992; **#278**]. Bernice Johnson Reagon's [1991; **#235**] response stressed the duty of historians to report accurately, not to take a PR approach for heroes and heroines, and pointed out the difficulties in straddling the Anglo–African American worlds.

Finding the offense is just the first step. There are many avenues for resolving the problem. For some, it would be helpful to have publishers support each other in efforts to keep track of known flagrant offenders. In 1907 Charles Towne [1907; **#1**] defended editors, acknowledging that no one can know everything that is in publication, nor can they assume that similarities in work necessarily mean plagiarism. To assist in keeping known plagiarists from continuing their work, Towne suggests a bureau, a central site for listing offenders. This list would be available to any who wanted to see it.

In journal and magazine publications, it is common practice among reputable publishers to note the offense in the next possible issue. Frequently, publishers will carry the controversy in the letters to the editor or in an editorial. For novels, it is possible that copies of the offending work may be pulled from the shelves. If the part in question is only a small part of the whole, the publisher may request the author to simply revise the section, or add appropriate acknowledgment and put the revision to press. In the news business, journalists and reporters are often fired if their work is not original [Fitzgerald, 1988; **#131** and Polilli, 1991; **#245**]. At other times, the accuser is left to fight alone. Editors for the *Ft. Worth Star Telegram* told Florence King, for example, that since Molly Ivins had not intentionally plagiarized her work, the thievery warranted no disciplinary action [Revah, 1995; **#603**]. The treatment of offenders is as varied as the accusations. Organizations treat each case individually, with each free to handle problems as seems appropriate to their situation.

For librarians, reporting the offender must be weighed against the right to privacy. In some cases, the personal safety of the accuser is also at risk [Anderson, 1994; **#468**]. Even more distressing to many voicing their concerns is the lack of responsibility educators take when they find evidence of plagiarism. The instructors fall short because they fail to confront the offender. It is easier to overlook the problem than to spend the time and energy documenting the source(s) and going through the bureaucratic channels dictated by the institution's policy. In short they are, through their example, condoning theft of the intellectual property by not enforcing the policies in place to punish such behavior. The hypocrisy of their lack of commitment is not lost on the students, who continue to turn in assignments written by others and research papers they have purchased from commercial vendors [Mano, 1987; #107] because they have no interest in excelling for personal growth, no fear of reprisal and no comprehension of the value of respecting the intellectual property of others. Until the campuses are willing to absorb the cost for prosecuting such behavior, the cheating will continue [Galles, 1987; #122].

Among faculty and researchers, the cost for being caught as a plagiarist may also reflect the hypocrisy. Researchers caught plagiarizing are frequently given the option to leave the institution quietly. This has led to some finding the accusation a road to promotion [Mallon, 1989; #149]. If the offender is well respected in the field, the whistle-blower may come under attack. Instead of censuring the robber, the community attacks the person whose work was used without proper acknowledgment. At the University of Hong Kong, a campus committee cleared Lam of any wrongdoing in using surveys created by co-worker Koo. Even though the courts ruled in Koo's favor, the administrators chose to side with their more favored colleague to maintain the status quo [Swinbanks, 1995; #541]. In other cases, if the plagiarism was found in government grant writing, the applicant may be required to submit documentation of sources along with any work to be published or may have to forego requesting grant money for a few years. Ohio State University professor Leo A. Paquette was barred from reviewing for 10 years when the panel found him guilty of using information for an NSF grant proposal he had gained when reviewing papers for the NIH [Zurer, 1994; #451].

Those accused of plagiarism both in and out of academia have varied responses when caught. For some, the first reaction is surprise; others offer excuses and explanations. When Eddie Cantor discovered that the winner in his "How Can America Stay Out of the War" contest copied his entry for an essay contest, the contestant surprised him with a twist on the rules. The winner thought the point was to enter the best work, not that it be original [*Time,* 20 April 1936; #36]. Gib Twyman, sports reporter for the *Kansas City Star* claimed that ideas he plagiarized came from a media lunch [*Editor & Publisher,* 15 January 1994; #421]. A Louisiana newspaper refused to publish an article by Jimmy Swaggart when they discovered that he had copied extensively in the work. Swaggart claimed the piece had accidentally been submitted and acknowledged that he had copied work by George Fossedal. In academia, Dr. Kenneth L. Melmon of Stanford stepped down as department chair when 24 percent of the textbook chapter he submitted for publication was found to come from another work. His first reaction was to be "stunned" that the acknowledgments had been excluded [Norman, 1984; #87]. His second defense was that he believed his editor had obtained the copyright permission [*Wall Street Journal,* 8 June 1984; #90]. Dean H. Joachim Maitre of Boston College profoundly apologized for taking material from Michael Medved of the *Boston Globe.* The material was used in a speech on the decline of morality in society.

Not all cases in academia are handled by committees and panels within the academic environment. When Pamela Berge found she was not receiving what she considered to be appropriate action, she set precedent by taking the University of Alabama–Birmingham and her former professor to court. Complaints are usually "bumped" to the next agency involved, in this case, the NIH. Under the False Claims Act, she sued the university for stealing her dissertation and won a judgment. For her trouble, she will receive $265,000 in damages and a recovery fee of 30 percent of the $1.65 million the University of Alabama must repay the U.S. government in grant money [Taubes, 1995; **#396**].

With so much material available in paper and electronic format, it is very difficult to not commit plagiarism. Most researchers rely on indexes for locating material already published on a given topic. Since not all articles and publications appear in indexes, it is important that questions about acknowledgment be handled with the utmost care. Accusers should give authors the opportunity to correct oversights before being accused of plagiarism because it is very difficult to regain their reputations if the accusations prove false. To prevent some of the possibility of unintentional plagiarism, D. M. Roy suggests that authors be required to list the literature consulted in their research process, journals be compelled to publish amendments to the references, and ombudsmen at grant-making agencies be appointed to assess claims of originality [Maddox, 1991; **#31**]. In this way, inadvertent copying would be caught and corrected before disgracing the person who thought his work was unique. Charles Yanikoski [1994; **#446**] reminds us of our responsibility when reporting suspected plagiarism. The accusation itself is damaging whether proven or not. Publicity for the cases should come after the decision has been made, not during the proceedings, to ensure that only those justly accused are subject to public censure. Accusations for political reasons cannot be condoned.

To detect and reduce acts of plagiarism, society relies on the ethical standards and behavior of those participating. It relies on reactions like those expressed by esteemed writer Harold Courlander (*The African*). When it was proven that Alex Haley (*Roots*) plagiarized his work, he stated, "Nobody really raised the issue of literary ethics, and Haley continued to receive honorary degrees…" [Reid, 1993; **#379**]. It is up to fellow authors, particularly those whose work was stolen, to condemn, not condone, the actions of the thief. The moral issue should not be evaded. Until plagiarists and acts of willful plagiarism are treated with disapproval, the practice will continue to erode the quality of works available [Shaw, 1982; **#76**].

4. Protecting One's Property

The one sure way of protecting your intellectual property is to never be successful [Lindey, 1952; **#34**]. The minute the idea becomes a concrete representation, the potential for others to use it or lay claim to it is there. It is important that writers and artists take steps to protect their interests, but not to the extent that paranoia stifles creativity [Wilson, 1990; **#200**]. The key is in planning. Make educated choices on how you want your work protected. Make legal agreements and contracts, and be willing to follow through to the courts if necessary to protect your interests.

For some the copyright issue may be settled by simply using software encoding devices that will stamp electronic data and detect any unauthorized changes to the original [Cipra, 1993; **#378**]. For others, societies such as ASCAP and Copyright Clearing Center are available to help collect royalties for musicians and writers. Photographers may submit their work to stock photography companies who serve as brokers for the photos [Franklin, 1994; **#519**]. Professional groups may be sources of information for tips on negotiating contracts with publishers, especially if the work is going to be held for access electronically [Schnuer, 1995; **#551**]. Businesses concerned with trade secrets should consider stressing the importance of company information and access and have policies governing expected behavior. Make customers aware that they are working with a company, not an individual customer representative [Arnott, 1994; **#526**].

In research, responsibilities and restrictions should be clearly identified in contracts among researchers, administration and private industry before the work begins. Leaving questions of publication and licensing rights until results are known to hold potential for the marketplace, can lead to misunderstandings and possible legal entanglements. The increased interest in indigenous plant varieties has increased the need to make more formal agreements with those in the region where the new varieties and species are found. As with other research having the potential for product development, making arrangements, licensing use and negotiating in advance for samples and information are the more efficient way of protecting the property of all involved. Discussion of conservation and cooperation at the onset may also discourage rival factions from delaying the process after work gets underway. No matter what path is chosen, the best defense for possible confrontation is accurate records, signed agreements with parties who have the authority to negotiate, and willingness to work out an equitable arrangement before it escalates to litigation [Geren, 1991; **#256**].

Internationally, one of the ways in which the originators of intellectual property are fighting the theft of their property is through international trade sanction. In the past, the signers of the Berne Agreement and other similar pacts relied on each country to respect the standards set by others. If offenses occurred, there was no way to force change or reparations. With GATT, the potential for employing economic trade sanctions on offenders has possibilities. Countries who want to be a part of the select trade circle, like Thailand, are beginning to enforce intellectual property rights and try the offenders.

Cultural, philosophical and economic pressures shape intellectual property laws. Such laws have been used to gain economic advantage, crush competition, achieve notoriety and gain free publicity. They have also protected reputations, encouraged discovery and provided the means for free flow of information.

Respect for intellectual property rights relies on the ethical conduct of all involved. Laws and international agreements are in place to set guidelines and concepts, but each accusation of infringement must be resolved on its own merits. This resolution may come through agreement among peers and professional organizations, directives from administrative offices or government agencies, or the state, federal and international courts. In any case, resolution is expensive and time consuming. As long as we hold a concept of intellectual property, there will be controversy on rights for that property. The controversy will spawn discussion of the benefits and fallacies of the system and ways to improve the process. A system that was instituted to promote creativity and secure a measure of payment for the labor of the originator has many inconsistencies. But, in the end, it does promote discourse, provide society access to information and protect the intellectual labors of many. As it evolves, it continues to provide the protection promoted by those who fashioned it.

The Annotated Bibliography

1. **Towne, Charles H. "Wanted—Black List Bureau."** *The Bookman* 24 (February 1907): 632–4.

   Suggests a central site to keep all informed of plagiarist activities. Amuses with a recounting of the Kipling spoof. Defends editors. No one can be expected to know all that appears in competitive publications and not all authors with similar stories plagiarized. Recounts a few incidents of the time to support his view.

2. **Samuel, Bunford. "Plagiarism Real and Apparent."** *The Bookman* 29 (April 1909): 201–5.

   A series of quotes from prominent authors, many in French, on their views of plagiarism. Not particularly reader friendly. Author concludes, "minds of men are strictly catenated in … knowledge, it seems to us that in matters of literature their connection … is rather that of a series of tangents held by a centre-heart…"

3. **Nathan, Jean N. "'Twice Told Tales' of the Magazines."** *The Bookman* 34 (January 1912): 481–4.

   Entertaining accounts of excuses given to editors by plagiarists when they are discovered. Responses from complete astonishment to claiming he copied in his sleep. Does not contain names to allow tracing cases.

4. **Maurice, Arthur R. "Concerning Literary Property."** *The Bookman* 43 (July 1916): 552–6.

   Comparison of stories illustrating the concept of a creative literary mind making free use of "ideas in the air." Good resource for studies of what plagiarism is NOT.

5. **"The New Type of Literary Criminal Who Has Produced a 'Plague of Plagiarism'."** *Current Opinion* 62 (February 1917): 125.

   Recount of an article by Robert H. Davis, prominent editor, appearing in *Bulletin of the Authors' League of America* in which Davis condemns the growing tide of plagiarism and the inability to stop it.

Plagiarists are described with begrudging admiration as artful intellectuals who prefer dishonest endeavors.

6. **Chew, C. "A Byron-Shelley Hoax."** *Nation* **107 (24 August 1918): 199–200.**
   The author brings what he considers to be reasons for believing *Narrative of Lord Byron's Voyage to Corsica and Sardinia during the year 1821…* to be a fabrication. Discusses personality traits displayed. A bit dry for the average reader.

7. **Keyserling, Hermenn. "Peter's Pence of Literature."** *The Saturday Review of Literature* **3 (April 1926): 378.**
   Count Keyserling suggests that copyright should not expire on exceptional works. Instead, a percentage of the royalties should go into a special fund to preserve the spiritual heritage. The money would be used to reward and encourage excellence. This fund should not be controlled by government as that would result in mediocrity. The average reader may find this article difficult to follow.

8. **Wright, Jonathan M. D. "Plagiarisms."** *Science* **53 (29 April 1929): 402–6.**
   The concept of plagiarism is not new to our culture. The use of the works of predecessors is rooted deep in our heritage. Allowing a little humor and courtesy into the fray when someone's work is suspect might be a more charitable approach. Scholarly writing style.

9. **"The Plagiarism Racket."** *The Nation* **129, no. 3355 (23 October 1929): 456.**
   Nearly one-half of all long-playing theatrical performances end up making some type of payment to persons claiming rights to the play. The author questions the value of copyright when so much is spent on settling frivolous lawsuits out of court. The law may make a victim of the author by "someone of whose work he has never heard."

10. **Salzman, Maurice.** *Plagiarism: The "Art" of Stealing Literary Material.* **Los Angeles: Parker, Stone & Baird, 1931.**
    [T. Mallon considers this work to be comprehensive but to have slim coverage of cases.]
    From a legal perspective in an easy style. Legal definitions followed by cases covering each point of the definitions. Focus is on motion picture industry and its ability to attract plagiarism cases. Chapter 4 includes the essay "Pigs Is Pigs and Plagiarists Are Thieves," by Ellis Parker Butler.

11. **Richardson, Eudora R. "The Ubiquitous Plagiarist."** *The Bookman* **73 (June 1931): 359–64.**

The source of the idea is of less value than the reworking and addition of beauty given by an author. Lists examples of derivative works of well known writers from 18th and 19th centuries. Helpful for persons interested in the scope of the "stealing" or those needing a starting point for deciding on a case to explore.

12. **Doran, George H. "What's in a Name?"** *The Saturday Review of Literature* **11 (13 April 1935): 617–8.**
    Publisher's belief that an ethical response when confronting plagiarists affords gain for all concerned. Discusses three situations in which he dealt with plagiarists in this manner, a minister, a successful novelist and a young author. Author carries a "belief in the goodness of man" tone throughout.

13. **Morley, Christopher. "Columns: Words and Musings by Morley: Echoes by McIntyre."** *Newsweek* **6, no. 1 (6 July 1935): 21.**
    Morley, author and critic for the *Saturday Review of Literature* points out to readers that the prose of well known and well paid columnist O. O. McIntyre closely resembles earlier works of Morley's. An example is included.

14. **"Columnist v. Columnist."** *Time* **26, no. 2 (8 July 1935): 38.**
    Well paid syndicated columnist Oscar Odd McIntyre is accused by Christopher Morley, writer for the *Saturday Review of Literature,* of borrowing phrases for McIntyre's book *The Big Town.* Morley mentions he has not minded McIntyre's occasional borrowing of a phrase for his weekly column, but objects to its landing on the bookshelf. Includes samples of exerpts for parallel comparison. McIntyre's editor accuses Morley of being a publicity hound as his column has little following compared to McIntyre's.

15. **"Biography and Plagiarism."** *The Saturday Review of Literature* **13 (4 January 1936): 8.**
    A reaction to *Frances Hackett v. United Artists, Alexander Korka and London Film Productions, Ltd.* on Hackett's *Henry the Eighth.* Author supports belief that historical biography can be plagiarized. History is a collection of facts. Historical novelists interpret those facts and have original impressions and interpretations of the incidents surrounding the facts.

16. **"Peace Piece."** *Time* **27, no. 16 (20 April 1936): 44–5.**
    Eddie Cantor's bout with a plagiarist. Cantor's contest winner for "How Can America Stay Out of the War" was found to have copied his essay entry. When confronted, the student stated he thought the point was to enter the best, not that it had to be original.

17. "Esquire Prints Another Story Already Printed." *Newsweek* **8, no. 7 (15 August 1936): 30.**

References two occurrences of plagiarism printed by *Esquire. The Perlu* paralleled *The Damned Thing* in a 1935 edition and *The Tale of Three Cities* bears remarkable resemblance to *The Eternal Triangle* published in *College Humor* in 1932. *Esquire* editor, Arnold Gingrich, suggested that the author inadvertently submitted both pieces without realizing the duplication.

18. "Catching a Plagiarist." *Publishers Weekly* **132 (6 November 1937): 1826.**

The use of the U.S. mail for fraudulent purposes brought John Kenneth Stalcup to justice. He was arrested in the midst of copying yet another article from a religious journal. The envelope was addressed and ready to send to one of the many publishers of religious journals who had published his plagiarized work in the past. Alfred D. Moore of *Classmate* discovered the fraud. This case is not covered in other citings.

19. Starbuck, A. "Experience Enriched by Reading." *English Journal* **27 (1938): 114–21.**

English teachers must stress originality and ideas when using a library term paper assignment to teach students. The artificial mechanical procedure of cards and bibliography only add to the possibility of plagiarism. Instead, students should be reading, analyzing, and sharing information about the topic of their paper as an ongoing study. The concept is again stressed in the 1990s.

20. "Important Plagiarism Decision." *Publishers Weekly* **(15 April 1939): 1423.**

Briefly discusses the outcome of the case of Edward Sheldon and Margaret Ayer Barnes *v.* Metro Goldwyn Pictures and Distributors. They claim their play *The Dishonored Lady* was used as a basis for *Letty Lynton*. The court decided that the sequence of events between the play and the movie were grounds for plagiarism, even though it was thought quite possible that the action was not intended. The law makes no provisions for unintended plagiarism.

21. Hastings, W. T. "Fourth Forger: William Ireland and the Shakespeare Papers." *The Saturday Review of Literature* **20 (24 June 1939): 16.**

Indicates *Fourth Forger* to be low quality with a number of areas in which Mair used material without giving proper acknowledgment to its source. Hastings was a member at Brown's English Dept. at the time he wrote the review. More informative for those researching forgery of Shakespeare than for plagiarism.

22. **"The Cow That Jumped Over the Channel."** *Newsweek* **18, no. 19 (10 November 1941): 33.**

    A description of a cow sent by a 10-year-old British boy to Ernest Brown, the British Minister of Health, so captured the Minister's attention that he read the piece publicly. Many news services, as well as Edward R. Morrow's CBS broadcast, repeated the work. It was later found to duplicate the writing of a German boy. A little respite involving boys from both sides during a World War. An exerpt from each text is printed. The pieces are similar enough to suggest that different interpretations of translators might cause the variation.

23. **Smith, Harrison. "Was 'Rebecca' Plagiarized?"** *The Saturday Review of Literature* **24 (29 November 1941): 3–4.**

    Author defends the honor of Daphne Du Maurier, stating the common theme of both *Rebecca* and *A Sucesora* by Carolina Nabuco are well-worn plots. The likelihood of Miss Du Maurier having opportunity to read Miss Nabuco's manuscript is extremely slight. The defense is an interesting example of a chapter in the diary of a plagiarism battle.

24. **Tigrett, John B., and Mitchell Dawson. "Hey! You Stole My Story."** *Saturday Evening Post* **215 (1 May 1943): 22+.**

    Entertaining style concisely describes the types of cases movie makers face on a regular bases. Plagiarism claims are prevalent in the industry. Reinforces the legal stance that ideas are rarely original. Most story lines fall in public domain. Details: vaudeville use of kinescope mixed with on stage performances; who "owns" Betty Boop's "boop-boop-a-doop;" Robert Sheets *v.* Warner Bros. (*The Road to Glory* with Fredrick March) in which Pinkerton's traced a typewriter to prove Sheets' guilt; Margaret Ayer Barnes and Edward Sheldon *v.* MGM (*Letty Lynton* from *The Dishonored Lady*).

25. **"Rutherford Montgomery Charged with Plagiarism."** *Publishers Weekly* **146 (9 September 1944): 918.**

    Author of outdoor series for boys and girls, Rutherford Montgomery is charged with plagiarism. John Holzworth claims that *Big Brownie* is too similar to his work, *Twin Grizzlies of the Admiralty Islands*. The *Big Brownies* was a Junior Literary Guild selection of the month. The selection committee chair was Eleanor Roosevelt. An average article containing a list of plaintiff and defendants with comments on feasibility of the charges.

26. **"Gill Made Sole Defendant in 'Big Brownie' Suit."** *Publishers Weekly* **146 (7 October 1944): 1488.**

    John M. Holzworth, author of *Twin Grizzlies of the Admiralty Islands* and *Wild Grizzlies of Alaska*, is suing Rutherford Montgomery. Holzworth claims Montgomery's *Big Brownies* takes from his works without authorization. This item became news because the Junior Literary Guild, with Eleanor Roosevelt as chairman of the selection committee, had recommended *Big Brownies* as its May 1944 selection. Brief comments about court jurisdiction between states is mentioned.

27. **Pollack, Channing. "The Plagiarism Racket."** *American Mercury* **60 (May 1945): 613–9.**
    Accusations of plagiarism are brought by shysters for profit and fame and non-professional writers who have no understanding of the probability of the similarity in anyone's work. Those accused suffer financial and emotional scars. Actual piracy is infrequent. Pollack had gone though a court case being accused of plagiarizing *The Fool*. Answered by Driscoll in July 1945.

28. **Driscoll, Arthur F. "The Plagiarism Racket: Reply."** *American Mercury* **61 (July 1945): 121–2.**
    Driscoll agrees with Channing Pollack that most plagiarism cases (99 out of 100) are false. Unlike Pollack, he thinks the accusers believe themselves wronged. There is not enough profit to be made to think otherwise. The number of cases has been reduced because courts preread for signs of copying and award sums to successful counsel. It appears to have an effect, even though the sums are rarely paid.

29. **Barzun, Jacques. "Strictly Personal: Quote 'Em Is Taboo."** *The Saturday Review of Literature* **28 (22 September 1945): 16–7.**
    On acknowledgments. The reason to give credit to an author and give the reader its source is shadowed by the need to prevent charges of copyright infringement by publishers who own copyright to the materials cited.

30. **Smith, Harrison. "The 'Rebecca' Case."** *The Saturday Review of Literature* **31 (7 February 1948): 18.**
    Author is pleased that Du Maurier was vindicated of all plagiarism charges and concerned that any successful author writing on a common topic puts reputation and personal finance at risk. There are so many "second-wife" novels out there, all with the potential for being challenged.

31. **Levy, Norman. "They've Stolen My Plot."** *The Atlantic* **184 (July 1949): 76–8.**
    Lawyer Levy gives a light overview to support the difficulties of proving plagiarism in the literary world. He points out that many want-to-be authors bring suit in hopes of financial gain from the success of

the author. Judge Woolsey cases are used as examples. He shows common source as the most productive defense.

32. **"This Is My Own Work."** *Senior Scholastic* **55, no. 8 (9 November 1949): 5.**
    A moral essay for young adults emphasizing that plagiarism is stealing. Students who copy won't ever be good writers because good writing comes from the personality of the individual. The plagiarist is "wearing the mask of other people."

33. **Cane, Melville. "Why Ask for Permission?"** *The Saturday Review of Literature* **33 (1 July 1950): 20–1.**
    Finds the fees publishers charge for permission to quote in another source for literary criticism to be against *fair use*. Publishers should be pleased for the free publicity. The only justified fees are for anthologies.

34. **Lindey, Alexander.** *Plagiarism and Originality.* **New York: Harper & Brothers, 1952.**
    [T. Mallon assesses this work as comprehensive but having slim coverage of cases.]
    A guide for those involved in plagiarism, this precisely written, easily read reference covers historical, ethical, legal and psychological aspects of plagiarism. Many case studies. Final chapter suggests ways to avoid the problem, with the ultimate being to never be successful. Excellent index listing names of works, artists and topics covered. Those specifically interested in playwrights and the motion picture industry in its first few decades might find Salzman's *Plagiarism: The "Art" of Stealing Literary Material* more helpful.

35. **Cerf, Bennett. "Heroine of the Month."** *The Saturday Review of Literature* **36 (7 February 1953): 7.**
    Virginia Kirkus is praised for her recognizing a galley of Robert E. Preyer Jr.'s *Position Unknown*, as being a word-for-word copy of Ernst Gann's *Island in the Sky*.

36. **"Can You Re-Sell Your Research?"** *Writer* **66 (August 1953): 262–4.**
    Ten editors respond to a writer's right to use the same research to write more than one article. Most accept the practice as long as articles are submitted for different audiences and editors are told of the other works. Editors come from a cross section of the field, from *Popular Mechanics* to *The Christian Advocate*. Actual letters are reproduced. Except for variation in style, all come to the same conclusions. No surprises here.

37. **Smith, Louis Charles. "Copying of Literary Property."** *Library Journal* **80, no. 1 (1 January 1955): 23–7.**

[A condensed version of the article. The original appeared in two parts in *Law Library Journal* August 1953 & 1954.]
Gives a clear overview of the need for photocopies for research versus the need for protection for the copyright holder. The concept of *fair use* is discussed; the creation of a policy agreed to by library and publisher is suggested. Author is senior attorney in the United States Copyright Office at the Library of Congress.

38. **"This Looks Familiar."** *Newsweek* **49, no. 7 (18 February 1957): 94.**
A case of plagiarism was settled on one publisher's (*Good Housekeeping*) assigning second publication rights to another (*The Saturday Evening Post*). Only the original author, Earl Fultz, seems to be the loser. The plagiarist, Eugene Pawley, is currently being sued for other past fraudulent deeds. Short exerpts from each work are included.

39. **Wolseley, Roland E. "Plan for Plagiarists."** *The Saturday Review of Literature* **41 (10 May 1958): 25.**
An exerpt from unfinished notes from English professor Frederick Welch submitted posthumously by Wolseley. The notes to students outline how to enjoy and be effective at plagiarism, and suggested responses to use when you are caught. Light reading.

40. **Stewart, Charles D. "A Pilfering by Poe."** *The Atlantic* **202 (December 1958): 67–8.**
Stewart offers similarities between Poe's *The Raven* and the raven from Charles Dickens' *Barnaby Rudge*. This is ironic as Poe was such an avenger on the topic of plagiarism.

41. **Ellis, H. F. "The Niceties of Plagiarism."** *The Atlantic* **203 (January 1959): 76+.**
Describes the lengths author Rider Haggard went to acknowledge sources for his ideas. It is an attempt to show that most of writing could be classed as plagiarism if enough research is done.

42. **Daniels, Edgar. "The Dishonest Term Paper."** *College English* **21, no. 403 (April 1960): 403–5.**
Suggests that carelessness to control students' work results in plagiarism. Instructors should clearly define the guidelines to prevent the "was never told" excuse, allow no "help" in papers turned in and have in-class writing to provide a base of comparison in ability levels.

43. **Ciardi, John. "The Case of the Happy Plagiarist."** *The Saturday Review of Literature* **44 (24 June 1961): 27.**
A pleasant personal account of an editor's brush with a plagiarist poet. Warns potential pranksters that plagiarism, no matter what the intent, is a crime.

44. **Weeks, Edward. "The Peripatetic Reviewer."** *The Atlantic* **217 (January 1966): 115–7.**
    Weeks comments that plagiarists, "if clever enough," will be successful in getting published because it is not possible for editors to have read everything. Readers are far more persistent and will recognize the crime. He mentions plagiarism of Don Robson. His 1962 Arthur Koestler Award winner *Young and Sensitive* was from *Fires of Youth* by Charles Williams.

45. **Poling, David. "Powell in the Pulpit."** *Saturday Review* **50 (22 April 1967): 86+.**
    Keep the Faith, Baby, by Adam Clayton Powell, is noted for its address of black issues, its noticeable absence of Vietnam, and its borrowing of sermons from Butterick and Lubbock. Similar style is discussed at great length in *Voice of Deliverance* by Kevin Miller in his work about Martin Luther King, Jr.

46. **"A Way with Words."** *Newsweek* **69, no. 18 (1 May 1967): 28–9.**
    Author points out surprising similarities between Congressman Adam Clayton Powell's collection of sermons, and those of a number of other ministers. Parallel examples are given.

47. **Boffey, Phillip M. "W. D. McElroy: An Old Incident Embarrasses New NSF Director."** *Science* **165, no. 3891 (25 July 1969): 379–80.**
    An incident in which a notable scientist did not rework taped notes before including them in a review. McElroy plagiarized the work of David S. Smith. When discovered, McElroy apologized and stated there was no excuse for his error. Apologies were made and an erratum slip sent out from the publishers of *The Journal of the Cell*.

48. **"Term Paper Hustlers."** *Time* **97, no. 16 (19 April 1971): 67.**
    International Termpapers, Inc., Quality Bullshit and other term paper supply companies are thriving. The ghost writers include professors from MIT and Harvard, boast the suppliers. They justify their enterprise by advertising that they take the stress off unimportant areas so students can learn, supply income to out of work Ph.D.s, and are only used for research. Campuses cannot find a legal way of shutting down the service as no plagiarism is involved at the supplier's level.

49. **Martin, R. G. "Plagiarism and Originality: Some Remedies."** *English Journal* **60 (May 1971): 621–5+.**
    Provocative article in which the author suggests that both teacher and student need to be reminded that originality is far more challenging and rewarding than plagiarism. Reminds that teachers, by "wanting" certain answers and giving assignments phrased to promote rote answers, are reinforcing the concept of plagiarism.

50. **Ace, Goodman. "The Writer: Men Who Sell Term Papers."** *Saturday Review* **54 (28 August 1971): 3.**
    Light article in which the writer chides himself for not having the foresight to charge his nieces and nephews for the papers and speeches he had written for them. Look at all the money made by Termpapers Unlimited—average cost is $16.00/paper.

51. **"On Normalizing Theft."** *New Republic* **166 (25 March 1972): 6.**
    What chance does an author have when publishers, McGraw-Hill in particular, are more interested in saving money than in protecting the integrity of the written word? The settlement of the *Memoirs of Chief Red Fox* case is used as an example.

52. **Rogers, Pat. "Defoe as Plagiarist: Camden's** *Britannia* **and** *A Tour Thro' the Whole Island of Great Britain."* *Philological Quarterly* **52, no. 4 (October 1973): 771–4.**
    Lists nine areas in which Defoe manipulated text to play down his reliance on other sources. This supports the suppositions of plagiarism made by Godfrey Davies in 1929.

53. **Ewell, Charles M. Jr. "Practical Plagiarism for Health Services Administration."** *American Journal of Public Health* **64, no. 3 (March 1974): 233–7.**
    Not about plagiarism. Discusses taking management practices from business to improve efficiency in health administration.

54. **"A Matter of Plagiarism."** *Time* **104, no. 12 (16 September 1974): 28–9.**
    Mikhail Sholokhov, Nobel Prize winner for Literature in 1965, is again accused of reworking *The Quiet Don* by Fyodor Kryukov, a Cossack writer who died in 1920, to produce his novel *The Quiet Don*. The accuser is Solzhenitsyn. The charge may prove embarrassing to the Kremlin, as Sholokhov has been favored in the capital. *The Quiet Don* is part of the curriculum in most Soviet schools. Solzhenitsyn calls to literary scholars to examine the work closely. See "Computer on the Don," *Scientific American*, February 1979, for one researcher's response.

55. **Kintner, Earl W., and Jack L. Lahr.** *An Intellectual Property Law Primer.* **New York: Macmillan Publishing Co., Inc., 1975.**
    Clearly written for the average reader. Information on law is dated, but the topics are well defined. Patents, trademarks, trade secrets, copyright, right of privacy and federal taxes are addressed. Excellent for initial overview. Appendix lists cases by type.

56. **Jackson, H. J. "Sterne, Burton, and Ferriar: Allusions to the** *Anatomy of Melancholy* **in Volumes Five to Nine of** *Tristram Shandy."* *Philological Quarterly* **54, no. 2 (Spring 1975): 457–70.**

Tristram Shandy was not plagiarism, but a clever manipulation of Burton's text aimed to point out the folly in Burton's *Anatomy*. The joke went undetected for 30 years until Ferriar pointed out the similarity but mistook the satire for plagiarism. Ironically, it took the scandal of Sterne's "plagiarism" to rejuvenate interest in Burton's *Anatomy*.

57. **Hess, Karen. "Recipe for a Cookbook: Scissors and Paste."** *Harper's* **251 (October 1975): 85–90.**
   Concept of plagiarism is included with other frailties of cookbooks such as errors in translation, willful substitutions, omissions and the lack of scholarship in most works. Author details culinary flaws in many cookbooks. Interesting for those interested in gourmet cooking, but might drag a bit for other readers.

58. **Stone, Edward. "The Buried Book:** *Moby Dick* **a Century Ago."** *Studies in the Novel* **7, no. 4 (Winter 1975): 552–62.**
   Shows the reader the many similarities of *Nimrod of the Sea; or The American Whaleman* by William M. Davis to *Moby Dick* by Herman Melville. The author discusses the climate of the time to point out the parallelisms may not have been noticed at the time of publication because *Moby Dick* was not widely read.

59. **"The Gripes of Academe."** *Time* **107, no. 19 (10 May 1976): 66+.**
   Passages author Gail Sheehy is accused by Roger Gould of plagiarism. Members of the behavioral science community concur that she used information from a number of her resources without giving appropriate credit. Sheehy and publisher Dutton settled out of court. Gould received $10,000 and 10% of the royalties.

60. **Malloch, A. E. "A Dialogue on Plagiarism."** *College English* **38, no. 2 (October 1976): 165–74.**
   An academic pseudo-discourse between instructors. Plagiarism breaks the contract between instructor and student. As instructors, it is their responsibility to assign work in which plagiarism cannot go undetected. Portrays the student as a victim of the system rather than one behaving unethically. Interestingly, the author chooses the personal pronoun "she" for the instructor and "he" for the plagiarist.

61. **Shapley, D. "Lewis of NBS Accused of Plagiarism."** *Science* **194, no. 4272 (24 December 1976): 1401.**
   Jordon D. Lewis, an official at the National Bureau of Standards, admits to taking the first 5½ pages of a 30 page keynote address from a report done by a Commerce Department advisory panel headed by Robert Charpie. Daniel V. De Simone, then secretary of that panel,

found the encroachment and wrote Lewis. De Simone voiced concern that persons using such reports are allowed to simply cite the panel, and not give credit to the individual members who created the work.

62. **Sullivan, Paul W. "News Piracy: An Interpretation of the Misappropriation Doctrine."** *Journalism Quarterly* **54, no. 4 (Winter 1977): 682–9.**
Although facts are in the public domain, the business of news is not. The author discusses legal precedent for protection of news articles. Main cases covered include: *International News Service v. Associated Press, Pottstown Daily News Publishing Co. v. Pottstown Broadcasting Co., Goldstein v. California, Sears, Roebuck & Co. v. Stiffel Company,* and *Compco Corp. v. Day-Bright Lighting.*

63. **Eissler, K. R. M. D. "A Challenge to Professor Roazen."** *Contemporary Psychoanalysis* **14, no. 2 (April 1978): 333–44.**
Roazen's work on Freud is challenged by the author. Eissler disagrees with Roazen's interpretations of many events and questions his sketchy documentation in his biographical work. Eissler, for example, after interviewing Weiss, a supposed victim of Freud's plagiarism according to Roazen, found that Weiss remembered no such incident. Suggested audience for this piece: those interested in "infighting" in academia, historical biography, or Freud.

64. **Zehner, Harry. "Plagiarism and Our Rubbery Copyright Laws."** *Saturday Review* **5 (24 June 1978): 28–30.**
Plagiarism is very difficult to prove. It requires proof of valid copyright, access of borrower to the work, and substantial similarity. Unfortunately, the victims are the readers, who, instead of original thought, get unoriginal "warmed over" ideas. Exposure is the only effective way to alert the public. Author illustrates how closely one author may "resemble" another with 6 samples of text appearing in works by noted social historian Stephen Birmingham. Each is followed by earlier works having the same phraseology. Mr. Zehner has effectively alerted his readers to Mr. Birmingham's questionable style.

65. **Ritchey, Lawrence. "The Untimely Death of Samuel Wesley; or, The Perils of Plagiarism."** *Music & Letters* **60 (January 1979): 45–59.**
Samuel Wesley's letters to *The Times* discounting his death in "about the year 1815" set into motion accusations of plagiarism against the offending *A Biographical and Historical Dictionary of Musicians* published by Messrs. Sainsbury and Co. The article contains colorful exerpts from letters of the time on the inaccuracy of the "death," the use of autobiography for many entries and commentary on the plagiarism.

66. **"Uprooted."** *Newsweek* **93, no. 4 (22 January 1979): 10.**

Alex Haley's success with *Roots* has brought with it lawsuits for infringement of copyright from Margaret Walker Alexander, author of *Jubilee*, and from Harold Courlander, author of *The African*. The cost of litigation was $600,000. Haley comments on the reasons for the litigation and his decision to stop writing.

67. **"Computer on the Don."** *Scientific American* **240, no. 2 (February 1979): 72+.**

Using computer comparisons of valid text, Geir Kjesaa, professor of Russian literature at the University of Oslo, has concluded that *The Quiet Don*, a widely read novel of the Don Cossacks, resembled works by its author Mikhail Sholokhov in word usage, repetition and vocabulary. This quells rumors that it was plagiarized from Cossack writer Fyodor Kryukov. Interesting summary of the process used for comparison.

68. **Stinson, Steve. "Organic Text Authors Charge Plagiarism."** *Chemical & Engineering News* **57, no. 52 (24 December 1979): 18, 20.**

Reports the pending lawsuit over the textbook *Organic Chemistry*. Morrison and Boyd with publisher Allyn & Bacon are charging T.W. Graham Solomons with publisher John Wiley & Sons with copyright infringement. Morrison and Boyd claim Solomons could not have written his text without using their book. The presentation and subject matter are too similar to be coincidental. Solomons claims they are bringing suit as a marketing ploy to curb sales so the Morrison and Boyd 4th edition will be successful.

69. **Greenway, John. "The Honest Man's Guide to Plagiarism."** *National Review* **31 (31 December 1979): 1624–6.**

Entertaining. Hopscotches through the centuries pointing out the attitudes and plagiaristic escapades of many well known writers from church fathers to Shakespeare to Chief Red Fox. May be used as a starting point or selection list for a student needing a research topic on plagiarism. Its sarcastic flavor does not fall into the category of being "politically correct."

70. **Broad, William J. "Would-Be Academician Pirates Papers."** *Science* **208, no. 4451 (27 June 1980): 1438–40.**

An entertaining, informative overview of a very clever con man and how he fooled the scientific community for over 3 years. The account of Alsabti, whose questionable credentials gained him entrance to numerous research laboratories, and gave him opportunity to steal and publish under his own name no less than 60 articles and reviews in prominent research journals worldwide. At the writing of this article his whereabouts are unknown. Publishers of the journals are divided on how to handle the plagiarism, retraction or no mention.

71. **Peer, Elizabeth. "Why Writers Plagiarize." *Newsweek* 96, no. 18 (3 November 1980): 62.**
[With Lea Donosky in London and George Hackett in New York.] Highlights the Epstein plagiarism of Amis' work. Brief quotes from psychiatrists suggest plagiarism to be common among creative people, an unconscious act or a cry for punishment for undeserved success. Lists a number of well known cases involving the famous.

72. **Rosen, R. D. "Epping." *The New Republic* 183 (15 November 1980): 13–14.**
Discusses many cases in which both obscure and known authors readily publicized their plagiarism to stir publicity for their work. The publicity in turn interested publishers in publication. The term "epping" evolved from Jacob Epstein's admitting to plagiarism and gaining fame from the incident.

73. **Phillips, Peter. "'Laboravi in Gemitu Meo': Morley or Rogier?" *Music & Letters* 63 (January 1982): 85–90.**
Compares bars, counterpoint, parts, etc. and concludes that it is likely that Thomas Morley let it be known that he was the composer of *Laboravi* and *Gaude Maria Virgo*. This would fit his pattern of borrowing from other composers of the day.

74. **Glatt, Barbara S., and Edward H. Haertel. "The Use of the Cloze Testing Procedure for Detecting Plagiarism." *Journal of Experimental Education* 50, no. 3 (Spring 1982): 127–36.**
A research study to determine the effectiveness of using the Cloze test, normally used for testing reading comprehension, in detecting plagiarism in students' work. The test relies on the unique linguistic patterns of the individual. The study grouped participants as non-black, black, and foreign. Results indicated that the test is a relevant indicator and can be used in conjunction with other factors to give substance to a teacher's impressions of plagiarism.

75. **Nelkin, Dorothy. "Intellectual Property: The Control of Scientific Information." *Science* 216, no. 4547 (14 May 1982): 704–8.**
An excellent article for those interested in the researchers' struggle over intellectual property rights and control. The author covers the philosophical conflict between pure and applied research when government funding and interests are involved in research. Gives examples of cases in which the courts decided whether or not data collected

by a researcher using funds from federal grant money should be released to the public or kept secret in the interest of national security.

76. **Shaw, Peter. "Plagiary."** *American Scholar* **51, no. 3 (Summer 1982): 325–37.**

As long as those in the literary profession continue to defend another's act of plagiarism, the moral status of literature will remain in question. Shaw illustrates his point with a discussion of how the literary community responded to Haley, Gardner, Epstein and Coleridge. How fellow authors, frequently those from whom the work was stolen, make excuses for the accused, condemn the accuser, and evade the moral issue. Plagiarism will continue to cause "devolution" in literature until the community treats plagiarists with disapproval and, if warranted by their public exposure.

77. **Fife, Stephen. "Meyer Levin's Obsession."** *The New Republic* **187 (2 August 1982): 26–30.**

Steps through a comparison for plagiarism in the play of *The Diary of Anne Frank* and concludes that Levin had very strong evidence that his work had been plagiarized. Implies Levin's anti-semitic concerns might have some basis. For readers interested in "walking through" the discovery process as well as those interested in the Levin *v.* Albert & Frances Hackett and Otto Frank case.

78. **Ostling, Richard N. "The Church of Liberal Borrowings: Plagiarism and Fraud Charges Rock the Seventh-Day Adventists."** *Time* **120, no. 5 (2 August 1982): 49.**

[Reported by Jim Castell/Washington and Dick Thompson/San Francisco.]

The divinely inspired writing and inherent honesty of Seventh-Day Adventist prophet Ellen G. White (1827–1915) have been called into question by Walter T. Rea. Rea has found much borrowing from other authors in White's works, even in those passages which described happenings in her visions. The church replies that the Bible is also compiled from pre-existing sources and supports White as an authoritative source for truth. Rea's book *The White Lies* records his findings and views.

79. **Carroll, Joyce A. "Plagiarism: The Unfun Game."** *English Journal* **71, no. 5 (September 1982): 92–4.**

Clever analogy. Plagiarism as a game of *Monopoly*. Also lists a number of the prominent cases of the 1970s and current theorists' ideas on motives of and deterrents for plagiarism. Suggests personalizing the writing process when teaching.

80. **Fromer, Paul. "Ghostwriting: A Borderline Deceit?"** *Christianity Today* **26 (September 1982): 12–4.**

    Attacks ghost authorship from the standpoint of not deceiving the reader. Suggests editors alert the reader by using "name withheld" and an explanation of why, or some indication that a pseudonym was used. If we trust in God we can trust each other. This foundation of trust and truth should be the basis of interaction with each receiving credit for his contribution. A unique article with a refreshing viewpoint.

81. **Kipkind, Andrew. "Kosinski Redux."** *The Nation* **235 (20 November 1982): 516.**

    More an essay on validity of the intentions of *Times'* reporter John Corry and the *Village Voice* in coverage of charges of plagiarism against anti-Communist Jerzy Kosinski than a piece on plagiarism.

82. **Bailey, Carl. "Eye on Publishing."** *Wilson Library Bulletin* **57 (December 1982): 320.**

    Publishing practices which increase pressures on staff to find new authors, and the "cookie-cutter" genre approach in publishing contribute to the rise in cases of plagiarism. This latest case of questioning whether or not enough acknowledgment was given by D. M. Thomas's *The Bronze Horseman: Selected Poems of Alexander Pushkin* seems a bit extreme to the author. Instead the question should be whether it contains enough originality.

83. **Johnson, Scott. "Research: Plagiary Is Only One Problem."** *The New York Times,* **9 January 1983, sec. 12, col. 1, p. 60.**

    Instead of stressing the importance of original thought and analysis of facts, our education system stresses the length of bibliography and footnotes when teaching research techniques. Under this concept, plagiarism becomes simply poor technique. Cases of plagiarist Napolitano and Lewis, and creator of false data Long are mentioned in the introductory paragraph.

84. **Carmack, Betty J. "Resolving an Incident of Academic Dishonesty: Plagiarism."** *Nurse Educator* **8, no. 1 (Spring 1983): 9–12.**

    Description and evaluation of steps taken by a nursing faculty member to address plagiarism on a team project. Breaches in academic honesty must be addressed and faculty need to be prepared to take action when incidents occur.

85. **Krevans, Julius R. "Intellectual Property Rights—A Modern Debate with Ancient Roots."** *Transactions of the American Clinical & Climatalogical Assn.* **96 (1984): 207–11.**

    The relationship between university research and industry must be acknowledged and managed. Concerns such as distorted research results to favor commercial enterprises, funds put toward the most profitable programs versus research to advancing science for the benefit of society are real and must be addressed. The fundamental differences in purpose between the two systems must remain intact. Guidelines with built in flexibility for case-by-case adjustments are suggested in the typical academic fashion. Appendix has an excerpt from *Guidelines for Disclosure and Review of Principle Investigator's Financial Interest in Private Sponsors of Research.*

86. **Trewin, Ion. "Auberon Waugh: Subliminal Plagiarism for *Lord of the Flies?" Publishers Weekly* 225, no. 2 (6 January 1984): 22.**
On the eve of William Golding's acceptance of a Nobel Prize in Literature, critic Auberon Waugh brought up the similarity of Golding's *Lord of the Flies* [1954] to an earlier English work by W. L. George, *Children of the Morning* [1926]. Golding does not remember reading the work. There is no suggestion of intended plagiarism, only of possible subliminal influence. Suggests that acknowledgment to descendants of George might be a considerate gesture.

87. **Norman, Colin. "Stanford Investigates Plagiarism Charge."** *Science* **224, no. 4644 (6 April 1984): 35–6.**
An account of the plagiarism of Kenneth Melmon, Chairman of the Department of Medicine, Stanford University. Melmon "says he was stunned" when he found the acknowledgments had been omitted. He claims Williams, now deceased, put pressure on him to include material he was working on for a forthcoming edition of a rival book. Goodman and Gilman's *The Pharmacological Basis of Therapeutics* and Williams' *Textbook of Endocrinology* are the texts involved. (See *The Wall Street Journal* June 1994 for another explanation from Melmon.)

88. **Adler, Reid G. "Biotechnology as an Intellectual Property."** *Science* **224, no. 4647 (27 April 1984): 357–63.**
Explains what constitutes a patent, trademark, copyright and trade secret as it may apply to biotechnology industries. Which protection is sought will depend on technological development, associated costs, security considerations and the type of subject matter needing protection. Some steps such as the National Productivity and Innovation Act of 1983 and the creation of the Court of Appeals for the Federal Circuit aimed at giving uniformity to patent infringement decisions are steps toward providing added protection for this industry in a world market. Notes cite court cases and applicable U.S. Codes.

89. **Berek, Peter. "The 'Upstart Crow,' Aesop's Crow, and Shakespeare as a Reviser."** *Shakespeare Quarterly* **35 (Summer 1984): 205–7.**

Supports the possibility that Greene's passages in *Upstart Crow* indicate accusations that Shakespeare began his career translating and revising plays and was a plagiarist.

90. **"Stanford Medicine Chief Quits Post After Censure."** *Wall Street Journal,* **8 June 1984, col. 4, p. 13(E).**
Dr. Kenneth L. Melmon stepped down as chair when a committee of peers found him guilty of "grossly negligent scholarship." Approximately 24% of a chapter of the text he wrote were found to come from another textbook. He states he thought copyright permission had been obtained by his editor.

91. **Williams, Sidney B., Jr. "Protection of Plant Varieties and Parts as Intellectual Property."** *Science* **225, no. 4657 (6 July 1984): 18–23.**
It is uncertain whether current patent protection will be enough to protect plant varieties, but the extent that plant breeding laws are being passed by countries indicates the perception of need developers have for such protection. The Plant Variety Protection Act of 1970 exists for those promulgated by seed in much the same way as the Plant Patent Law, the Townsend-Purnell Act of 1930, protects those produced asexually. The PVPA generally covers food, the Plant Patent is used for nonfood crops. Varieties of all kinds and particularly parts of plants, may be protected under the General Patent Law or by filing them as trade secrets. Possible areas of contention such as registration of variety names, trademarks and the Farmers' Crop Exemption are mentioned.

92. **Berghel, H. L., and David L. Sallach. "Computer Program Plagiarism Detection: The Limits of the Halstead Metric."** *Journal of Educational Computing Research* **1, no. 3 (1985): 295–315.**
Scholarly. Detecting plagiarism in programs from computing science students is increasingly difficult and labor intensive. Development of an effective software to detect plagiarism is needed. The use of metric quantitative methods appears to be useful, but the Halstead features have no unique or practical properties to make them singularly good indicators for detecting program similarities. The study was conducted using Ottenstein's n-tuple profile procedures for comparison. Programs are included in the appendix. Notes.

93. **Mawdsley, Ralph D.** *Legal Aspects of Plagiarism.* **Kansas: Nolpe, 1985.**
Plagiarism should be handled within each educational institution to best prepare students for life beyond the *fair use* walls. Allowing students to commit plagiarism puts academic honesty in jeopardy and opens the faculty and institution to possible copyright infringement lawsuits should the student or faculty use the plagiarized work in

publications. Contains cases and examples for defining plagiarism and copyright infringement. Discusses student assignments under *fair use.*

94. **Noble, June, and William Noble.** *Steal This Plot.* **Vermont: Paul S. Eriksson, 1985.**
Most of this work discusses the concept of plot versus story. There are only 13 plots—vengeance, persecution, catastrophe, self sacrifice, love/hate, survival, the chase, grief and loss, rebellion, betrayal, rivalry, discovery/quest, ambition—and a limited number of story spicers—deception, mistaken identity, unnatural affection, criminal action, suspicion, suicide, searching, honor/dishonor, material well-being, authority, making amends, conspiracy, rescue. We are all products of those before us. Borrowing a little is tolerated, copying a lot is not. Contains questions and answers forum for ways to protect your plot before publication and ways to avoid infringing on another's rights. Discusses some cases. Bibliography and Index.

95. **Sokolov, Raymond. "The Case of Johanna's Quail."** *Natural History* **94 (February 1985): 90+.**
B. Olney accused Richard Nelson of duplicating wording from his recipe book. Sokolov criticizes Olney's work also, suggesting more information on sources of recipes in his work was warranted.

96. **Chaney, Jerry. "Editors, Teachers Disagree About Definition of Plagiarism."** *Journalism Educator* **40, no. 2 (Summer 1985): 13–6.**
A casual survey indicating that both academics and editors have varying ideas about what constitutes plagiarism in journalism. Use of graphics and pictures seem to result in the greatest differences. Three of 75 educators' policies cite borrowing pictures as plagiarism compared to 76 percent of editors. Other topics include use of wire service information, proof and punishment, and prevention.

97. **Owens, R. Glunn, and E. M. Hardley. "Plagiarism in Psychology— What Can and Should Be Done?"** *Bulletin of the British Psychological Society* **38 (October 1985): 331–3.**
Suggests that difficult though it may be to report and investigate accusations of plagiarism, we should be making the attempt and praising institutions who resolve the issue publicly. He also notes the efforts of editors of *Journal of the Experimental Analysis of Behavior* who send reprints of a publication to all co-authors and authors cited in the publication. Mentions Alsabti and Soman as cases in which institutions failed the community by not publicly denouncing the plagiarists. Perhaps the Society should begin investigation activities before the government gets involved as it has with congressional hearings in the United States.

98. **"Notes and Comment."** *The New Yorker* **61 (21 October 1985): 30.**
Writer speaks out at the lack of scrutiny most pay to what they read. This author was more concerned that none seem to have noticed that his comments describing rain on the Continental Divide closely resemble those of Steinbeck in *Travels with Charley.* The awareness also brought to mind the difficulty in proving innocence if accused of plagiarism and the condemning attitude of the public toward the accused.

99. **Fass, Richard A. "By Honor Bound: Encouraging Academic Honesty."** *Educational Record* **67, no. 4 (Fall 1986): 32–5.**
Although indexed under plagiarism, this article concerns the broader topic of academic honesty. Students today come with a different set of standards—the end justifies the means. It is the responsibility of the faculty and administration to agree on policy, promote compliance and be honorable examples to students.

100. **Elmer-Dewitt, Philip. "A Victory for the Pirates?"** *Time* **128, no. 16 (20 October 1986): 86.**
The format of computer software lends itself to ease of copying and making illegal copies. Software vendors' attempts to protect their products have led instead to an angry customer base. Software manufacturers are now trying lawsuits against offenders in an attempt to protect their interests and are adding services for legitimate users to promote legal purchase of the products.

101. **Hertz, Neil. "Teacher and Plagiarist."** *Harper's* **273 (November 1986): 24+.**
[From "The End of the Line." Originally appeared in Yale French Studies, No. 63.]
Essay on the ritual condemnation of plagiarism found in Cornell's *A Writer's Responsibilities* pamphlet. Laborious reading for the general reader.

102. **Riordan, Catherine A., and Nancy A. Marlin. "Some Good News About Some Bad Practices."** *American Psychologist* **42, no. 1 (January 1987): 104–6.**
Survey done to measure perceptions of APA members of "frequency, wrongness, and recommended sanctions for unethical research." Two scenarios followed by questionnaires were used. Results indicated that plagiarism was thought to warrant more formal university action than false data. Those who knowingly committed the offense should be dealt with more severely.

103. **Shea, John. "When Borrowing Becomes Burglary."** *Currents* **13, no. 1 (January 1987): 38–42.**

Using the promotional material from another institution can financially impact that college or university, but, as the survey by CASE shows, plagiarism is thought of in degrees of borrowing among those in institutional advancement. Many excuses concerning time restraints and expertise are given. Most do not consider it a serious concern. Some felt that the borrower was more likely to lose as the information would be less suitable for that institution. Becoming active in professional organizations, awareness of plagiarism, and self censorship are suggested to combat the trend. A Statement of Ethics is included.

104. **Green, Kenneth C., and Steven W. Gilbert. "Software Piracy: Its Cost and the Consequences."** *Change* **19, no. 1 (January/February 1987): 46–9.**
College and university campuses must accept responsibility for educating its society in software copyright, encourage self regulation against software piracy and work with vendors to secure appropriate site license agreements to protect the rights of commercial vendors in promoting and developing software products. If we are to have educational products available, we must show that we are responsible clients. The idea promoted by a *Wall Street Journal* article that campuses are a poor market because of high rates of piracy and availability of student programs is contested.

105. **Fanning, Diedre. "Invisible Property."** *Forbes* **139, no. 6 (23 March 1987): 104.**
Bankruptcy law has not kept pace with business. Reversion rights on intellectual property are not honored if the owning company declares bankruptcy. The distributions fall to the judge in the bankruptcy court. Many companies, among them Madic Corp., Librizol Enterprises, Japan Steel Works, have suffered financial loss when companies they negotiated with for intellectual property rights went bankrupt. Until the laws are changed, negotiate with suppliers who are financially sound or buy the product outright instead of licensing.

106. **Klass, Perri. "Turning My Words Against Me."** *The New York Times Book Review* **92 (5 April 1987): 1, 45–6.**
A writer/doctor explains her reactions to accusations of plagiarism and incompetence from a psychotic "stalker." The accuser sent letters to publishers, the hospital, and the press to try to discredit her. Against recommendations from a psychiatrist, the author decided to make the story public. Her justification was that being a writer, she had little choice. Her words belonged to her, not another. The tone is a bit sensational, but does give an unusual accounting of one accused of plagiarism.

107. Mano, Keith D. "The Cheating Industry." *National Review* **39, no. 10 (5 June 1987): 50, 52+.**

Selling term papers commercially has become part of the institutional structure. Advertisements appease guilt by denigrating the need for learning to write. These businesses could not survive if the schools dealt more harshly with students by expelling them, but that interrupts the cash flow based on per student funding and might require schools to actually *teach* writing.

108. "Swaggart Column Nixed." *The Christian Century* **104 (17 June 1987- 24 June 1987): 552.**

A Louisiana newspaper refused to print an Easter Sunday contribution (article) from Swaggart, claiming he copied major portions of it from an article written by George Fossedal. Swaggart stated the article was sent accidentally, and stated he had copied the material.

109. DeLoughry, Thomas J. "Widespread Piracy by Students Frustrates Developers of Computer Software." *Chronicle of Higher Education* **33, no. 48 (12 August 1987): 1, 31+.**

Pirating software among campus students and faculty concerns the software developers. Attempts to correct the problem include trying to dissuade students and faculty by changing attitudes toward pirating, reducing costs of software and prosecuting those who make illegal copies. Many are optimistic that changes are occurring. Kenneth A. Wasch, executive director of Software Publishers Association is not one of them. EDUCOM has proposed the Software Initiative to assist in software distribution for higher education and stresses the importance of respecting intellectual property rights in this area as we do in other formats.

110. Holden, Constance. "Researcher Accused of Plagiarism Resigns." *Science* **237, no. 4819 (4 September 1987): 1098.**

Plenum Press has withdrawn Raymond J. Shamberger's 1984 book *Nutrition and Cancer* after Colin Campbell pointed out that the work was taken from a National Academy of Science 1982 Report. Shamberger, head of the enzymology section at the Cleveland Clinic Foundation, resigned as of June 30. He could not be reached for comment. Campbell considers it the most "serious case of plagiarism" he has ever heard.

111. Dyson, Esther. "Sue 'Em? or Love 'Em?" *Forbes* **140, no. 5 (7 September 1987): 307.**

The best strategy in the computer world is to share. Datapoint did not let Arcnet go beyond their control while Metcalf allowed Xerox to license Ethernet design freely. The market rewards innovation and open competition.

112. **"A Case of Plagiarized Passion?"** *Newsweek* **110, no. 12 (21 September 1987): 35.**
Brief aside in an article about Joseph Biden's run for the presidency. Gives parallel quotations from Neil Kinnock and Biden.

113. **Safire, William. "No Heavy Lifting."** *The New York Times Magazine,* **27 September 1987, sec. 6, p. 12+.**
Speech writers have taken from other orators as a matter of course. Exerpts from speeches by FDR, Winston Churchill, Nixon and others are given to illustrate the practice and use of oratory style. But, Safire states, times have changed; acknowledgment is the current practice. Joseph Biden was a victim of that change.

114. **Borger, Gloria. "On Trial: Character."** *U.S. News & World Report* **103, no. 13 (28 September 1987): 26–7.**
Compares Robert Bork hearing for Supreme Court Justice with the misadventures of Joseph Biden, the Judiciary Committee Chair. It is a question of character, Bork in the intellectual realm, Biden in the personal.

115. **Fotheringham, Allan. "Peccadillos and Presidents."** *MacLean's* **100 (28 September 1987): 68.**
Biden did nothing other great orators have not done; he borrowed from the best. Article consists primarily of examples of quotes stolen by FDR, Reagan, Trudeau, and Jack and Robert Kennedy.

116. **Kaus, Mickey. "Biden's Belly Flop."** *Newsweek* **110, no. 13 (28 September 1987): 23–4.**
An interesting portrait of how the media affect the political scene. They took the opportunity given them by Biden's plagiarized speech and used it to expose his flaws, his history of plagiarism and lies about his accomplishments. For comparison, Al Gore's theft of a speech getting little attention and Ted Kennedy's having a fellow student take an exam for him at Harvard in "stressless scholarship" were cited. Suggests the demise of the Biden campaign might end the Democrats 20 years of trying to mold potential candidates into "ersatz Kennedys."

117. **McDonald, Marci. "A Candidate's Character in Question."** *MacLean's* **100 (28 September 1987): 24+.**
Voices surprise that Biden's character should be questioned. He, among the candidates, seemed the most safe, a family man. Mentions that the leaks may have come from opposing democrats and a possible White House source. Biden's history of plagiarism gave the impression of style without substance. Includes some exerpts for comparison.

118. **Shapiro, Walter. "Biden's Familiar Quotations."** *Time* **130, no. 13 (28 September 1987): 17.**
     [Reported by Michael Duffy/Washington.]
     A quick summary of the areas that brought Biden's campaign to a halt. Also raises the question of exposure of Biden's transgressions having been planned, political perhaps? See *Newsweek*, same date, for a similar twist.

119. **Kessler, Brad. "Biden's Truth."** *Nation* **245 (3 October 1987): 328–9.**
     Sees Joseph Biden's plagiarism as part of the general media packaging of politicians. Since ideologies are no longer marketed, the objective is to destroy the candidate by damaging the image. Also discusses the invisible backing by Phillip Morris of an advertisement to oppose a ban on smoking. All part of anonymous political packaging.

120. **Hunt, George W. "Of Many Things."** *America* **157, no. 9 (10 October 1987): 202.**
     Light article. Gives origins of the words "plagiarism" and "quote" and quotes on literary stealing written by famous authors—Seneca, Hawthorne, Wilde, etc. Hunt claims Senator Biden's predicament inspired him.

121. **Walsh, Michael. "Has Somebody Stolen Their Song?"** *Time* **130, no. 16 (19 October 1987): 86.**
     Explains that most songs derive from other tunes or classical pieces. Musicians have always borrowed from one another's works. That Morris Albert's *Feelings* is not original should not come as a surprise. Walsh lists a number of current songs which have come under copyright infringement, as well as classics which spawned current pieces.

122. **Galles, Gary M. "Professors Are Woefully Ignorant of a Well-Organized Market Inimical to Learning: The Big Business in Research Papers."** *Chronicle of Higher Education* **34, no. 9 (28 October 1987): B1, B3.**
     Selling research papers is big business. Article gives ways in which the companies avoid prosecution such as the disclaimer, "for research only." They are still in business because campuses make prosecuting students cost prohibitive. Administration and faculty must unite to curb the practice.

123. **DeConcini, Dennis. "Protecting Against Patent Piracy."** *USA Today (Periodical)* **116 (November 1987): 25–6.**
     American industry needs support from our government to compete in the world market. DeConcini covers his attempts and those of fellow senators to support intellectual property rights for foreign markets

through legislation. Among these, a 10 year copyright protection on designs that are "distinctive and original," exclusion of the need to prove injury from infringers and allowing suit for damages if a manufacturer uses their patented process without proper compensation.

124. **Friend, Tad. "Wishing It Was Just the Thought."** *Harper's* **275 (December 1987): 68–9.**
The author gives a brief accounting of the greeting card industry, its look and prose. A single sentence mentions Blue Mountain Arts winning a "tradedress infringement" suit against Hallmark, forcing Hallmark to recall 83 of its cards. No specific details of the "look" causing the suit are given.

125. **Wiegner, Kathleen K. "When the Going Gets Tough, the Tough Go to Court."** *Forbes* **140, no. 14 (28 December 1987): 36–7.**
During the 1960s and 1970s computer companies' primary interest was getting the new products on the market as soon as possible. The fierce competition it brought has triggered fights over intellectual property. Litigation has been spurred by the Copyright Act of 1976 and the Semiconductor Chip Protection Act of 1984. Too much litigation may slow down the marketplace, but knowing that the courts will enforce rights also gives confidence to contracts and licensing agreements.

126. **St. Onge, K. R.** *The Melancholy Anatomy of Plagiarism.* **Maryland: University Press of America, 1988.**
The basis of scholarship is to search for the truth. It is founded in the principle that scholars should receive tenure to protect their pursuit of truth no matter where that search leads. Many on academic campuses today do not follow the traditional definition of scholarship. Their work does not contribute in originality or consequences, but has instead been linked to personal advancement and monetary gain. Institutions have replaced honor and integrity with image. Until the focus on scholarship and truth return to the academic environment, there is little hope of minimizing incidences of plagiarism. The way in which we are taught by copy and imitation in reading and writing without mention of the evils of stealing ideas contributes to an ignorance and an acceptance of plagiaristic styles. Uses Biden and Bork as examples for the misuse of power. Attacking plagiarism is as good a place as any to begin revitalizing academic ethics. Index.

127. **Lottman, Herbert R. "'Blue Bicycle' Faces Plagiarism Charges in France and U.S."** *Publishers Weekly* **23, no. 2 (15 January 1988): 27.**
Trust Bank Co., owners of the copyright for *Gone with the Wind*, are

suing author Regine Deforges of *The Blue Bicycle*, and its French and U.S. publishers. Claims did not surface until "*Blue*," originally written as part of a series of take-offs on classics, became a best-seller in its own right. A California judge allowed the distribution of the work citing "tardy filing" as one reason. Bank Trust Co. intends to pursue the claim.

128. **Jackson, Louise A., Eileen Tway, and Alan Frager. "Teacher, Johnny Copied!" *The Education Digest* 53 (February 1988): 39–41.**
[Originally published in *The Reading Teacher*.]
Causes for plagiarism from children include: internalizing a memorized piece; competing for recognition; inability to synthesize material; an adult mistaking a copied piece for an original poem by the child. Suggests teacher's need to explain "ownership" of writing and other remedies to curtail the process.

129. **Wood, Christopher. "A Tale of Twin Spinsters." *Maclean's* 101 (15 February 1988): 59.**
[With Philip Grenard in Sydney and Barbara MacAndrew in Charlottetown.]
Maureen Garvie, in reviewing Colleen McCullough's *The Ladies of Missalonghi* remembered a novel read in childhood written by the author of *Ann of Green Gables,* Lucy Maud Montgomery. The similarities to *The Blue Castle* were undeniable. McCullough insists the book to be her own creation; the similarities are merely remembrances of a favored novel she read as a child. Montgomery heirs are considering a copyright infringement lawsuit against McCullough. Potential earnings are a factor in this discovery of possible plagiarism as McCullough's success with *The Thorn Birds* ran into the millions of dollars.

130. **Safire, William. "The Player's the Thing." *The New York Times,* 21 February 1988, sec. 137, pp. 14–5.**
In *Marxian Plagiarism* Safire has a discussion with historian/professor Mrs. Bea Kristol (Gertrude Himmelfarb) about the origins of a few marxisms ("nothing to lose but their chains…," "religion being the 'opium' of the people…," etc.) Light, typical Safire.

131. **Fitzgerald, Mark. "Chicago Tribune Correspondent Forced to Resign." *Editor & Publisher* 121, no. 11 (12 March 1988): 16.**
Jonathan Broder of the *Chicago Tribune* was considered a hardworking journalist, an extraordinary reporter. He was forced to resign when it was discovered that he had used the idea, imagery and wording of Joel Greenberg, a reporter from the *Jerusalem Post*. Although fellow reporters protested, editor James Squires held firm. Plagiarism cannot be tolerated even from reporters of Broder's caliber.

132. **Tavris, Carol. "Cryptomnesia: Crimes of the Unconscious."** *Vogue* **178, no. 4 (April 1988): 46.**
Brief. Mentions the study by Brown and Murphy on cryptomnesia. Inadvertent plagiarism is a normal result of the memory process, but it does not make hearing your ideas expressed by another any more pleasant.

133. **Fitzgerald, Mark. "Drama Critic Is Reassigned After Admitting to Plagiarism."** *Editor & Publisher* **121, no. 14 (2 April 1988): 17, 57.**
Covers reporter David Hawley's (*St. Paul Pioneer Press Dispatch*) admitted plagiarism and his responsible action to admit the misconduct and accept the consequences. After receiving a letter from a reader, Hawley admitted his plagiarism from a 1982 review by Frank Rich to the editor and submitted his resignation. Hawley was reassigned to the features section. Includes excerpts from the *Notice to Readers* printed next to Hawley's final review.

134. **Posner, Ari. "The Culture of Plagiarism."** *The New Republic* **198 (18 April 1988): 19–20+.**
Ghostwriting. Politicians, researchers, journalists, Supreme Court justices, persons in all walks of life, now rely on "researchers" and professional writers to complete articles, books, speeches and opinions for them. A benefit: ghostwriters can command recognition and higher pay. A loss: the public reads thoughts that might be similar to that of the "author." Has many paragraphs of specific "authors" and their ghostwriters. An interesting and informative starting point for those researching the topic of ghostwriters and plagiarism.

135. **Blum, Debra E. "U. of Minnesota Chief Quits Job Candidacy in North Dakota Amid Plagiarism Charges."** *Chronicle of Higher Education* **34, no. 36 (18 May 1988): A15, A20.**
Richard J. Sauer has withdrawn his application for President of North Dakota State University. He states the controversy over his admitting to plagiarizing parts of his speeches, though inadvertent, has caused a division on campus he would not be able to overcome. Quotes indicate Sauer uses standard plagiarist excuses, "inadvertent ... poor judgment ... sloppy." He has not withdrawn applications for two other positions.

136. **"U. of Minnesota Chief Back in Presidential Race."** *Chronicle of Higher Education* **34, no. 37 (25 May 1988): A2.**
Announcement that Richard Sauer has resubmitted his application for the university's presidency at the request a of North Dakota State University official.

137. **Sonnenfeldt, Helmut. "Summit Speak."** *New Republic* **198, no. 22 (30 May 1988): 18–19.**
Recounts the practice of drafting summit meeting communiques by staffers on all sides before the meetings take place. It saves time and is generally accurate in the spirit of the meeting if not the actual content.

138. **Tennant, Anne W. "Sixteenth-Century World Views."** *Americas* **(July/August 1988): 38–43.**
Maps of Mexico City and Cuzco, Peru created in 1528 in Germany were "stolen" from Italian maps. Reproductions of Bordone's Italian maps were accidentally reversed North to South. For 225 years the readers still had misconceptions of the areas covered by the maps as the error was just repeated, not corrected.

139. **Blum, Debra E. "Plagiarism in Speeches by College Presidents Called 'Capital Offense' and 'Ultimate Sin.'"** *Chronicle of Higher Education* **34, no. 46 (27 July 1988): A11, A12.**
Bandwagon flavor to this article. Various university presidents hawk the importance of acknowledging sources. Article prompted by the Sauer affair.

140. **"Master's Degree Revoked in Plagiarism Case."** *Chronicle of Higher Education* **34, no. 47 (3 August 1988): A2.**
Brief. Western Michigan University has revoked Libyan citizen Mustafa S. al-Ghariani's doctoral degree. The dissertation for his MA had been plagiarized from fellow Libyan Ali Shembesh. This is the first time the university has revoked a doctorate.

141. **Raloff, J. "R&D Highlights of the Trade Bill."** *Science News* **134, no. 7 (13 August 1988): 101.**
Provisions to remove proof of injury as a requirement to ban infringing imports, and allowances for suing those companies making and distributing products made by patent infringers are included in the Omnibus Trade Bill awaiting President Reagan's signature.

142. **Ljungquist, Kent, and Buford Jones. "The Identity of 'Outis': A Further Chapter in the Poe–Longfellow War."** *American Literature* **60, no. 3 (October 1988): 402–15.**
Gives evidence that Lawrence Labree, editor of the New York *Rover*, is the infamous Outis, supporter of Longfellow in the Longfellow-Poe plagiarism controversy. His conclusions are based on the similarity between the information available to Labree and the commentary by Outis. Refutes the idea that Poe himself was Outis. Poe's comments indicated he was unfamiliar with topics Outis discussed, and seemed

unaware of the web of proof Outis was building in support of Longfellow. Contains a brief chronological series of events summarizing the Poe-Longfellow clash.

143. **Newcomb, Peter. "The New Aristocracy."** *Forbes* **142, no. 7 (3 October 1988): 114–7.**
The entertainment industry has become a new wealth haven. Much of this has been possible since the courts recognized a persona as intellectual property, and as such, eligible for royalty payments for use. Wealth for the stars, with no overhead. Clear profit. The "big" money is no longer confined to Wall Street and the auto industry. Entertainment is a top money-maker. Includes a list of the top 40 Hollywood incomes. Includes a sidebar mentioning digital sampling and visual replication as issues for the courts.

144. **Moore, Thomas H. "Colleges Try New Ways to Thwart Companies That Sell Term Papers."** *Chronicle of Higher Education* **35, no. 11 (9 November 1988): A1, A36.**
Campuses are combating students buying term papers by advertising that copies of the catalogs are being kept on file, suggesting changes in writing assignments to include in class exercises, removing posted advertisements and giving specific guidelines to foreign students.

145. **Alexander, James D. "Lectures: The Ethics of Borrowing."** *College Teaching* **36, no. 1 (Winter 1988): 21–4.**
Stresses the importance of instructors showing by example. Their lectures should follow the same rules for giving recognition to the ideas of another as they expect their students to follow.

146. **Culliton, Barbara J. "Harvard Psychiatrist Resigns."** *Science* **242 (2 December 1988): 1239–40.**
Discusses discovery of plagiarism and subsequent resignation of Harvard's Shervert H. Frazier, psychiatrist-in-chief of McLean Hospital and professor in their medical school. Harvard's response indicates its concern for retaining intellectual property rights.

147. **Leo, John. "The Crimson Copycat."** *U.S. News & World Report* **105, no. 23 (12 December 1988): 90.**
Publish or perish and the volume of publications on the market that are "not actually meant to be read," are blamed for increasing incidents of plagiarism and mediocre research. The case of plagiarism by psychiatrist-in-chief of Harvard's McLean Hospital Shervert Frazier is discussed along with references to a number of other cases (Cyril Burt, Galileo, Newton, Alsabti) covered in *Betrayers of Truth: Fraud and Deceit in the Halls of Science*, by William Broad and Nicholas Wade.

148. **DeLoughry, Thomas J. "Self-Detection Programs Help Students Deal with Plagiarism."** *Chronicle of Higher Education* **35, no. 16 (14 December 1988): A14.**
Brief. Describes using Glatt Plagiarism Teaching Program to assist students in learning what plagiarism is.

149. **Mallon, Thomas.** *Stolen Words: Forays into the Origins and Ravages of Plagiarism.* **New York: Ticknor & Fields, 1989.**
Mallon has chosen to cover a sample of cases of plagiarism in depth, to give not just the facts, but impressions and reasons for actions given by those involved in the conflicts. Throughout, the inability to punish the offender is evident. Cases include: Victorian novelist Charles Reade, an avid promoter of international copyright laws while he plagiarized authors on the continent; Jacob Epstein, son of a well known publisher; Sokolov, a history professor in the 'publish or perish' setting; and a suit against TV show *Falcon Crest*. Citations given, but not categorized.

150. **Agres, Ted. "Archaic Patent File System Strangles U.S. Inventiveness."** *Research & Development* **31 (January 1989): 23–4.**
The U.S. Patent & Trademark Office is overhauling the system which has been operating in much the same way since Thomas Jefferson first initiated it. Complaints of delays of up to 18 months and unavailability of 27% of the files at any given time has prompted the measure. Costs for the computer conversion venture are rising. The project is already 3 years behind and millions of dollars over budget. The computer access is currently only open to the public on two terminals in the Patent Office. Thomas Giammo, head of the project, expresses concern that dial-up access is too costly and might be in conflict with commercial products.

151. **Goldberg, Michael. "Fogerty Wins Unusual Self-Plagiarism Suit."** *Rolling Stone***, no. 543 (12 January 1989): 15.**
After spending "about $400,000 more than the song earned," John Fogerty was found not guilty of self-plagiarism. Fantasy, Inc., owners of the rights to *Run through the Jungle* and most other songs composed for Creedence Clearwater Revival, claimed Fogerty plagiarized that piece when he created *The Old Man Down the Road* under a Warner Bros. label. A verdict of guilty could have put a shadow on any composer's right to grow and continue in his style as his career progresses.

152. **"Lamarck, Dr. Steele and Plagiarism."** *Nature* **337, no. 6203 (12 January 1989): 101–2.**
The charges of plagiarism brought by Dr. E. J. Steele against Dr. John

Cairns are not about copying. They are questions of using another's idea without recognition of the originator. Since the original idea in the research has yet to be proven, validation of plagiarism is, to the author, validating the disputed data as well. Steele's lack of understanding of this basic scientific research principle is shameful, and brings the public image of scientific research up for ridicule.

153. **Merickel, Mark L. "The Educator's Rights to Fair Use of Copyrighted Works."** *West's Education Law Reporter* **51, no. 3 (13 April 1989): 711–24.**
Gives guidelines for educators to assist them in determining appropriate procedures for following copyright laws. Provides two examples and case law citations for each.

154. **Brown, Alan S., and Dana R. Murphy. "Cryptomnesia: Delineating Inadvertent Plagiarism."** *Journal of Experimental Psychology* **15, no. 3 (May 1989): 432–42.**
A research study in which subjects were asked to recall what they considered the source of their idea. Plagiarism resulted the in three categories of generation, recall-own, and recall-new. The subjects were most likely to use the words and ideas of the person who spoke just before them and think they were their own. The authors use George Harrison's composing of *My Sweet Lord* from *He's So Fine* as an example of inadvertent plagiarism. References cases of colleagues. Scholarly.

155. **Cleveland, Harlan. "How Can 'Intellectual Property' Be 'Protected'?"** *Change* **21, no. 3 (May/June 1989): 10–11.**
Electronic storage and transmission give us a perfect time to evaluate our concept of intellectual property rights. Information cannot be owned; knowledge cannot be exchanged. Instead we should be considering information as commonly shared. The incentive for creativity is contained in the atmosphere of developing new ideas to benefit the organization and the enterprise.

156. **Fisher, Francis Dummer. "The Electronic Lumberyard and Builders' Rights."** *Change* **21, no. 3 (May/June 1989): 12–21.**
The current copyright system, based on print, needs to be reevaluated in light of electronic medium. The purpose of intellectual property right protection is to encourage creativity. In the electronic realm, the means of protection through policing of copying does not make sense as use and reuse of materials may involve ideas not remotely connected to the original creation. Since there has been little study on whether copyright promotes creativity, the premise of monetary compensation may not be an accurate one. The academy of higher education cannot

leave decisions of intellectual property rights and controls to the "copyright industry." Freer access to expressions of ideas will benefit both education and commerce.

157. **Garcia, D. Linda. "Rethinking Communications Policy."** *Change* **21, no. 3 (May/June 1989): 28.**
    Suggests that universities be involved in revising communications network policies as well as intellectual property issues.

158. **Gilbert, Steven W., and Peter Lyman. "Intellectual Property in the Information Age: Issues Beyond the Copyright Law."** *Change* **21, no. 3 (May/June 1989): 22–8.**
    Electronic communications are causing us to rethink our definitions of authorship and property in education. Scholars must be active participants in the discussion or they may find that the legal and economic influences have drawn the regulations without consideration for teaching and scholarly concerns. Speaks of cooperation needed among booksellers, libraries and computing facilities and the software publishers. Stresses the need to respect the intellectual property of others as technology brings an ease to thievery not possible with printed materials. Calls for organizations to work together to identify problems and devise solutions. Article rehashes common themes.

159. **Kahin, Brian. "Software Patents: Franchising the Information Infrastructure."** *Change* **21, no. 3 (May/June 1989): 24.**
    The software industry is edgy about having patents in an industry that has been subject to copyright. Any one computer software application may have as many as 10,000 components subject to patent, making the patent process expensive, time consuming and frequently inaccurate. Current court decisions have allowed computer processes to be patented when the equivalent manual process was not. These basic procedures for information flow are corrupted when subjected to patent. It is questionable whether this serves the common good. Schools and universities should be actively involved and prepared to influence decisions on the place for patents in computer software development.

160. **Fields, Howard. "IIPA Targets 12 Pirate Nations, Including China."** *Publishers Weekly* **235, no. 19 (12 May 1989): 106, 8.**
    Lists estimated dollar losses to U.S. companies incurred from illegal copying of textbooks and computer manuals in China, Singapore, Egypt, India, Indonesia, Korea, Malaysia, Nigeria, Saudi Arabia, Taiwan and Thailand.

161. **Hunt, Morton. "Did the Penalty Fit the Crime?"** *The New York Times,* **14 May 1989, sec. 6, col. 1, pp. 36–7+.**

Documents the case of Dr. Shervert Frazier from the discovery, documenting and reporting of the plagiarism by graduate student Paul Scatena to Frazier's forced resignation and reinstatement. The plagiarism was well documented by both Scatena and the faculty committee appointed to investigate the allegations. Many felt that since Frazier had contributed so much to the field of mental health, was quite effective in fund raising, and had a successful practice that his punishment by Harvard and McLean's Hospital was too harsh, minimizing the importance of ownership of ideas. Others believed it an appropriate, swift handling of poor scholarship in an area where personal integrity is essential. The report puts the case in context, describing the negative atmosphere surrounding the scientific community because of many recent cases of misconduct in enterprises funded by government tax dollars and subsequent funding. Outsiders gauge their perceptions of the community by these cases.

162. **Blum, Debra E. "A Dean Is Charged with Plagiarizing a Dissertation for His Book on Muzak."** *Chronicle of Higher Education* **35, no. 35 (19 May 1989): A17.**
American Sociological Association on behalf of Jerri Husch has concluded that Stephen H. Barnes' *Muzak: The Hidden Messages in Music* unfairly appropriated Ms. Husch's dissertation. In response, the publisher has issued a second edition containing complete documentation. The ASA is not appeased. Gives a brief overview of both sides of the case.

163. **Dwyer, Paula. "The Battle Raging Over 'Intellectual Property'."** *Business Week* **(22 May 1989): 78–9+.**
[with Laura Jereski in Boston, Zachary Shiller in Cleveland, Dinah Lee in Hong Kong, and bureau reports.]
Control of patents is becoming a company's major asset and is a leading factor in deciding which areas of research they pursue. Litigation is expensive, but recent court ruling favoring the patent holder has encouraged companies to pursue violations of patent rights. An increase in accepted percentage of royalties from 1% to as much as 5% by Intel for its microprocessor can result in millions of income dollars. There is a less pleasant side to the increase in cries of violation. In developing nations, it may not be wise to pursue violators. Incurring trade sanctions from Brazil resulted in their teaming with other third world nations to successfully block an inclusion of intellectual property standards in GATT. At home, smaller industries may find larger companies using charges of infringement as a tactic to destroy the competition by delaying production until the case is settled.

164. Hammonds, Keith. "Don't Bury Software's Promise in a Legal Bog." *Business Week* **(22 May 1989): 83.**

Hammond urges that major companies not be given too tight a control on their product lines. It will stifle development and prevent smaller software companies from competing.

165. Culliton, Barbara J. "NIH Sees Plagiarism in Vision Paper." *Science* **245, no. 4914 (14 July 1989): 120–2.**

Lost data, fuzzy memory of events, a co-worker claiming evidence of wrong-doing all intertwined in the presentation of evidence. NIH investigation has requested that C. David Bridges be banned from receiving federal monies and from serving on any NIH review bodies for the next 10 years. It concludes that Bridges violated the sanctity of peer review by using information he gained while reviewing Robert R. Rando's work. Bridges denies the charges, stating his research paralleled that of Rando. Sidebar bullets political issues stirring from the scrutiny by congressional committee versus academia highlighted by this case.

166. Palca, Joseph. "New Round in Dingell v. NIH?" *Science* **245, no. 4916 (28 July 1989): 349.**

Representative John Dingell questions why the NIH did not accuse C. David Bridges of fraud since they found that he had stolen ideas from Robert R. Rando, falsified dates in data, and possibly created false data. Their response: the decision was in the hands of Department of Health and Human Services Inspector General. He also questions why *Science* editor, Daniel Koshland, did not investigate when he learned there were problems with Bridge's article. The response: the issue was one of references, not plagiarism.

167. Seymour, Jim. "Jim Seymour." *PC Magazine* **8, no. 14 (August 1989): 79–80.**

Software programmers have worked to get consistency in the look and functionality of the different software packages. Litigation, for example, from Apple over the *trash can* icon, may force manufacturers to stop moving toward consistent, easier to use products.

168. Avram, Henriette D. "Copyright in the Electronic Environment." *Educom* **24, no. 3 (Fall 1989): 31–3.**

Reports conclusions of the Library of Congress Network Advisory Committee regarding revisions of copyright. After describing the accolades of the committee, Avran lists questions before the committee and conclusions reached by the 5 subcommittees assigned to work on the questions. Conclusions were (1) the current copyright system works, (2) the dynamics of electronic environment make administering of the law difficult, (3) monitoring fair use is problematic, and (4) better definitions are needed for database compilation, derivative works, ownership and compensation for intermediaries.

169. **Martin, Brian. "Fraud and Australian Academics."** *Thought and Action* **5, no. 2 (Fall 1989): 95.**
Describes highly publicized cases and failure of peer review. Comments on the influence powerful figures have in the right to pursue investigations within the community.

170. **Cosgrove, Stuart. "In Praise of Plagiarism."** *New Statesman & Society* **2, no. 65 (1 September 1989): 38–9.**
Theft of art is a tradition, not just in written word, but music, dance and painting. Quotes from Bertolt Brecht, "The first-law of creativity is theft." Discusses the Festival of Plagiarism. Some might find the article a bit vague and disjointed.

171. **Hild, John. "Piracy and Protection."** *Editor & Publisher* **122, no. 35 (2 September 1989): 22PC, 39PC.**
The honor system is not working in regulating software copyright. Companies are not keeping tight controls. The prices on software are being regulated by piracy, not by developers and consumers balancing need and development costs. In the long run, all will lose if piracy flourishes because it damages incentives to develop new and better products.

172. **Dyson, Esther. "Intellectual Property."** *Forbes* **144, no. 6 (18 September 1989): 202.**
It is time for this country to reduce the unpredictability in copyright and patent laws for software. Copyrights cover the "look and feel" of the product while patents cover the functionality, but investors are shy about risking venture capital because there are no definite accepted guidelines. Concerning patents, it is time for the government to streamline the patent registry process by speeding up entry and adding persons knowledgeable in software to their staff.

173. **Lindley, David. "Plagiarism: Justice Not Seen to Be Done?"** *Nature* **341, no. 6241 (5 October 1989): 376.**
C. David Bridges asserts that he has been deprived of his grant and future grants by the NIH and DHHS without having the opportunity to present evidence to defend himself. Since there is no legal right to receive federal grant monies, there is no legal redress in place for questioning their withdrawal. Trickett of DHHS says if "Bridges has a case it will be heard."

174. **"Back with the Wind: Mon Dieu! Has Scarlett O'Hara Gone Continental?"** *Time* **134, no. 15 (9 October 1989): 51.**

Margaret Mitchell's family is suing novelist Regine Deforges and the publishing company she owns. The claim, that *La Bicyclette Bleue* plagiarized *Gone with the Wind*. Deforges admits to using much from the first 100 pages, but then claims to have launched her own story of a heroine in Vichy France. If found guilty, payments to the Mitchell heirs could mount to over $16 million.

175. **Fields, Howard. "Commerce Dept. Seeks Reports of Copyright Abuse in China."** *Publishers Weekly* **236, no. 15 (13 October 1989): 13.**
To assist in deciding if trade sanctions should be imposed against China, the U.S. Department of Commerce is asking companies to report any violations of intellectual property rights.

176. **Berry, John N., III. "The Price of Rights."** *Library Journal* **114, no. 17 (15 October 1989): 4.**
U.S. libraries must become active in the negotiation of information rights and money in order to protect access rights for all. European practices require the libraries to pay public lending money as compensation for copyright owners and authors. Our library budgets cannot afford to support this concept.

177. **Pitta, Julie. "The Fall of Adam?"** *Forbes* **144, no. 8 (16 October 1989): 287.**
Adam Osborn is being sued for infringement on a software he developed which is similar to Lotus 1-2-3. Legal costs and drop in sales will bankrupt his Paperback Software International.

178. **Lasswell, Mark. "Crossing 'The Thin Blue Line'."** *Rolling Stone***, no. 563 (19 October 1989): 30.**
Randall Dale Adams has sued Errol Morris for the right to control his own life. Morris is the producer and director of *The Thin Blue Line*, the film which brought about Adams' release from prison. Morris contends that he paid the agreed upon amount of $10 dollars by Federal Express at Randall's instruction and has a signed receipt as proof. The author suggests that lawyers are the reason for the case. Morris says he is "all too happy" to return the rights to Adams.

179. **Gordon, Ian J. "Plagiarism."** *Nature* **341, no. 6244 (26 October 1989): 682.**
Brief. Plagiarism and fabrication are not equally damaging. Fabrication is misleading; plagiarism introduces redundancy.

180. **Blum, Debra E. "Dean Accused of Plagiarism Leaves His Job at Eastern New Mexico U."** *Chronicle of Higher Education* **36, no. 11 (15 November 1989): A23.**
University of Eastern New Mexico is unwilling to state whether

Stephen H. Barnes left voluntarily or has been fired. The departure followed a faculty review of allegations of plagiarism brought by the American Sociological Association. The ASA is still demanding that Barnes' publication be recalled.

181. **Gunnerson, Ronnie. "How to Protect Your Products and Ideas."** *Home Office Computing* **7 (December 1989): 38+.**
The best form of insurance for protection of intellectual property is filing with the federal government for patent, trademark or copyright protection. Trademark should be used for brand names, symbols and product design, copyright for original works and trade secrets for business information and formulas.

182. **Palmieri, Anthony III. "Intellectual Property and the Pharmaceutical Scientist: A View from the Other Side."** *American Journal of Pharmaceutical Education* **53, no. 4 (Winter 1989): 353–5.**
Academics and industry can provide mutual benefits if the industry is assured that care will be given for intellectual property rights over public disclosure. This joint effort is the most effective way to move a potential product to public availability. Palmieri reminds the reader that patents are to prevent others from using a product, not promote its usefulness. Excellent reading.

183. **Prettiman, C. A. "Calderon, Richard Savage, and Christopher Bullock's 'Woman Is a Riddle'."** *Philological Quarterly* **68, no. 1 (Winter 1989): 25–36.**
Scholarly article. Analysis of Christopher Bullock's play, *Woman is a Riddle* [1716]. Similarities and differences among it, the Spanish *La Dama Duende* by Calderon, and Richard Savage's, *Love in a Veil* are explored. Speaks of historical practices, opportunity and probability. Notes.

184. **Reilly, William J., Jr. "Intellectual Property and the Pharmaceutical Scientist: An Industry Perspective."** *American Journal of Pharmaceutical Education* **53, no. 4 (Winter 1989): 351–3.**
Author formerly worked in academia and is now in industry. The main focus for research in industry is financial and is in conflict with ideals of academia. By controlling cost on the academic side and adhering to the "Rules of Scholarship" from industry's viewpoint, a workable, mutually profitable arrangement can be made. Gives researchers practical strategies for getting contracts.

185. **Zatz, Joel L. "Intellectual Property: An Academician's Perspective."** *American Journal of Pharmaceutical Education* **53, no. 4 (Winter 1989): 46–50.**

Patents can mean money for you and your institution and should be given serious consideration. Care should be given to the initial contract agreements, record keeping (especially in recording dates), confidentiality versus publication and responsibilities of team members to other organizations that might bring confusion of ownership. Audience is university faculty, but it does clearly present a definition of patents for general public use.

186. **Feldman, Gayle. "SSP Top Management Roundtable: Whither Intellectual Property?"** *Publishers Weekly* **236, no. 23 (8 December 1989): 34.**
An overview of the 8th annual Society for Scholarly Publishing Top Management Roundtable The focus: implications of the electronic network to scholars, publishers and librarians. Value added, peer review, tracking, compensation and possible alternative configurations such as university controlled networks were highlighted.

187. **Seecof, Benjamin. "Scanning into the Future of Copyrightable Images: Computer-Based Image Processing Poses a Present Threat."** *High Technology Law Journal* **5:2 (1990): 371–400.**
Copyright laws need revision to accommodate the ease and speed of copying and scanning that has emerged with digital imaging technology. Covers issues such as traditional means for proving copyright infringement, concerns of photographers, publishers and hackers in using images from the network resources, and possible modification to current tests to cover digital reproduction of still images. Possible modifications might include using Cohen's similarities and proof of copying plus access, but using similarities as seen by the "ordinary observer" and moving burden of proof of copying to the plaintiff. Makes a brief comparison with digital sampling in music, and suggests a national registry for collecting royalties for images. Notes.

188. **Feinberg, Robert, and Donald Rousslang. "The Economic Effects of Intellectual Property Right Infringements."** *The Journal of Business* **63, no. 1 (January 1990): 79–90.**
Based on data collected from U.S. International Trade Commission, the authors estimate cost of piracy to business versus cost benefits for consumers. Losses in profits are less than indicated by studies which measure losses in sales alone, but even taking into account the benefit to consumers in lower item pricing, the infringement cannot be condoned. The caveat indicates other factors such as loss of potential investor capital and high enforcement costs must also be considered. Mathematical formulas comprise much of the article.

189. **Blum, Debra E. "American Historical Association Toughens Its Guidelines for Handling Charges of Plagiarism or Other Misconduct."**

Chronicle of Higher Education **36, no. 17 (10 January 1990): A15, A18.**

The society has agreed to publish findings on misconduct cases in their monthly newsletter once the cases have been resolved. Names of persons found guilty of misconduct may be published. It is hoped that this will encourage high ethical standards among those in the profession.

190. **McDowell, Jeanne. "He's Got Their Number, Almost."** *Time* **135, no. 4 (22 January 1990): 50.**

The judge ruled in favor of Art Buchwald in his suit against Paramount for recognition that *Coming to America* credited to Eddie Murphy was too similar to Buchwald's original screen play *It's a Crude, Crude World* submitted to Paramount in 1983, but Buchwald may have difficulty collecting his 19% of the net for the $300 million hit. Hollywood bookkeeping rarely finds any net profit in its endeavors.

191. **"There's No Business Like Show Business."** *U.S. News & World Report* **108, no. 3 (22 January 1990): 14.**

Although figures do not match the *Time* account [January 23, 1990] of this case, both give little hope that Art Buchwald will see much of the money settled by the courts for his rights to a percentage of *Coming to America*. The brief article shows various ways Hollywood movie industry accounting can parcel out money to itself to give the illusion that no profit occurred.

192. **Hirsch, Jerry. "More on Shockley."** *Nature* **343, no. 6259 (15 February 1990): 587.**

Not relevant for plagiarism. Just a few omissions on Shockley's personal life the author wanted to point out.

193. **Harris, Kathryn. "Coming to the Money."** *Forbes* **145, no. 4 (19 February 1990): 179.**

Brief. Lawyer Pierce O'Donnell has won the plagiarism suit against Paramount Communications, Inc. for Art Buchwald and Alain Bernheim. *Coming to America* was considered similar enough to a 1983 option they had given to the studio. The question now is how to recoup the $1 million legal fees. Unless net profit from the film can be found, O'Donnell is only entitled to 40% of Paramount's $250,000 fee to Buchwald.

194. **Marshall, Eliot. "Academy Sued on 'Plagiarized' Diet Report."** *Science* **247, no. 4946 (2 March 1990): 1022.**

Victor Herbert and James Olson have charged the National Academy of Science with copyright infringement. Both had been members of a committee working on Recommended Dietary Allowances for the 9th ed. Due to controversy over dosages of vitamins A and C, the report was not published. When put under pressure to account for the use of the funds, both the $600,000 of the original monies and an additional $160,000 from NIH, the Academy produced the 10th edition. Herbert and Olson argue that the 10th was created by editing and updating the work of the 9th's manuscripts. Herbert is requesting $300,000 plus royalties of 5% of sales.

195. **"Wonder Cleared in Recent Song Plagiarism Lawsuit."** *Jet* **77 (12 March 1990): 61.**
Stevie Wonder was cleared of plagiarism charges for song *I Just Called to Say I Love You.* Lloyd Chiate's side is not mentioned in this article. His attorney claims bias against the unknown versus the star and is calling for a mistrial. (See *Jet* September 7, 1992, for additional information on the lawsuit.)

196. **Rowe, Richard R. "Democracy and the Marketplace of the Mind."** *Bulletin of the American Society for Information Science* **16, no. 4 (April/May 1990): 26–8.**
Freedom to access information is the cornerstone of democracy. Those who work in the information industry have an obligation to promote this access. Rowe suggests the adoption of an Information Bill of Rights internationally and the restructuring of intellectual property rights to ensure that free competition also includes access to the ideas of the minority. Government funding should be available for researchers to gather information not necessarily profitable but needed to reflect a balanced coverage.

197. **Hart, Jeffrey. "Lethal Sensitivity."** *National Review* **42, no. 7 (16 April 1990): 43.**
Expresses concern that the universities are using campus disciplinary policy to punish conservative students and promote "sensitivity." As an example he describes the trials of Andrew Baker at Dartmouth. Sally Sedgwick, professor of one of his philosophy seminars, accused Baker of suspected plagiarism with no sources to substantiate the charges. One of his essays was just better than the others and she "had a hunch." The committee ruled "failure to cite" and suspended him for 2 terms. Threat of lawsuit reinstated him, but the "failure to cite" is still on his record.

198. **Byron, Christopher. "From Molehill to Mountain."** *New York* **23, no. 21 (28 May 1990): 16, 19.**
This author tracks the highlights of Dr. Heidi Weissmann's accusations of plagiarism against former mentor Dr. Leonard M. Freeman

over a series of lecture handouts. The author mentions that the plagiarism suit may have been prompted by Weissmann's sex discrimination suit against her employer, Montefiore Medical Center. The saga continues with Weissmann accusing Freeman of tax evasion. A cry which has been picked up by a little known group, the National Coalition. Their main purpose appears to be attacking corporations' ties with academia.

199. **"The Sudden Rediscovery of a Long-Forgotten Kid's Tale Has Britain Abuzz: Did Fergie Fudge Her Budgie Book?"** *People Weekly* **33 (11 June 1990): 54.**
London magazine *Private Eye* reports similarities between *Budgie at Bendick's Point*, a children's book written by the Duchess of York, and *Hector the Helicopter*, a story published in 1964 and written by Arthur W. Baldwin. Publisher Simon & Schuster dismisses the charges stating there are common themes in many such books.

200. **Wilson, John M. "How to Protect Your Script."** *Writer's Digest* **70, no. 7 (July 1990): 30–2+.**
Uses the Art Buchwald case against Paramount for *Coming to America,* Michael Montgomery's case against Hal Needham and Robert Levy (*Smokey and the Bandit*) and Paul Schrader's (*Blue Collar*) sharing profits with a young writer as an example of ways in which plagiarism accusations are handled in Hollywood. Urges novice writers to protect their work, but not to let paranoia stifle creativity. Possible theft is a part of the creative person's life. Gives suggestions for protecting one's work.

201. **Dyson, Esther. "Information, Bid and Asked."** *Forbes* **146, no. 4 (20 August 1990): 92.**
AMIX (American Information Exchange) is introducing a marketplace for buying and selling information. Products may be product surveys or Wall Street research. The information may exist or may require compiling. Cost is negotiated among subscribers—buyers and sellers.

202. **Kruse, H. H. "Mark Twain's** *A Connecticut Yankee:* **Reconsiderations and Revisions."** *American Literature* **62, no. 3 (September 1990): 464–83.**
Kruse only briefly mentions the plagiarism by Twain of *The Fortunate Island and Other Stories* by Max Adeler (Charles Heber Clarke) in creating *The Connecticut Yankee in King Arthur's Court*. The majority of the article speaks "Yankee" in it's historical perspective and of Twain's need to have the public's awareness of the work aroused before publication. Twain's concern that the Proclamation of the Republic speech given by the Yankee might be considered plagiarized

from the Manifesto of the Republican Government of Brazil was one
area discussed.

203. **Allen, Paula Gunn. "Special Problems in Teaching Leslie Marmon
Silko's *Ceremony*." *American Indian Quarterly* 14, no. 4 (Fall 1990):
379–86.**
As a member of both cultures, having been raised Pueblo and educated white, the author expresses the emotional and ethical dilemmas
of teaching about Native American traditions. To whites, information
is linked to freedom; to Native Americans, sharing knowledge with
those not in the group may bring harm to loved ones. Students are
drawn to her classes to learn about topics she cannot discuss without
violating an ethical bond to her culture. She uses the disasters that
befell the Pueblo when they told tribal history and lore to Elsie Clews
Parsons as an example.

204. **Garcia, D. Linda. "Information Exchange: The Impact of Scholarly
Communication." *Educom* 25, no. 3 (Fall 1990): 28–32.**
From the legal perspective, copyright laws are adequate to cover electronic format and transmission. Universities, however, should look
beyond the intellectual property questions. They should view the issue
in the context of the societal impact on access, privacy, security and
liability, and plan accordingly. The 1986 study by the Office of Technology Assessment is covered.

205. **Hennipman, P. "An Old Case of Plagiarism: Pierson Eclipsed by
Schwarzkopf." *History of Political Economy* 22, no. 3 (Fall 1990):
539.**
A case from the 1800s. German political economist, A. Von Schwarzkopf was acclaimed in his country for his excellent work on the Italian economist Custodi collection. The acclaimed work was actually
a translation of the work done by an internationally renown economist and banker, N.G. Pierson. Schwarzkopf's deceit was noticed by
Pierson and by Cossa, another well known economist of the day. Ironically, the ideas have been preserved through the German's reputation,
not through Pierson's.

206. **Schmidt, Arno. "The Ascher Case." *Southern Humanities Review* 24,
no. 4 (Fall 1990): 323–36.**
[Translated with introduction and notes by Thomas Ringmayr.]
Edgar Allan Poe's *Fall of the House of Usher* is shown to parallel *The
Robber's Castle* by Heinrich Clauren. Many examples of similar phrasing and plot construction are given. Schmidt does not condemn Poe,
but praises his skill in taking a mediocre plot and turning it into a
thriller. The introduction describes Schmidt's literary accomplishments

and style, a style he compares to Joyce, Carroll, and German expressionists. The flow of the article might be a bit difficult for those not used to long paragraphs with little punctuation, but the coverage is worth the effort for those interested in Poe or articles accepting plagiarism as a legitimate aspect of creative writing.

207. **Ostling, Richard N. "A Hero's Footnotes of Clay."** *Time* **136, no. 22 (19 November 1990): 99.**
Clayborne Carson, selected by Coretta King to compile her husband's works, discovered and documented extensive plagiarism in the works of Martin Luther King. Carson's concern that the plagiarism not overshadow King's accomplishments is evident in his caution in bringing the information forward. Boston University, where King was given a doctorate based on the plagiarized dissertation, is investigating. (Better coverage on Carson and King is found in articles by Babington [Jan 1991], Garrow [June 1991] and Reagon [June 1991]).

208. **"Widow of Scholar Whose Work King Copied Says Husband Deemed It Trivial."** *Jet* **79 (26 November 1990): 5.**
Dr. Jack Boozer hoped discovery that Martin Luther King plagiarized his doctoral dissertation from Boozer's dissertation would never be made public. From a report in *The New York Times* quoting Mrs. Boozer's statements that her husband had been a great supporter of Dr. King.

209. **Willinsky, John. "Intellectual Property Rights and Responsibilities: The State of the Text."** *The Journal of Educational Thought* **24, no. 3A (December 1990): 68–82.**
Suggests the importance of including the foundations of intellectual property as a necessary part of a complete education in literacy. Gives historical examples of defamation, obscenity and copyright. Stresses that educators are giving students an introduction to the "word trade" and have an obligation to lay the foundations of intellectual property concepts in that introduction.

210. **Morrow, Lance. "Kidnapping the Brainchildren."** *Time* **136, no. 24 (3 December 1990): 126.**
An essay in which the author brushes reasons and traits found in the plagiarist. Mentions a personal incident, Martin Luther King, Senator Joseph Biden and the copying of school children. There's a sadness in the words.

211. **Gimlin, Hoyt. "Americans' Search for Their Roots."** *Editorial Research Reports* **4, no. Article 20 (14 December 1990): 714–26.**
A false hit. Refers briefly to Haley's *Roots*, as an impetus for many to trace ancestry. No commentary on plagiarism.

212. **Corn, David. "A Non-Rascal Thrown Out."** *The Nation* **251, no. 21 (17 December 1990): 768, 70.**
A tribute to Democratic Congressman Bob Kastenmeier of Wisconsin for his efforts in 1976 to revise the Copyright Laws to include *fair use* and public access. He introduced a bill extending the same access accorded to published works to unpublished works such as letters and diaries. The bill was stopped in the Senate by the computer software industry. Other political accomplishments were discussed.

213. **Basombrio, Ignacio. "The Uruguay Round and Intellectual Property."** *Copyright Bulletin* **25, no. 2 (1991): 15–7.**
Economic growth for countries to the South is dependent upon establishing themselves in international markets. To this end they are participating in various international discussions to outline and support the needs of the underdeveloped nations. The proposal resulting from these talks stresses a more equitable distribution of technological advances, a stance more in accord with a multilateral effort, copyright protection without prejudice and property rights balanced with societal needs.

214. **Bradley, Clive. "The Role of GATT in Intellectual Property."** *Copyright Bulletin* **25, no. 3 (1991): 11–5.**
In an effort to curb international piracy, economic "experts" who have little knowledge of actual trade practices in copyright and patent goods, may influence GATT to accept a doctrine of international exhaustion. The doctrine would replace the current licensing practices with an "open market" policy. The articles most damaging are #6 which states a copyright holder cannot control the resale of copies, and #43 which enables GATT to override contracts seen to be too restrictive. Enacting these changes would damage international trade and availability of products as well as curb the rights of the owners to make a reasonable profit from their investment.

215. **Committee on the Judiciary House of Representatives.** *Computers and Intellectual Property.* **Washington, D.C.: U.S. Government Printing Office, 1991.**
Serial No. 119—Hearings before a subcommittee.

216. **King, Rufus C. "The "Moral Rights" of Creators of Intellectual Property."** *Cardozo Arts & Entertainment Law Journal* **9, no. 2 (1991): 267–301.**
Scholarly. Although Congress agreed to adopt the Berne Convention protections on intellectual property, it has, with the exception of adopting the Visual Artists Rights Act of 1990, side-stepped the issue of protection of "moral rights." King progresses through the logic of

rights and privileges, and moral versus legal rights. He concludes that the Strong Right of Attribution, compelling another to acknowledge authorship of one's work, is not a justifiable moral or legal right. The Strong Right of Integrity, alteration of the work resulting in loss of the originator's reputation or honor, is and should be an enforceable legal right.

217. **Oppenheim, Charles. "Legal Issues for Information Professionals: Some Recent Developments."** *Information Services & Use* **11, no. 1-2 (1991): 73–85.**

From the European view. Librarians and information providers are left in the unenviable position of trying to guess what the law may rule as *reasonable* or *substantial* in copyright regulation. The new Copyright Act in the UK allows "fair dealing" only for individuals. It excludes libraries and institutions except under limited circumstances. The uneasiness of software companies and publishers has put information providers in an awkward position of being responsible for rules that are not possible to police. A current directive concerning software databases, aimed at protecting the privacy of individuals against mailing lists and credit agencies, could make work in libraries impossible. It requires persons to be notified if their name is put into a database and, if accessed by a third party, that the person be notified and asked if their name be used again. The rule could be applied to card catalogs and authors. Oppenheim also discusses liability for accurate information in databases.

218. **Raymond, Chris. "Martin Luther King's Plagiarism: Moral Issues for Researchers."** *The Education Digest* **56, no. 5 (January 1991): 40–3.**

[From the *Chronicle of Higher Education*.]

Traces the discovery and disclosure of Martin Luther King's plagiarism. Clayborne Carson's concern that information be presented in its historical context, the university community's concerns about sensationalism detracting from the importance of King's contribution and hesitation at being the one to publicize the misconduct, and suspicions of a cover-up by Boston University are suggested as reasons for the delay in publishing the information.

219. **Lazare, Daniel. "The Kandell Case."** *Columbia Journalism Review* **29 (January/February 1991): 6+.**

If reporters cover a similar topic and interview the same people but use the information to write independent works, is it plagiarism if there are similarities between those two works? The *Wall Street Journal* fired editor and reporter Jonathan Kandell when John W. Kiser III, author of *Communist Entrepreneurs* accused Kandell of plagiarism. Kandell is suing the *Journal* for libel. He does have personal notes from interviews to show independent research and members in the profession who attest to his honesty. The article brings up pertinent points on boundaries for defining plagiarisms within journalism.

220. Babington, Charles. "Embargoed." *The New Republic* **204 (28 January 1991): 9–11.**
Tracks the excuses and "correct politics" involved in suppressing the plagiarism of Martin Luther King by mainstream media— *The New York Times, Washington Post, Atlanta Journal/Constitution, The New Republic. Wall Street Journal* finally came forward and printed the story. Gives statements by Clayborne Carson, head of the research group compiling the papers, explaining how he evaded the plagiarism issue.

221. Eng, Paul. "Collaring the Copycats of the Campus." *Business Week,* **no. 3197 (28 January 1991): 70A.**
Brief. Spotlights Barbara Glatt's software for detecting plagiarism. Glatt believes her software is appropriate not only for the classroom, but to assist business and the courts. The software is based on the premise that those who copy cannot recreate the product.

222. McLeod, Jonah. "Let's Stop This Family Feud." *Electronics* **64, no. 2 (February 1991): 4.**
Texas Instruments Inc. is using the International Trade Commission in addition to civil court to curb the competition. TI is asking the ITC to prohibit import of chips created in foreign manufacturing facilities by their competitors. This ploy puts the competitors at a disadvantage by threatening their preferred tariff and tax benefits if they do not contract with TI for royalty rights.

223. Weber, Samuel. "The Patent Battle Takes an Ugly Turn." *Electronics* **64, no. 2 (February 1991): 51–6.**
Times have changed. During the rapid development in the 1970s, no infringement claims in the computer industry were upheld. Adding protection to software in the 1980 Copyright Law revisions, the Semiconductor Protection Act of 1984, and protection against copying masks in 1985 has brought licensing of intellectual property rights to the forefront. Businesses like Texas Instruments are suing computer chip suppliers and computer manufacturers for infringement, and enjoying huge royalty payments and licensing fees. TI holds over 5000 patents, collecting over $600 million per year for the company coffers.

224. **"Was He Really Bruno Borrowheim?"** *Newsweek* **117, no. 7 (18 February 1991): 75.**
Anthropologist Alan Dundes accuses famed psychoanalyst Bruno Bettleheim of plagiarism. Dundes claims *The Uses of Enchantment: The Meaning and Importance of Fairy Tales*, 1976, contains much from an earlier work by Julius E. Heuscher. Heuscher is more inclined to give the benefit of the doubt. He thinks Bettleheim might simply have read and internalized the work. Heuscher's reaction is quite common among scholars who find their work used by another.

225. **Ferrero, Bonnie. "Samuel Johnson and Arthur Murphy: Curious Intersections and Deliberate Divergence."** *English Language Notes* **28 (March 1991): 18–24.**
Murphy borrowed heavily from Johnson's *Miscellaneous Observations on the Tragedy of Macbeth* when he put together his essay *Macbeth*. The difference came in Murphy's adding "the Liver of a blaspheming Jew," a reference omitted by Johnson. Historical context is discussed.

226. **Rees, Warren, Nancy Freeman Rohde, and Richard Bolan. "Legal Issues for an Integrated Information Center."** *Journal of the American Society for Information Science* **42, no. 2 (March 1991): 132–6.**
Mentions copyright protection for any databases created using the copyright material of others but adding organizational value. The majority of the article does not apply to intellectual property. It covers right to privacy, misrepresentation, products liability and defamation.

227. **Stanberry, Kurt. "The Changing World of International Protection of Intellectual Property."** *Publishing Research Quarterly* **(Spring 1991): 61–77.**
Gives brief overviews of the Berne Convention, Universal Copyright Convention and Madrid Union's handling of copyright and trademark protection. It also covers GATT, WIPO and IFRRO solutions to violation of intellectual property rights world-wide and the difficulties in obtaining compliance from Asian and South American nations. Without some guarantee of protection of intellectual property it is difficult to convince free market economies to invest in underdeveloped nations. GATT, with some enforcement possibilities through trade sanctions for offenders will more than likely be the preferred mechanism for this protection.

228. **Weber, Robert. "Copyright in the Electronic Age."** *Publishers Weekly* **238, no. 14 (22 March 1991): 52–3.**
Publishers want to know how they will be compensated and how

access will be controlled and measured for items housed in electronic format. Those in education, business and research are interested in a *fair use* for the information. The fixed fee approach, specialized databases with restricted access, and exceptions proposed by EDUCOM are discussed.

229. **Grassmuck, Karen. "Institutions' Limits on Sharing of Research Findings Prompt Debate; Chilling Effect on Science Predicted."** *Chronicle of Higher Education* **37, no. 31 (17 April 1991): A31–3.**
Universities and research institutes are becoming more restrictive in sharing their research findings, adding clauses reserving rights to any commercial use of the research. Protesters of the practice claim it stifles research sharing, but Baylor College and Scripps have found many willing to collaborate under these restraints. Main objectors appear to be the NIH and Harvard. Martin Kenny of UC at Davis claims that outcry over restrictions is merely "the pot calling the kettle black." Taking advantage of the patent process is giving universities access to funding for additional research.

230. **"British Library Begins Copyright Cleared Service."** *Library Journal* **116, no. 8 (1 May 1991): 18–9.**
The British Library has agreed to comply with fees to the Copyright Clearance Center through the British counterpart the Copyright Cleared Service. The move was primarily due to the international document delivery system they are marketing, as single copies for research does not violate British copyright law. As serial subscription prices soar, libraries are using alternate markets to provide articles for their patrons. The British Library provides such a service.

231. **Maddox, John. "Another Mountain from a Molehill."** *Nature* **351, no. 6321 (2 May 1991): 13.**
Plagiarism is a very serious matter as is theft of intellectual property. But so is making groundless accusations. As the amount of research material becomes greater, it is more difficult to locate early research done by those in other fields which may overlap. Researchers must rely on indexing done by bibliographers for databanks; some literature might be missed. Descriptions of D. M. Roy of the Materials Research Laboratory claims against Patricia A. Bianconi, Jun Lin and Angela R. Strzelecki are given as an example. Roy advocates requiring authors to list the literature research process, journals be compelled to publish amendments to the references and ombudsmen at grant-making agencies be appointed to assess claims of originality.

232. **Carson, Clayborne, Peter Holloran, Ralph E. Luker, and Penny Russell. "Martin Luther King Jr., as Scholar: A Reexamination of His**

Theological Writings." *Journal of American History* 78, no. 1 (June 1991): 93–105.

A tedious series of quotes interspersed with text. Downplays the importance of King's plagiarism by extolling his accomplishments, stressing that King chose to be a preacher, not an academic. Puts some of the responsibility on King's mentor, DeWolf for not being diligent in recognizing the use of other's works. Nears condescending in their attempt to be fair.

233. Garrow, David J. "King's Plagiarism: Imitation, Insecurity, and Transformation." *Journal of American History* 78, no. 1 (June 1991): 86–92.

In contrast to Carson's report, Garrow depicts King's academic years as a bit frivolous and going for the "paper" rather than being a serious scholar. King's personality seemed more in line with that of a plagiarist, i.e., able to do the work, insecure about his ability, more interested in the credentials than the scholarship. The Civil Rights movement gave King's life a mission, a sense of meaning that had been lacking in the earlier years.

234. Higham, John. "Habits of the Cloth and Standards of the Academy." *Journal of American History* 78, no. 1 (June 1991): 106–10.

Uses the handling of Martin Luther King's plagiarism to again stress the need for responsibility among the academic community and particularly the AHA to uphold its standards and to publicize misconduct. Actions by the academy should not be swayed by fear of litigation as with Sokolow, nor romanticized as Keith Miller did of King. They should be exposed and documented as was done with the King Papers.

235. Reagon, Bernice Johnson. "Nobody Knows the Trouble I See"; or, "By and By I'm Gonna Lay Down My Heavy Load." *Journal of American History* 78, no. 1 (June 1991): 111–9.

Addresses the Martin Luther King issue from a cultural perspective. It is the duty of historians to record accurately, not just give a pristine PR gloss to heroes and heroines. Discusses straddling cultures and the differences between Anglo academic success based on original findings in data and African-American based on original sound and intonation. Article will be a helpful addition for those researching King and cultural differences in assessing originality, but not those interested in facts on fraud and misconduct cases.

236. McCarroll, Thomas. "Whose Bright Idea?" *Time* 137, no. 23 (10 June 1991): 44–6.

Intellectual property has become a highly guarded corporate asset. As much of a company's wealth lies in its ideas and inventions, guarding against the lucrative pirate industries both at home and abroad has become an integral part of doing business. Lawsuits are more common both nationally and internationally as the rights of the patent owner are more stringently enforced in the courts. The impact is felt in supporting organizations as well. Legal offices are specializing in trademark and patent law; insurance companies are offering intellectual property insurance. There is concern in the software industry that such controls will stifle product development, but reassurance that rights will be protected also stimulates research and development in all industries.

237. **Grassmuck, Karen. "Gatorade Brings U. of Florida $17-Million—and 5 Court Actions."** *Chronicle of Higher Education* **37, no. 39 (12 June 1991): A25–6.**
A thirst quenching product created by Dr. Robert Cade and fellow researchers at U. of Florida is again raising the property rights claims made by the licensed owner of Gatorade. The Gatorade trust claims that Cade's new drink, TQII, is a variant of his original product. No participants were available for comment. Provides a brief history of licensing and royalties (approximately $8 million for each researcher and $17 million for the university) from Gatorade.

238. **Flanders, Bruce L. "Barbarians at the Gate."** *American Libraries* **22, no. 7 (July/August 1991): 668–9.**
Yet another crisis. Copyright infringement made easy by electronic storage and communication of information. Librarians can help protect intellectual property rights by increasing public awareness and supporting government enforcement of property rights, but they must also guard access for the economically disadvantaged. Briefly describes examples of downloading and manipulating files by infopreneurs, musicians and researchers.

239. **"Maitre and Morality."** *Time* **138, no. 2 (15 July 1991): 25.**
Dean H. Joachim Maitre of Boston College of Communication acknowledges and profoundly apologizes for plagiarizing from articles by Michael Medved of the *Boston Globe*. Ironically, the theme of the speech was society's moral decline. (See Cunningham, Nov 1991, for a different slant on this case.)

240. **"Japan News Chief Resigns After Plagiarism. (Kyodo New [sic] Service; Shinji Sakai)."** *The New York Times,* **19 July 1991, sec. A, col. 2, p. 7(N)9(L).**
Brief. Discovery that writer Hidetoski Okada had plagiarized a series of 51 medical articles has resulted in his dismissal and the resignation of Shinji Sakai, president of Kyoto News Service, Japan's largest agency. The agency is examining ways to restore its integrity.

241. **Easterbrook, Gregg. "The Sincerest Flattery."** *Newsweek* **118, no. 5 (29 July 1991): 45.**

There has been a rash of reported plagiarism cases and the author has become one of the victims on that list. A Stanford professor stole (he claims computer error) pages for a textbook. Easterbrook briefly recounts his battle. He also lists the names of many current plagiarism cases listed in the bibliography.

242. **Henry, William A., III. "Recycling in the Newsroom."** *Time* **138, no. 4 (29 July 1991): 59.**

[Reporting by Minal Hajratwala/New York.]

Plagiarism breaks the implicit contract that journalists have with readers, that the information given is factual and based on the writer's experience. Article discusses cases of reporter Fox Butterfield from the *Boston Globe* and Laura Parker of the *Washington Post*'s Miami Bureau. Both quoted from interviews they had not personally conducted.

243. **Carroll, Jerry. "Plagiarism: Publish and Perish."** *Globe and Mail* **3 (10 August 1991): D5.**

There seems to be an increase in plagiarists getting caught. A quick summary lists current cases of plagiarism across journalism and academia and the penalties each plagiarist received.

244. **"Plagiarism Chic."** *U.S. News & World Report* **111, no. 7 (12 August 1991): 10.**

Gives "tongue-in-cheek" rating for current plagiarism charges. Rating depends on who steals from whom. Reader must be aware of current cases. Article is useless unless reader is looking for cartoons, anecdotes, etc.

245. **Polilli, Steve. "Fired for Plagiarism."** *Editor & Publisher* **124, no. 33 (17 August 1991): 14, 44.**

Accounts the firing of reporter Kate Sherrod of the *Fort Worth Star-Telegram* on charges of plagiarism. Sherrod claims her challenges to management were the real reason for the firing. Harral, editorial director states plagiarism issue was the only reason for the dismissal. Curiously, the author chooses to solicit a quote from Molly Ivins who will herself be named a plagiarist a few years later. Contains a brief parallel exerpt and stresses Sherrod's efforts in the battered women's arena.

246. **Blanden, Michael. "Technology: Plagiarism, Piracy and Profit."** *The Banker* **141, no. 787 (September 1991): 41–2.**

[This abstract was written from a full text electronic version from UMI.]

The European Commission has adopted the Berne Convention rules on copyright to give consistency and competitive advantage for Europeans in the international software marketplace. This is not an ideal way of handling it. Revisions were made to address "reverse engineering," third party maintenance and development of inter-operable systems. The ECIS in the UK are concerned that the regulations favor major suppliers. Negotiations are still possible.

247. **Branscomb, Anne. "Common Law for the Electronic Frontier."** *Scientific American* **265, no. 3 (September 1991): 154–8.**
There is little common law to provide precedent and much discussion about regulating computer networks. Privacy issues as more personal data is being collected and stored, protection against malicious mischief and unwanted entry, and a fear of censorship and the hindering of the free flow of information are major areas of concern. Mentions *Prodigy's* contention that they have the right to filter, the Sundevil federal computer indictments, *Revlon v. Logisticon, Inc.* where access to the computer system was suspended due to non-payment, and the Weld and Silber political campaign involving altered video tapes.

248. **Chapman, Wayne K. "Milton and Yeats's 'News' for the Oracle: Two Additional Sources."** *English Language Notes* **29, no. 1 (September 1991): 60–4.**
Scholarly. Voices some comparisons of Yeats and Milton. Familiarity with *News for the Delphic Oracle* and Milton's works a must to follow these comments.

249. **Goldberg, Morton David, and Jesse M. Feder. "China's Intellectual Property Legislation."** *The China Business Review* **18 (September/October 1991): 11.**
In response to pressure from the international trade community, China has amended the Chinese Copyright Law and Implementing Regulations, but the changes allow many loopholes. Unpublished foreign software is not protected. Software is not considered "literary works," it is a special class, which allows appropriation of structure, and users to make a "limited number" of copies without specifying the boundaries of "limited." It is also incompatible with the Berne Convention in its registration policies. Substantial changes will have to be made before it is acceptable for foreign trade.

250. **Belich, Vladimar. "A Russian Perspective: The Author's Right of Innovative Pedagogics."** *Action in Teacher Education* **13, no. 3 (Fall 1991): 53–5.**
Outlines the work of the Department of Pedagogical Patents Authority. The department proposes training for pedagogues in analysis of

pedagogical activities, development of skills in describing their contributions in order to apply author's rights to their innovations and organization of pedagogical innovations. Once compensated for the innovation, the innovation would be freely available to others in the field for their use and additions.

251. **Garfinkel, Simon L., Richard M. Stallman, and Mitchell Kapor. "Why Patents Are Bad for Software."** *Issues in Science and Technology* **8, no. 1 (Fall 1991): 50–5.**
Registering software patents appears to be stifling creativity instead of promoting research and development. The Patent Office may take up to 3 years to process an application. The researchers are not skilled in the computer area. Their decisions on "prior art" are haphazard at best or bent to interests of large companies and patent attorneys. Unfortunately the Advisory Commission on Patent Law Reform (U.S. Patent and Trademark Office Subcommittee) has no representatives from the software industry who will express doubts about the need to patent software.

252. **Nemchek, Lee R. "Copyright Compliance by Law Firms (17U.S.C. & 108): An Ethical Dilemma for Librarians."** *Law Library Journal* **83, no. 4 (Fall 1991): 653–84.**
Contrary to the information published in the King report 1982 which stated that for profit libraries made considerable effort to comply with the Copyright Act, the survey done by this author indicates that law firms are not particularly interested in copyright compliance when they photocopy. The survey did find, however, that photocopying is not being used in the law libraries surveyed to substitute for subscriptions; areas in which they do not comply is more likely due to ignorance of the law rather than an intent to cheat publishers of profits. Ethical difficulties facing librarians is discussed. Includes the survey questionnaire and a bibliography covering copyright issues and libraries.

253. **Perrit, Jr., Henry H. "A Value-Added Framework for Analyzing Electronic and Print Publishing."** *Electronic Networking: Research, Applications and Policy* **1, no. 1 (Fall 1991): 18–22.**
Discusses the impact of electronic storage on publishing and the value added in information products. Legal issues involved in the shift from paper to electronic are addressed.

254. **Kanner, Bernice. "Double Takes."** *New York* **24 (9 September 1991): 20–1.**
Copycat advertising is accepted as long as the copy does not dilute the impact of the original. Energizer Bunny, Pillsbury Doughboy and

Stolichnaya's vodka are among those discussed. Duplication is double edged. Customers want conformity, but too much similarity may result in a canceled contract.

255. **Lottman, Herbert R. "Two Hachette Trade Imprints Fight Each Other in Plagiarism Suit." *Publishers Weekly* 238, no. 42 (20 September 1991): 22.**
Yes, one faction of a publishing group can sue another in the same group for plagiarism. Durand of Fayard brought Grasset to court over passages in *Dieu et la science* charging passages were taken from *La Mélodie secrète* by Trinh Zuan Thuan. The court awarded modest damages and a request for Grasset to credit Fayard's publication in future editions. The Grasset book also borrowed heavily from *L'Univers: Dieu on hasard* by American author Michael Talbot.

256. **Geren, Gerald S. "Preparing Intellectual Property Suits." *Design News* 47, no. 18 (23 September 1991): 188.**
Litigation on intellectual property matters is a fact of life but should be avoided if at all possible. Court cases are expensive, time consuming and rarely profitable. Outcomes are unpredictable. If you find yourself in a potential dispute, gather facts and relevant legal information to allow you to analyze the problem. Determine a position that will not be harmful should you have to go to court. Try to settle the problem through redesign, licensing, ceasing to sell, etc.

257. **Cooper, Carolyn C. "Making Inventions Patent." *Technology & Culture* 32, no. 4 (October 1991): 837–45.**
Preface to other articles in the issue. Summary given for each entry. Also contains an addendum which addresses gaps in the Patent Office files caused by fires in 1836 and 1877 and the office's attempts to restore the data that was destroyed.

258. **_____. "Special Construction of Invention Through Patent Management: Thomas Blanchard's Woodworking Machinery." *Technology & Culture* 32, no. 4 (October 1991): 960–98.**
Historically, guarding patents has been a management nightmare requiring fierce watchfulness and confrontation. Only the most skilled in politics and persuasion survived for our history books. The patent system did not decide ownership of an invention, ownership was decided in the courts. Cases of Blanchard's lathe and Gorham's silver pattern are used to illustrate how patents influence the products created in industry. Includes illustrations. For those interested in the development and power of industry during the 19th century, also read Usselman's article on railroad patents printed in this issue.

259. McCracken, Ellen. "Metaplagiarism and the Critic's Role as Detective: Ricardo Piglia's Reinvention of Roberto Arlt." *PMLA* **106, no. 5 (October 1991): 1071–82.**
Scholarly. Suggests that the reader must read *Homenaje a Roberto Arlt* and *Luba* as a continuum. Describes the way in which the reader must interact and decipher meanings hidden in false paths and traps set by Piglia in his mixture of parody and metaplagiarism in tribute to Arlt.

260. Usselman, Steven W. "Patents Purloined: Railroads, Inventors, and the Diffusion of Innovation in 19th-Century America." *Technology & Culture* **32, no. 4 (October 1991): 1047–75.**
Railroads became successful by including employee innovation as part of the natural progression within manufacturing. The innovation was valued as a company asset. These advances were shared among all railroads. This prevented any one railroad from running the risk of patent lawsuits in the courts. These patent pools also benefited the railroad suppliers, as innovations from the railroad staff could be applied to other markets as well. The entire concept was effective, controlling and, contrary to the concept of patent monopolies, inspired innovation and investment. Also discusses the Tanner case and the Bureau of Inventions. An informative analysis and well worth the reader's time whether the interest is in patents or the impact of the railroads on American industry and legislation.

261. Hurley, Mark J. "Centesimus Annus." *America* **165, no. 12 (26 October 1991): 291–2.**
From the Vatican's delegate to the World Intellectual Property Organization Convention in Washington, May 1989. The focus was on protection for design of computer technology. Praise was given to the Vatican for its call for an agreement based on justice, equity and charity for the underdeveloped nations. The benefits of accruing from the exchange and transfer of intellectual property must apply to all. No additional details about the conference are mentioned.

262. Harris, Jr., Arthur S. "Writing Too Well." *Writer's Digest* **71, no. 11 (November 1991): 7.**
Editors may question an unknown author whose work appears to be too well written. This is understandable and to be expected with the many publications today. The author suggests courteous answers to phone calls and professional letterhead and business cards.

263. Maggs, Peter. "Post-Soviet Law: The Case of Intellectual Property Law." *Harriman Institute Forum* **5, no. 3 (November 1991): 1–8.**
There is historical precedent in both Russia and its neighboring states for protection of intellectual property rights. The USSR conformed

to the Universal Copyright Convention of Paris, the Berne Convention, the Nice Agreement, the Strasbourg Agreement and the Budapest
Treaty. Under these agreements, the successor state is obliged to retain
a system of copyright, patents, trademark and unfair competition laws.
Baltic states, although not bound as Soviet states, retain the obligations of treaties formed before their becoming part of the USSR. Their
major concern should be the re-establishment of patent and trademark offices as those patents under the USSR are not binding in the
Baltic states. The article details the history of intellectual property
rights in the Soviet Republic.

264. **Marcus, Steven J. "A Splash of Cold Water."** *Technology Review* **94
     (November/December 1991): 5.**
     The recent exposure of fraud and misconduct among researchers in
     academia should not cause too much alarm. It only shows that they
     are flawed and driven by profit motive like most of us. It seems appro-
     priate that they and their institutions benefit financially from their
     research and work done in conjunction with the private sector just as
     we benefit from their discoveries.

265. **Turow, Scott. "On Intellectual Property."** *Society* **29 (November/
     December 1991): 73–5.**
     It is the author's right to decide whether his work should or should
     not be published. Altering Copyright Act Section 107 to eliminate the
     distinction between published and unpublished works would threaten
     that authority. It is also counter to the copyright premise that the
     owner may use or exclude his property as he sees fit. Writers have
     many reasons for not moving a piece to publication. By allowing the
     possibility that another might use these works, we are encouraging
     the destruction of many original works.

266. **Cunningham, Mark. "A Boston Massacre."** *National Review* **43, no.
     21 (18 November 1991): 25–6.**
     Summary of the attack on Boston University's professor Joachim
     Maitre by the *Boston Globe*. A case of the media creating a story on
     innuendo and unnamed sources. His plagiarism, which he states was
     unintentional, got more coverage than that of Martin Luther King.
     Cunningham suggests that the subject of his speech, attacking debas-
     ing elements of our culture, was on trial, not his use of another's
     script.

267. **Case, Tony. "Dealing with Ethical Dilemmas."** *Editor & Publisher* **124,
     no. 47 (23 November 1991): 17, 42.**
     A brief summary of the Associated Press Managing Editors (APME)
     conference in Detroit. Speakers suggested that the rise in recent cases

of plagiarism has occurred partly through lack of "guidelines" on conduct and partly from economic pressures to deliver a product which will keep the reader's attention. Ethical dilemmas of propaganda versus responsible reporting facing journalists out of country were also mentioned.

268. **Brown, Alan S., and Hildy E. Halliday. "Cryptomnesia and Source Memory Difficulties."** *American Journal of Psychology* **104, no. 4 (Winter 1991): 475–90.**
The report of an academic study of cryptomnesia (inadvertent plagiarism) resulting from not remembering the appropriate source of the information/idea. Findings support earlier studies indicating that the phenomenon does exist, that it is "separate from conscious recollection" and that the source is more likely to be someone speaking before the individual, not after. An article written by academics for an academic publication. Jargon abounds. References.

269. **Magnus, Elisabeth. "Originality and Plagiarism in** *Areopagitica* **and** *Eikonoklastes."* *English Literary Renaissance* **21, no. 1 (Winter 1991): 87–101.**
Milton, in his *Areopagitica* and *Eikonoklastes*, gave plagiarism a Reformation flavor. In *Eikonoklastes* his denouncing of Charles I included the King's stealing the ideas and thoughts from the people and using them to claim his authority and power. In *Areopagitica* a person's value is based on work and personal discovery; original labor is stressed. Persons must be intellectually active, forever challenging beliefs and ideas to pursue truth.

270. **Raines, Lisa. "Protecting Biotechnology's Pioneers."** *Issues in Science and Technology* **8, no. 2 (Winter 1991): 33–9.**
Raines believes the Patent Trade Office should use the *Mancy* case as a basis rather than the *Durden* when reviewing patent applications for biotechnology. "*Durden* deals with a *process of making* an end product, whereas *Mancy* refers to a *process of using* starting-materials." She also points out inconsistency in patent regulation for starting-material patents. Although unauthorized use of starting-materials consititutes patent infringement, it does not prevent other companies from using the materials overseas and exporting the finished products to the United States. Legislation to reverse use of *Durden* is pending, but has opposition from the generic drug industry and the patent lawyers who claim the change would lead to "automatic" process patents and uncertainty in the law. Their vested interest is obvious.

271. **Galen, Michele. "Is It Time to Reinvent the Patent System?"** *Business Week* **(2 December 1991): 110–11+.**

[With John Carey in Washington, Stephanie Anderson Forest in Dallas, Joan O'C. Hamilton in San Francisco and bureau reports.] Ironically, changes in patent laws a decade ago are contributing to problems with slow processing and high costs from courts ruling in favor of patent owners. This trend may be negatively effecting U.S. competitive edge in world markets today. Its "first to invent" clause is being reviewed to see if the European "first to file" concept might be more suitable for today's market and result in additional incentive to develop ideas into finished products.

272. **Stone, Richard. "Court Test for Plagiarism Detector?" *Science* 254, no. 5037 (6 December 1991): 1148.**
    Feder and Stewart's "plagiarism machine" has been used to help determine the extent to which *Plastic Surgery* [1990] edited by Joseph G. McCarthy repeats the earlier edition *Reconstructive Plastic Surgery* [1977] edited by John Marquis Converse. McCarthy and Converse collaborated on an earlier, non-published version of the work. McCarthy has given, he states, recognition to Converse in the preface. The Converse heirs do not agree. Stewart and Feder have found a 57% overlap from the samples they have taken from a number of chapters. Suggests the numeric format may be welcomed in the gray area of plagiarism.

273. **Rogers, Gerard F. "Reporting on Intellectual Property." *Editor & Publisher* 124, no. 49 (7 December 1991): 14T, 19T+.**
    Reporters' lack of understanding of the topic, results in confusing, imprecise reporting. As examples, DeCosta's battle with CBS and Viacom for recognition of rights to Paladin and "Have Gun, Will Travel," Gerber versus Beech-Nut, and AMD's battle for use of computer term "386" are discussed.

274. **Begley, Sharon. "Open Season on Science." *Newsweek* 118, no. 25 (16 December 1991): 65.**
    [With Mary Hager in Washington.]
    The National Academy of Science is under fire from both the Dingell congressional committee, which has questioned its financial situation, and from former committee member Dr. Victor Herbert who is claiming copyright infringement on an RDA report which the NAS published. A portion of the report was created by Herbert while he served on an earlier NAS committee. Much of the data was taken from the work done by that earlier committee.

275. **Dreyfuss, Rochelle C. "A *Wiseguy's* Approach to Information Products." *The Supreme Court Review* (1992): 195–234.**
    Our new products require new law combining the provisions for

patents and copyright. The law should allow flexibility for various product groups and be viewed as a continuum based on copying. Use current Trademark law as an example for types of coverage. Build exceptions into the system to protect free flow of information where needed. To create a groundwork for his proposal, the author examines the *Bonito Boats, Inc. v. Thunder Craft Boats, Feist Publications, Inc. v. Rural Telephone Service Co.*, *Simon and Schuster v. New York State Crime Victim Board* (Criminals may not profit from their crimes) cases as examples of the gaps left using current law. He argues that costs incurred in compiling information resources are legitimate and should be given consideration beyond "facts are public domain" to encourage compilation of new materials. Notes include many legal citations.

276. Howard, Rebecca Moore. "A Plagiarism Pentimento." *Journal of Teaching Writing* **11, no. 2 (1992): 233–45.**
Suggests that students "patchwriting" is not plagiarism. It is their attempt to move toward acceptance into their respective disciplines by imitating the writing styles of those already in those fields. It may also be used when students are immature or uncomfortable with the material about which they are writing. Refers to the Brown, Day, Jones and the Sherrod studies on summary writing and copy-deletion.

277. Information Technology Association of America. *Using Software: A Guide to the Ethical and Legal Use of Software for Members of the Academic Community*. **Washington, DC: Inter-university Communications Council (EDUCOM), 1992.**
Gives an outline of restrictions and *fair use* of commercial, shareware, freeware and public domain software. Answers commonly asked questions.

278. Miller, Keith D. *Voice of Deliverance: The Language of Martin Luther King, Jr. and Its Sources*. **New York: The Free Press, 1992.**
Miller finds King's "borrowing" (Miller's euphemism for plagiarism) to be in character with the traditions of the folk preacher and many ministers. His staunch defense of King is admirable, if a little arrogant. But his point that King accomplished his goals for justice in a segregated America by combining the words of others with his oratory skill does give a positive slant to the "borrowing." Examples of the parallel writings (Mays, Hamilton, Bosley, Gandhi, Brooks, Butterick, Fosdick) are included with detailed explanations of how the works of these preachers and theologians reflected or influenced King's philosophy. Extensive notes and an Index. More a discussion of the folk pulpit and white Protestant theology during the 1950s and 1960s than of plagiarism, but an extensive research endeavor.

279. **U.S. Congress, Office of Technology Assessment.** *Finding a Balance: Computer Software, Intellectual Property, and the Challenge of Technological Change.* **Washington, D.C.: U.S. Government Printing Office, 1992.**
[Report number OTA-TCT-527.]
The report examines the current system of copyright and patent protection for computer software. It places emphasis on the business of intellectual property protection versus the need to promote technological advancement. Includes a summary of a draft for the Uruguay Round of Multilateral Trade Negotiations as it applies to software copyright and related rights, and details the European Economic Community's Directive on Legal Protection for Computer Software. The report explains issues in a format familiar to most researchers. It may be a bit overwhelming for a general interest reader. Notes.

280. **Marshall, Eliot. "Statisticians at Odds Over Software Ownership."** *Science* **255, no. 5041 (10 January 1992): 152–3.**
Leland Wilkinson of SYSTAT accuses Pawel Lewicki of StatSoft of plagiarizing his software statistical calculation program. Wilkinson claims opportunity, as Lewicki requested a copy of the program for review three years before Lewicki's own product hit the market. The case is being discussed on e-mail; it has not gone to court. The listserv commentary has been as much for difficulties and flaws in the products as about the plagiarism issue. With "bugs" identified, improvements are being made in both software packages.

281. **Fitzgerald, Mark. "Royko: Boston Globe Columnist Is Ripping Me Off."** *Editor & Publisher* **125, no. 3 (18 January 1992): 9, 45.**
In his ongoing rivalry with Mike Barnicle of the *Boston Globe*, Mike Royko of the *Chicago Tribune* accuses Barnicle of lifting the theme from his annual Christmas column. Barnicle counters that the idea is hardly original.

282. **Polilli, Steve. "More Plagiarism Incidents Plague Texas Daily (Fort Worth Star-Telegram)."** *Editor & Publisher* **125, no. 3 (18 January 1992): p11.**
Brief accounts of 3 incidents of plagiarism at the *Fort Worth* (Texas) *Star-Telegram* involving veteran reporters James Walker, Bill Youngblood and Kattie Sherrod.

283. **Lepkowski, Wil. "Impact of Intellectual Property Violations."** *Chemical & Engineering News* **70, no. 4 (27 January 1992): 29–30.**
Summary of a paper by University of Pennsylvania economist Edwin Mansfield to the National Research Council on the patterns of investment

of U.S. industry in developing countries who have weak intellectual property laws. His findings stated that the more research intensive the industry, the more they are damaged by weak laws in another country. Countries like India, Thailand, Brazil and Nigeria were simply not considered for contracts. He also concluded that direct investment was not affected by status of intellectual property laws, but that little data was currently available concerning effects of intellectual property law. Conclusions on the effects of weaker or stronger laws on innovation could not be drawn without extensive data collection.

284. **Graham, Lamar B. "Unbelievably Barnicle." *Boston* 84, no. 2 (February 1992): 13.**
Graham, in a casual style, supports Royko's claims that Barnicle plagiarized his work for his Christmas "Mary and Joe" story appearing in, among others newspapers, the *Globe* Dec. 22, 1991. Gives parallels for text comparison, along with references to other questionable pieces from the pen of Barnicle.

285. **Mooney, Carolyn J. "Critics Question Higher Education's Commitment and Effectiveness in Dealing with Plagiarism." *Chronicle of Higher Education* 38, no. 23 (12 February 1992): A13, A16.**
Recent increase in publicized plagiarism cases has prompted societies and academic institutions to reevaluate and in some cases establish policies on plagiarism. Many still feel the cases are inadequately handled. Questions arise about definitions, whether intent should be considered, who has authority to levy sanctions and whether offenses should be made public. Cases mentioned include: Oates, Gallmeier, Sokolov.

286. **_____. "Plagiarism Charges Against a Scholar Can Divide Experts, Perplex Scholarly Societies, and Raise Intractable Questions." *Chronicle of Higher Education* 38, no. 23 (12 February 1992): A1, A14+.**
An example of an author acknowledging some but not all of the contributions taken from another's work. Charles P. Gallmeier case is discussed as well as ways academics handle charges of plagiarism. There are strong supporters on both sides. The case involves 2 universities and 3 professional societies. In the end, no decisive conclusions were drawn. The author gave a well mapped summary of the 3+ year ordeal.

287. **Stearns, Laurie. "Copy Wrong: Plagiarism, Process, Property, and the Law." *California Law Review* 80, no. 513 (March 1992): 513–53.**
Considers using contract law to deal with plagiarism and copyright infringement as plagiarism deals more with process and audience expectations, areas argued under contract negotiations. Copyright law

offers only an owner to property consideration. After a thought pro-
voking article, the author cautions that laws necessarily bring restrictions and may be counter to the creative process. Perhaps the traditional avenues are best after all.

288. Simone, Joseph T., Jr. "Improving Protection of Intellectual Prop-
      erty." *The China Business Review* 19 (March/April 1992): 9–11.
      A Memorandum of Understanding signed by the Ministry of Foreign
      Economic Relations and Trade has given the Chinese a reprieve from
      pending trade sanctions. The MOU addresses intellectual property
      rights in patent, trademark, trade secret and copyright laws. The agree-
      ment moves China closer to compliance with the Berne Convention,
      requires enacting of unfair competition in compliance with Article
      10bis of the Paris Convention, and an enacting of trade secret legis-
      lation. There is some question that the Ministry had authority to sign
      the document.

289. Heller, James S. "The Public Performance Right in Libraries: Is
      There Anything Fair About It?" *Law Library Journal* 84, no. 2
      (Spring 1992): 315–40.
      Clear overview of public performance issues and how they affect
      libraries. The major focus is on home and classroom viewing of video-
      recordings versus viewing in the library. Stresses that public libraries
      do come under the exemption if they meet the *fair use* criterion in sec-
      tions 107 and 110 of the copyright law, but that the premise has not
      been challenged in court. Suggests that since this is a gray area,
      libraries must have written policies and guidelines for their staff to
      protect the rights of the user as well as the rights of the copyright
      owner.

290. Perrin, Noel. "How I Became a Plagiarist." *American Scholar* 61, no.
      2 (Spring 1992): 257–9.
      A Dartmouth professor blames his lack of follow through when he dis-
      covers that an editor has combined a paragraph from Richard Henry
      Dana with his own writing in preparing an article for the travel section
      of the *New York Times*. He had included the clip as a suggested sidebar
      for the article. Angry readers were quick to point out the plagiarism.

291. Tepper, Laurie C. "Copyright Law and Library Photocopying: An
      Historical Survey." *Law Library Journal* 84, no. 2 (Spring 1992):
      341–63.
      Library copying has been an established practice for library patrons.
      Access to information is a main reason for libraries to exist. Concern
      for this copying was not an issue until the machine became part of

standard library equipment. The author covers the Copyright Acts of 1909, Gentleman's Agreement of 1935, establishment of CONTU in 1974, the Copyright Revision Act of 1976, the Copyright Clearance Center, and many court cases which influenced copying practices. Promoting the dissemination of ideas is the primary reason for copyright. By lending works without charge, U.S. libraries play an important role in that process.

292. **Koshland, Daniel E., Jr. "The Race for 'Gold' in Research."** *Science* **255, no. 5049 (6 March 1992): 1189.**
[Editorial.]
A compromise among international patent laws would benefit all concerned. The United States should shift to the "first to file" principle used by other nations, and other nations should respect a grace period for those concerned about publication time frames. These changes could provide a more formal structure needed in our world but retain some of the cooperative ventures found among researchers.

293. **Wilson, David L. "The War of the Statistical-Software Companies: a Feud Over Competing Programs Gets Ugly."** *Chronicle of Higher Education* **38, no. 28 (18 March 1992): A23.**
Leland Wilkinson, president of SYSTAT Inc., battles Pawel Lewicki, co-founder and major stockholder of StatSoft Inc., charging that StatSoft took software innovations from other sources to create his company's product and denigrated SYSTAT to market StatSoft. Lewicki is charging slander and threatening a lawsuit. Mentions plagiarism, but is more concerned with the validity of the statistical output of the software and the replies and rebuttals.

294. **Berger, Jerry. "Plagiarism—The Unspoken Evil of the Newsroom."** *Editor & Publisher* **125, no. 13 (28 March 1992): 40, 33.**
A random survey of newspapers suggests that most either have policies for ethical conduct in place or feel that professional journalists should not need to have such guidelines written down any more than should a minister. Mentions the Maitre, Butterfield, Parker and Sherrod cases.

295. **Betts, Donald D. "Plagiarism."** *Canadian Journal of Physics* **70, no. 5 (May 1992): 289.**
A statement of retraction. The editor found an article by Fu-bin Li published in their journal in 1990 to be a plagiarism of an article published two years earlier by Archarya and Narayana Swamy. He denounces plagiarism as damaging to the soul, depriving an author of recognition, and eroding the integrity of science.

296. St. Clair, Gloriana. "Intellectual Property." *College and Research Libraries* **53, no. 3 (May 1992): 193–5.**

Determination needs to be made on whether *fair use* does stimulate creativity while giving equitable reward to the creators. Ease of copying is eroding both author and publisher profits; cultural differences make enforcement difficult. This is especially true in the scholarly community. St. Clair suggests that the law should be modified to recognize the needs of education and libraries. All materials produced using federal money should be included under *fair use*. Librarians are encouraged to stimulate discussions among faculty and administration regarding intellectual property issues.

297. Sterling, Gary. "Plagiarism and the Worms of Accountability." *The Education Digest* **57 (May 1992): 54–6.**

[Condensed from Reading Improvement, Fall 1991.]
Plagiarism inhibits real learning and damages the student-teacher trust. Sterling recounts his efforts to inspire his students to critical thinking through discussions on plagiarism.

298. Marshall, Eliot. "Intellectual Property: A New Wrinkle in Retin-A Dispute." *Science* **256, no. 5057 (1 May 1992): 607–8.**

University of Pennsylvania has become much more enthusiastic about the accomplishments of Albert Kligman, medical faculty member and patent holder of Retin-A, now that they have come to an agreement with Johnson & Johnson and Kligman on a percentage of shared profits. Marketers estimate the product could earn from $600 million to $1 billion per year.

299. "NAS Sizes Up Scientific Misconduct." *Science News* **141 (2 May 1992): 303.**

National Academy of Science has released its report on misconduct in science. It defines misconduct in science as "fabrication, falsification or plagiarism in proposing or performing research, or in reporting findings." Article is a summary, and useful in researching misconduct in science, but not plagiarism specifically.

300. Greenberg, Daniel S. "Cool Response for Academy's Misconduct Study." *Lancet* **339, no. 8803 (16 May 1992): 1219–20.**

Greenburg is less than pleased, as is the NSF, with a report from the National Academy of Science. After 2 years and $888,000, the study, which was intended to clarify issues of scientific misconduct and suggest appropriate action, reported in typical bureaucratic language and did nothing but narrow the definition of misconduct in an unwelcome direction. They classified tampering with the research of another to be vandalism and, therefore, outside the jurisdiction of the definition.

301. Bennett, Scott, and Nina Matheson. "Scholarly Articles: Valuable Commodities for Universities." *Chronicle of Higher Education* **38, no. 38 (27 May 1992): B1–3.**
Publishers see scholarly writing as a commodity to sell; some scholars see it as knowledge to share. The copyright owner makes the decision on which path is taken. The authors suggest that the university community should manage copyrights as a resource and should bargain with publishers for *fair use* rights for scholarship to help curtail high costs of prestigious journals.

302. Barreiro, Jose. "The Search for Lessons." *Akweikon Journal* **9, no. 2 (Summer 1992): 18–39.**
Native American cultures respect the right of certain groups within the culture to have knowledge not given to all. It is enough that their knowledge contributes to the well being of all. In working with native community cultures, the right have been racist and repressive, the left paternalistic and manipulative. Descriptions of various environmental projects from crop-burning in the rain forests to collecting eagle feathers are given as examples of the conflict between ideas of the indigenous community versus the white community, and the gains made when Native populations are involved in conservation ventures.

303. Beahm, George. "A Literary License to Steal." *Publishers Weekly* **239, no. 26 (8 June 1992): 72.**
Brings back the concept discussed by Count Hermann Keyserling [April, 1926] of unlimited copyright to an author's work but with a capitalist's twist. He does not advocate a foundation for the royalties, but states the heirs have a right to the royalties in the same way as a business is inherited. Why should authors, musicians and artists be forced to give away their rights when others are not. Beahm also points out that less scrupulous publishers claim copyright to books they have reprinted that are in public domain. This, to him, is a license to steal.

304. Hilts, Paul. "Through the Electronic Copyright Maze." *Publishers Weekly* **239, no. 26 (8 June 1992): 35–7.**
Digital information does not fit well into current copyright laws. It encounters problems in *fair use* under both the right to compensation and control of reproduction as definitions of author, publisher and editor are less distinguishable. Author, publisher and library are impacted. To ensure an equitable arrangement between scholarly publications and the research community, publishers and researchers must decide what their roles are and participate with Congress in drafting future intellectual property laws that support that role. The article pinpoints ease of copying, the impact of interlibrary loan on subscriptions,

the right to control use of one's work, support costs for universities doing "cheap" electronic publishing and changes in licensing agreements signed with publishers as examples of areas which need addressing.

305. **Fein, Esther B. "They Wrote a Book with His Words."** *The New York Times,* **24 June 1992, sec. C, col. 4, pp. 15, 20(L).**
Homemaker and fan of Dean Koontz, Linda Kuzminczuk, caught the similarities between *Phantoms* and *The Crawling Dark,* a novel written by Dawn Pauline Dunn and Susan Hartzell who write under the pen name of Pauline Dunn. Koontz was "stunned" by the news. Settlement to Koontz included a half page ad in *Publishers Weekly* announcing the withdrawal of *The Crawling Dark* and of *Demonic Color* also a Dunn/Hartzell copycat of *Phantoms.* The advance money was turned over to Koontz to cover legal fees. This case is unusual as accusations of plagiarism are generally brought against the better known author.

306. **Dolnick, Edward. "The Great Pretender."** *Health* **4, no. 77 (July/August 1992): 31–40.**
A false lead. Discusses pathological liars. Mentions that one in five liars have been arrested for theft, forgery or plagiarism.

307. **Reid, Calvin. "Two Novels from Zebra Withdrawn for Plagiarism."** *Publishers Weekly* **239, no. 30 (6 July 1992): 8.**
Dean Koontz brought legal action when a fan alerted him that *Phantoms* had been plagiarized. Zebra has withdrawn *Crawling Dark* and *Demonic Color* both by the writing team of Dawn Pauline Dunn and Susan Hartzell, pseudonym, Pauline Dunn. Walter Zacharius, CEO of Zebra Books, comments on how difficult it is for publishers to spot such problems. They rely on the integrity of the author. He also reminds that many plagiarists just move to a new pen name when discovered.

308. **"Degree Revocation Invalid."** *The Citation* **63, no. 15 (1 August 1992): 179.**
Because the Board of Regents of New Mexico State University alone has the power to withdraw Ph.D.s, the withdrawing of a degree by the faculty and officers was not considered valid. Hand v. Matchett 957 F.2nd 791 (10th Cir, Feb. 25, 1992.).

309. **Eisenberg, Rebecca S. "Genes, Patents, and Product Development."** *Science* **257, no. 5072 (14 August 1992): 903–8.**
The National Institutes of Health has filed for patents on over 2750 partial complementary DNA sequences of unknown functions. The reasoning given is to promote product development by giving patent protection early in the discovery process. Many in industry disagree with

that premise and express concerns that patents at this stage will only add to the difficulties of negotiating licensing and will slow product development. The Industrial Biotechnology Association, representing 80% of U.S. investment in biotechnology, is urging the NIH to put the sequences in *public domain*. Discusses whether NIH filing meets the *utility* and *not obvious* requirements needed to patent an item.

310. **"Policing Thoughts."** *Economist* **324, no. 7773 (22 August 1992): 55–6.**
Control of intellectual property rights is big business. In the GATT talks, U.S. negotiators used it as a bargaining tool for leverage in negotiating on agriculture and services. In 1980, the dam opened when it became possible to patent living things. The NIH has interfered with foreign researchers' willingness to collaborate with American counterparts by patenting human genes. In 1982, America created a new court for dealing only with patent appeals. In 1990 the U.S. surplused $12 billion in the ideas trade. The latest advance/problem is the ability to patent software. This area is of special concern, as patents, unlike other intellectual property rights, do not recognize independent simultaneous discovery.

311. **Venuti, Lawrence. "The Awful Crime of I.U. Tarchetti: Plagiarism as Propaganda."** *The New York Times,* **23 August 1992, sec. 7, col. 1, p. 7.**
Points out that the plagiarizing of I. U. Tarchetti may have been a deliberate attempt at scoffing at the bourgeoisie. His *The Elixer of Immortality* is a copy of Mary Shelley's *The Mortal Immortal*. Suggests the role of translator is plagiaristic as they strive to make the foreign sound native.

312. **Shakow, David J. "Computers and Plagiarism."** *Journal of Legal Education* **42, no. 3 (September 1992): 458–60.**
The ease with which a student may plagiarize by downloading from electronic sources such as LEXIS and WESTLAW requires instructors to make it very clear to students what is expected of them, to monitor what they do and to stress ethical standards to discourage plagiarism.

313. **Sharkey, Paulette Bochnig. "Telling Students About Copyright."** *The Education Digest* **58, no. 1 (September 1992): 66–8.**
A simple, clear explanation of copyright. What is it, what does it cover, how long does it last and what happens to violators?

314. **Came, Barry. "Death in a Classroom: A Lone Gunman Terrorizes a University."** *Macleans* **105 (7 September 1992): 44–5.**
Vengeance appears to be Valery Fabrikant's motive for murdering fellow professors at Montreal's Concordia University. Fabrikant accused

college administrators of having sinister motives for denying him tenure, and his colleagues of financial corruption and plagiarism. The article has nothing on plagiarism. It carries a message of gun control.

315. **"Stevie Wonder Didn't Steal Song, Appeals Court Rules."** *Jet* **82 (7 September 1992): 27.**
Court of Appeals rejected the argument that the trial judge was biased and upheld an earlier court decision [*Jet* March 12, 1990] that Stevie Wonder did not plagiarize *I Just Called to Say I Love You* from Lloyd Chiate's song *Hello, It's Me/I Just Called to Say*. The songs were "not substantially similar." Brief, but contains the key facts from the March 1990 case.

316. **Anderson, Christopher. "NIH CDNA Patent Rejected; Backers Want to Amend Law."** *Nature* **359, no. 6393 (24 September 1992): 263.**
Patent for over 2,000 CDNA sequences filed by the National Institutes of Health was rejected by the U.S. Patent Office. The grounds, that they are "obvious." Many of the sequences were already published. The mistake was in the NIH using 15mers as the standard instead of 30 or even 50 now claimed by some researchers as being the needed base for originality. The NIH has 3 months to refile a revised application.

317. **Mundell, Ian. "OST Rows with Tide in Report on Intellectual Property."** *Nature* **359, no. 6393 (24 September 1992): 264.**
Brief. The first report from the newly established British Office of Science and Technology voices concern that students be aware of intellectual property issues and the rewards for its exploitation in the form of patents. The usefulness of this approach is questioned. Companies in the pharmaceutical industries look to the government researchers for basic research, not innovations. "It is what they are good at."

318. **Kahin, Brian. "Scholarly Communication in the Network Environment: Issues of Principle, Policy and Practice."** *Electronic Library* **10, no. 5 (October 1992): 275–86.**
A preliminary paper defining intellectual property issues to be discussed in a joint policy and procedures effort by Harvard's Information Infrastructure Project and the Coalition for Networked Information, an NSF grant based group. Discusses computer conferencing, joint authorship, derivative works and implied consent. Explains site license, international access and control. Extensive notes and suggested readings.

319. **Reissman, Rose. "Gabriel's Poem."** *Educational Leadership* **50, no. 2 (October 1992): 88–9.**

How does an elementary teacher handle a student who has plagiarized? This author called Gabriel aside, quietly got him to admit the wrong, and encouraged his creating his own poetry. The author wishes to share her positive approach with her readers.

320. **Burd, Stephen. "Proposed Changes in Patent Laws Would Cripple Universities' Licensing Efforts, Scientists Say."** *Chronicle of Higher Education* **39, no. 7 (7 October 1992): A21, A25.**
Discusses the effects of the U.S. adopting the *first to file* procedures for patents, as is the practice with most other nations, and abandoning its current *first to invent* policy. Supporters insist that we must conform to international procedures to be competitive. An opposer, Edward L. MacCordy who recently resigned from the Commerce Department's advisory panel when his opposition was excluded from the departmental report, stated his fears that even with a *prior-user rights* clause, university researchers would no longer be sought out for research and development. The *prior-user rights* clause would make it impossible to claim the exclusive rights for licensing needed to contract with many companies. Others in the academic community are less inclined to see any damage resulting from the change.

321. **Carlson, Bob. "Protecting Intellectual Property Without Stifling Research."** *Computer* **19, no. 11 (November 1992): 87–90.**
Stresses the importance of not punishing developers for using reverse engineering and computer code disassembly.

322. **Weisband, Suzanne P., and Seymour E. Goodman. "International Software Piracy."** *Computer* **19, no. 11 (November 1992): 87–90.**
[Sidebar by Bob Carlson. *Protecting Intellectual Property without Stifling Research* stresses the importance of not punishing developers for using reverse engineering and computer code disassembly.]
On the local front, laws intended to protect intellectual property rights on software are now being used to create an economic advantage while intimidating innovation. In the foreign market, protection against theft of the property through piracy is still a major issue. The authors suggest 5 policy adoptions to help regulate the foreign market: (1) adjust prices to fit the foreign market, (2) define exceptions, (3) encourage local software production, (4) educate consumers on legal and ethical issues, and (5) reassess copyright controls on software.

323. **Thompson, N. J. "Intellectual Property Materials Online/CD-Rom: What and Where."** *Database* **15, no. 6 (December 1992): 17–20, 22–24, 26–34.**
Summaries and evaluations of on-line and CD-ROM databases used exclusively for intellectual property issues. Discusses copyright,

patent and trademark products, and gives search tips to warn the user of flaws and false hits in retrieving from those databanks covered. International coverage. Defines scan, phonetic, and design searching. Includes Lexis and Westlaw for legal cases. The article is a helpful introduction to types of resources available and their reliability/unreliability factors even though some of the product lines may have changed since 1992.

324. Pemberton, Gretchen A., and Mariano Soni, Jr. "Mexico's 1991 Industrial Property Law." *Cornell International Law Journal* **25 (Winter 1992): 103–30.**

Discusses the need for intellectual property protection in Mexico (U.S. losses were estimated at from $43 billion to $61 billion in foreign markets between 1986–91), the law as it existed before the 1991 Industrial Property Law, and the changes and problems still apparent in the new law. Covers patents, utility models and industrial designs, trademarks, trade names and commercial advertisements (slogans), and trade secrets. Suggests changes in political structure in 1994 might impact the intellectual property protection climate currently in effect under Salinas.

325. Peterson, Kirstin. "Recent Intellectual Property Trends in Developing Countries." *Harvard International Law Review* **33 (Winter 1992): 277–90.**

Developing countries have intellectual property needs not met by the current system, particularly in medicinal plants and genetic materials for the seed and insecticide industries. Allowing plant collection and sharing collective knowledge within the indigenous society without adequate compensation decreases the value and discourages conservation and teaching of the techniques. A number of groups are forming solutions. G-15, administered by India, is forming a gene bank for herbs and medicinal plants. The U.N. is proposing renting sections of rain forest to researchers. Private industry is working out agreements with local governments in ways similar to its agreements with universities. These efforts show the willingness of developing nations to control their resources.

326. Stopp, Margaret, and Harry Stopp, Jr. "The Enforcement of University Patent Policies: A Legal Perspective." *Journal of the Society of Research Administrators* **24, no. 3 (Winter 1992): 5–11.**

Uses the *University Patents, Inc. v. Kligman,* a 1991 case, to illustrate the difficulties that can arise under the Patent and Trademark Law Amendments Act of 1980 if responsibilities and obligations are not clearly stated between researcher and university. Although the case was settled out of court, it did bring out that the courts expect the university to track patentable activities among its researchers. The researchers are not responsible for reporting the activity to their employer.

327. **"All in the Mind."** *The New Yorker* **68, no. 43 (14 December 1992): 46.**
Recounts *Time*'s political correspondent Michael Kramer's use of sentences written a month earlier by Charles Fried. Kramer apologized saying the borrowing was not a conscious act.

328. **Dwyer, Dan. "Universities, Intellectual Property and Litigation: A View From the Sidelines."** *Australian Universities' Review* **36, no. 1 (1993): 25–7.**
At university, lack of litigation to date should not cause complacency about intellectual property matters. The greatest deterrent is a willingness to battle for your rights, while realizing that most issues do not warrant the cost involved in legal confrontation and should be resolved by other means.

329. **Gering, Thomas, and Helwig Schmied. "Intellectual Property Issues: Technology Licensing—Cost Versus Benefits."** *Higher Education Management* **5, no. 1 (1993): 100–10.**
A study suggesting that European universities should be as monetarily successful in registering patents and university licensing as have their counterparts in America. Patent registration is a means for securing R&D investments and generating income for further development of products. Merging research and industry will benefit the public by giving more opportunities for R&D, and allowing new product development. Overall licensing fees collected in America in 1990 was over $100 million.

330. **Ricketson, Sam. "Intellectual Property Rights in the Australian University Context: An Overview."** *Australian Universities' Review* **36, no. 1 (1993): 5–7.**
Intellectual property covers 9 areas—patents, circuitry, plant varieties, designs, copyright, live performance, trademarks, unfair competition and trade secrets. Gives an overview of how university currently handles ownership, and suggests modifications. These points of discussion include expansion of current policy to cover all areas listed above, and to ensure payment and proper acknowledgment to university persons for their work. The article does not bring up new issues, but does give a concise, well organized overview of the basics.

331. **Saunders, David. "The Intellectual Property of Academics as Teachers, Scholars or Researchers."** *Australian Universities' Review* **36, no. 1 (1993): 2–4.**

Acknowledges the difficulties in resolving copyright limitations in an academic setting. Areas impacting change include: open learning; novel arrangements for working with indigenous populations; legal decisions. In academia teachers face conflicts between the rights of author-ownership for their work and educational interests in using their work. Especially in commercial ventures, this can be resolved by creating minimum standards of protection with groups who have similar needs, not by abolishing the restrictions.

332. **Smith, Madeline, and Richard Eaton.** *Documents in the Case of Georges Lewys v. Eugene O'Neill, et al.* **New York: Peter Lang Publishing Inc., 1993.**
A chronological account of the court recordings [May 1929-March 1934], beginning with initial filing of Lewys' complaint. O'Neill's comments were pieced, for ease of reading, from several of the original documents filed with the courts. Closing arguments and Judge Woolsey's Opinion are printed in their entirety. The court held in favor of O'Neill. Appendix includes brief biographies of Judge Woolsey and the lawyers involved.

333. **Dillon, John. "Intellectual Property."** *Canadian Forum* **71, no. 816 (January 1993): 11–12.**
Canada's Mulroney government amended it's Copyright Act to include software as "literary works," compulsory licensing in return for royalties of sound recordings, and a weakened compulsory licensing for plant breeders. NAFTA and TRIPS appear to be moving away from licensing toward monopolies. Monopolies would result in increased costs for generic drugs, farmers paying royalties for seed if they saved seeds from current crops, and the erosion of rights for society in general. Licensing patents and taxing to fund research should be given greater support; pressures of foreign trade agreements should be given less consideration.

334. **Buzzelli, Donald E. "The Definition of Misconduct in Science: A View from NSF."** *Science* **259, no. 5095 (29 January 1993): 584–85+.**
Indexed under plagiarism only because the writer discounts the National Academy of Science in their limiting the definition of misconduct in science to "fabrication, falsification, or plagiarism." The author argues persuasively that the phrase "other serious deviations" included in the NSF definition are required to allow debarring of federal monies from other forms of unethical conduct in scientific research.

335. **Nobile, Philip. "Uncovering Roots."** *Village Voice* **38, no. 8 (23 February 1993): 31–38.**
Alex Haley's *Roots* called literary hoax. Discussion.

336. **White, Edward M. "Too Many Campuses Want to Sweep Student Plagiarism Under the Rug."** *Chronicle of Higher Education* **39, no. 25 (24 February 1993): A44.**
Plagiarism should be dealt with as an educational issue, not just a disciplinary problem which discourages teachers from bringing charges. The current system should be revised to stress individual thought. It should not put such emphasis on passively adopting another's ideas.

337. **Hilts, Philip J. "When Does Duplication of Words Become Theft?"** *The New York Times* **142, no. 49, 285 (29 March 1993): A10(L).**
A discussion of the definition of plagiarism using exerpts from the Oates case as a sample of how differing concepts would interpret the case. "Stolen Words: Forays into the Origins and Ravages of Plagiarism" (Thomas Mallon, Penguin, 1991) and "The Logic of Rhetoric and Exposition" (H. Martin and R. Ohmann, 1958) are cited as sources for definitions used at Vassar and Boston University respectively.

338. **Pisacreta, Edward A. "Distance Learning and Intellectual Property Protection."** *Educational Technology* **33, no. 4 (April 1993): 42–4.**
Reminds readers that distance learning requirements may differ from the standard photocopy issues faced in a traditional classroom. Educators should identify areas of possible copyright issues, meet with legal counsel to set up guidelines and train participants in the issues before engaging in distance learning. Lists sections of copyright law that have traditionally applied to performance and duplicating in an educational setting.

339. **Stone, Richard, editor. "Feder and Stewart, Historian Trade Charges."** *Science* **260, no. 5105 (9 April 1993): 151.**
Stephen Oates challenges the accusations of plagiarism brought by Walter Stewart and Ned Feder. He states that they would be plagiarists if the "plagiarism machine" were used against their own work. A decision by the AHA regarding Oates' work stated that "insufficient acknowledgment" had been given to a work by Benjamin Thomas, but that it was not a case of plagiarism. These results were published approximately a year before Stewart and Feder began their investigations.

340. **Magner, Denise K. "Historian Who Was Accused of Plagiarism Faces New Complaint."** *The Chronicle of Higher Education* **39, no. 32 (14 April 1993): A19, A20.**
Feder and Stewart brought a complaint of plagiarism to the AHA against Stephen Oates, noted historian, for his biographies of Lincoln (175 samples), Falkner (200 incidents) and King (140 phrases). Mr. Stewart's statement of Mr. Oates, that "he slices his copying into finer

pieces than any scientific plagiarist of which we're aware." In an earlier review of Oates' work on Lincoln, the AHA had concluded that
Oates had not given appropriate acknowledgment, but had not committed plagiarism. The case has triggered the reevaluation of the Association's Statement on Plagiarism. The Association insists the need for
revision was based on more than just this incident.

341. **Anderson, Christopher. "NIH Fraudbusters Get Busted."** *Science* **260,
no. 5106 (16 April 1993): 288.**
The office of NIH researchers Walter Stewart and Ned Feder has been
closed after nearly 20 years of investigation and research. Those who
question the level of scholarship and methods of the pair in their pursuit of fraud in research, David Baltimore among the more avid opposition, state the move was long overdue. Ironically, the closure
occurred because they stepped from the scientific community to
examine the works of an historian, Stephen Oates, for possible plagiarism. Oates lodged a complaint to members of Congress, Health
and Human Services Secretary Donna Shalala, and the NIH inspector general, stating that it was improper use of federal resources to
investigate his works as he is a private citizen with no funding from
federal coffers. They agreed.

342. **Wheeler, David L. "2 NIH Researchers Are Told to Stop Investigating Fraud and Plagiarism."** *The Chronicle of Higher Education* **39,
no. 33 (21 April 1993): A16.**
After 10 years of investigating scientific misconduct, Walter Stewart
is being reassigned in the NIH as a research chemist. His co-worker
Ned Feder will be transferred to the grant review offices. The reason
given, their work was too far from the mission of their department.
The scientists had been given excellent work reviews during those 10
years. The reassignments came after Stephen Oates, an historian the
investigators had charged with plagiarism, complained to their administrators that the pair had misused government resources in investigating him. Oates was not funded by federal grant monies nor is he
a scientist.

343. **Mervis, Jeffrey. "NIH Takes Stewart and Feder Off the Misconduct
Beat."** *Nature* **362, no. 6422 (22 April 1993): 686.**
After over 10 years of investigation of scientific misconduct, the NIH
has chosen to close the office of two controversial scientists, Walter
Stewart and Ned Feder. Reasons given for this decision include: the
creation of the Office of Research Integrity's filling the need for their
services; the NIDDK (National Institute of Diabetes and Digestive and
Kidney Diseases) was told to reduce its work force by 30 positions and

this department was considered expendable; and, although not directly mentioned in the official letter of reassignment, that the Oates investigation was outside the scope of the department. Concern is expressed that there will be no one to fill the gap in the investigative work, as the ORI deals only with investigating complaints and proposing appropriate sanctions.

344. **Davis, Bernard D. "The New Inquisitors."** *The Wall Street Journal* **CCXXI, no. 80 (26 April 1993): A12(E)**
The scholarly community has need of whistle-blowers to protect the integrity of research, but the rights of the accused must also be protected. In the cases of Stephen Oates and Dr. Baltimore brought forward by Mr. Stewart and Dr. Feder (whose interest in misconduct arose after less than successful careers in biological research) initial questions of misconduct were not supported by later more extensive research into the matters in the true scientific tradition. We must be cautious of the recriminations brought by zealots and those with political agendas.

345. **Gray, Paul. "The Purloined Letters."** *Time* **141, no. 17 (26 April 1993): 59–60.**
A step by step summary of the case brought against Stephen B. Oates, noted historian, for his work *With Malice Toward None*. Includes the results found when Stewart and Feder used a work that had already been subjected to scholarly scrutiny to test their new software "plagiarism machine." Gives excerpts for the reader to scrutinize, reminding the public that theft of ideas is still a serious matter, and not just an academic debate.

346. **Hardigg, Viva. "Breaking Up the Gang."** *U.S. News & World Report* **114, no. 16 (26 April 1993): 22.**
Brief. Stewart and Feder have been ordered out of their offices by the NIH. Stephen Oates, noted historian, claimed they were beyond their responsibilities in using their software "plagiarism machine" to analyze his writings. Robert Bray, one of Oates' accusers, commented that we need more people checking for these acts of misconduct, not less.

347. **Marsh, Richard L., and Gordon H. Bower. "Eliciting Cryptomnesia: Unconscious Plagiarism in a Puzzle Task."** *Journal of Experimental Psychology* **19, no. 3 (May 1993): 673–87.**
Scholarly. Expands on the research done by Brown and Murphy. Their three experiments found a higher rate of cryptomnesia (inadvertent plagiarism) than in the Brown and Murphy study. The work is referenced with comments about correlations to other similar studies recently completed by colleagues.

348. Goode, Stephen. "Trying to Declaw the Campus Copycats." *Insight on the News* **9, no. 18 (3 May 1993): 10–13+.**
Plagiarism on campus is on the increase. Mentions the Oates case, Miller's justification for M. L. King, and selling term papers. Quotes Minsky's suggestion that the university's registering patents lessens their concern with origination as long as they get ownership, and Shamoo's suggestion that research be audited by persons outside academia and government to promote ethical scholarship and rebuff the "old-boy network" that protects its own. Glatt plagiarism software may be useful for detecting plagiarism in students' work.

349. Hilts, Philip J. "Institutes of Health Close Fraud Investigation Unit." *The New York Times* **CXLII, no. 49,322 (5 May 1993): A21(L)**
The office of Dr. Stewart and Dr. Feder, self appointed investigators of fraud in the scientific community, is being closed, their files sealed, and their 'plagiarism machine' software put into storage. Congressman Dingell, long a supporter of their efforts, expressed concern for the need of Health and Human Services to continue to supply such investigative services into allegations of misconduct. Dr. Lawrence, acting deputy director of the NIH, stated that the quality of their work in pursuing misconduct allegations was not in question, only that it was outside the boundaries of the purpose of the Institute. The pair gained national recognition for their work in uncovering fraud perpetrated by Dr. John Darsee. Their writings exposing the ineffective procedures for investigation resulted in many institutions, Harvard among them, invoking new standards of scientific conduct.

350. Greenberg, Daniel S. "Reassignment for NIH's Fraud Hunters." *The Lancet* **341, no. 8854 (8 May 1993): 1204.**
A concise synopsis of the investigative careers of Ned Feder and Walter Stewart at the NIH. Points out their success in attracting national attention to allegations of misconduct among the scientific community on such cases as David Baltimore, Robert Gallo and Stephen Oates, while 'ruffling a few feathers,' among them Senator Paul Simon, on the Washington scene.

351. Magner, Denise K. "Historian Charged with Plagiarism Disputes Critics' Definition of Term." *Chronicle of Higher Education* **39, no. 36 (12 May 1993): A16–A20.**
Historian Stephen Oates is viewing the publication of his upcoming book on Clara Barton with trepidation. Former works on Lincoln, Martin Luther King, Jr., and William Faulkner have all come under attack for plagiarism on grounds many supporters feel were unfounded. Critics state his accusatory response brought about much of the difficulties

he now faces. Viewpoints on definitions of plagiarism, varying from reuse of descriptive adjectives to copying of entire paragraphs to the intent to steal ideas, are brought forward. Article gives a well stated, concise overview of the stages of the Lincoln case.

352. **Wheeler, David L. "Did 2 Who Fought Research Fraud for NIH Go Too Far?"** *Chronicle of Higher Education* **39, no. 36 (12 May 1993): A16, A18.**
The NIH offices of Walter Stewart and Ned Feder will be closed after their 10 years of effort in identifying and examining cases of misconduct and fraud in scientific research. Their current employer, the National Institute of Diabetes, Digestive and Kidney Diseases states their investigation of the works of Stephen Oates, noted historian, was too far outside the scope of the mission of the organization. Supporters and critics of the investigative techniques state their opinions of the work done by these men and the need for such scrutiny.

353. **"French Banker Plans Lawsuit Over Allegation of Plagiarism."** *The New York Times,* **20 May 1993, sec. A, col. 2, p. 3.**
Brief. Jacques Attali (*Verbatim*) is accused by *Le Nouvel Observateur* of using at least 43 quotes from the works of Nobel prize winner Elie Wiesel's accounts of his 5 years as aide to President Mitterrand. Attali is suing the weekly magazine for libel.

354. **"NIH Fraud Busters Refuse to Accept Transfer."** *Chemical & Engineering News* **71, no. 21 (24 May 1993): 24.**
Walter Stewart and Ned Feder have chosen to take annual leave to rally support for protesting their new assignments at the National Institute of Diabetes, Digestive & Kidney Diseases. To emphasize his objections, Stewart has gone on a hunger strike. The investigative team were transferred to new positions after historian Steven Oates and members of the Washington community raised objections on the relevancy of their investigation of possible plagiarism in Oates' works. Rep. John D. Dingell, although he had requested their services in the past, has written to Dept. of Health & Human Services Donna Shalala for details, but appears to be less than enthusiastic about assisting their cause.

355. **Bray, Robert. "The Dreaded 'P(Lagiarism) Word'."** *The Wall Street Journal* **CCXXI, no. 101 (25 May 1993): A15(E).**
[Letters to the Editor in response to Bernard Davis' "The New Inquisitors," April 26, 1993.]
As the person who first documented the similarities between Oates and Benjamin Thomas' works, Bray questions the validity of the committee who cleared Oates of suspected charges. Many, he states, simply

allowed their names to be put on the document without reading the works being questioned. The AHA is also criticized for hiding behind a euphemistic phrase, "derivative to a degree requiring greater acknowledgment" and not specifically stating plagiarism. Feder and Stewart are supported for their efforts.

356. Swan, John. "NIH Fraud Researchers Deserve Support." *Chronicle of Higher Education* **39, no. 38 (26 May 1993): B3, B4.**
[Letter.]
Support for the efforts of Stewart and Feder in trying to detect unlawful practices in science. With the increase of information in electronic format, the need for services like theirs becomes more evident. Although the 'plagiarism machine' may not be able to establish clear cases of misconduct, such as those suggested in the works of Stephen Oates, the technique still has value in many contexts.

357. Jameson, Daphne. "The Ethics of Plagiarism: How Genre Affects Writers' Use of Source Materials." *Bulletin of the Association for Business Communication* **56, no. 2 (June 1993): 18–28.**
A bit redundant, but gives a clear expression of how genre and audience influence the definition of plagiarism. Gives examples of how academic environments require different levels of documentation from the business community. Corporate America is similar to the pre-Renaissance ideals. Sources are not as important as the final product. Individuals are not given credit for contributions and are expected to build from the groundwork of others. It is the responsibility of business communication instructors to bridge the differences and give their students the background needed for the workplace. Gives instructional strategy. Notes.

358. Hilts, Philip J. "Fraud Sleuth on a Fast Over a Halt to Inquiries; a Government Analyst of Scientific Fakery Seeks Reinstatement." *The New York Times* **CXLII, no. 49,439 (1 June 1993): C1, C10.**
Walter Stewart has gone on a hunger strike. The NIH, he protests, halted their investigative work without due process. In addition to being removed from their work, Stewart and co-worker Ned Feder are banned from discussing any work done during the last five years at the Institute. Neither will be allowed to participate in an upcoming conference on plagiarism in which their work will be discussed. Besides the Oates' case which brought about this measure, Stewart and Feder investigated a number of cases including: the David Baltimore case, and two cases in which Donna Shalala, current Secretary of Health and Human Services, had an active role in impeding their investigative efforts. The quality of their work does not appear to be

the issue. Other whistle-blowers around the country are expressing support for Stewart, reaffirming that, as Ernest Fitzgerald, whistle-blower on Air Force contract fraud put it, "[Whistle-blowers] don't even get the same consideration as suspected sex offenders..."

359. **Magner, Denise K. "History Association to Probe Accusations of Plagiarism Against Stephen Oates."** *Chronicle of Higher Education* **39, no. 39 (2 June 1993): A12–14.**
The AHA will be investigating new charges brought by Mr. Stewart and Mr. Feder against Mr. Oates. These charges will cover, not the Lincoln work, but his works about Martin Luther King, Jr. and William Faulkner. Charles S. Yanikoski, a supporter of Oates' work, states that Feder and Stewart would also be guilty of plagiarism if their works were examined by their own criterion. (See Stone, April 1993 for similar comments.) The AHA has revised their definition of plagiarism, as more time was being devoted to the letter rather than the spirit of the statement. They have divided the concept into two categories—plagiarism and misuse. Exerpts of the AHA document appear on page A14.

360. **Dingell, John D. "Shattuck Lecture—Misconduct in Medical Research."** *The New England Journal of Medicine* **328, no. 22 (3 June 1993): 1610–15.**
Does not cover plagiarism. Gives an overview of misconduct in science and the investigative role played by the Congressional Subcommittee on Oversight and Investigations. Prominent cases of fraud in research are summarized.

361. **Holzer, Harold. "Beware All Writers—You May Be Next."** *The Wall Street Journal* **128, no. 108 (4 June 1993): A13 (W).**
[Letters to the Editor. Response to "The Dreaded P(lagiarism) Word" by Robert Bray, May 25, 1993.]
As a committee member, Holzer refutes the charges of being a pawn in the Oates' case and considers the accusations to be an insult to those scholars who have participated and simply don't agree with the accusers.

362. **Oates, Stephen. "Beware All Writers—You May Be Next."** *The Wall Street Journal* **128, no. 108 (4 June 1993): A13 (W).**
[Letters to the Editor. In response to Mr. Bray, "The Dreaded P(lagiariam) Word," May 25, 1993.]
Supports the verdicts of the committee and the integrity of its members. Indicates that all can be guilty of plagiarism if "phrased plagiarism" is used to define the concept instead of the Lindley standard currently accepted by most scholars. Any scholar, particularly the more prolific, will be open to media attacks labeling them plagiarists.

363. **"Revenge on Two Whistle-Blowers."** *The New York Times* **CXLII, no. 49,352 (4 June 1993): A30.**
[Letters.]
Suggests that the crackdown by the NIH with the approval of Donna Shalala, Secretary of Health and Human Services, on the activities of Walter Stewart and Ned Feder, smacks of vengeance more than good management practices. Stewart and Feder have been barred from accessing their personal files both during and off working hours and advised that they not speak of their investigative work. This prevents them from speaking at an upcoming conference on plagiarism. The sanctions are the result of their zealous crusade against misconduct, a campaign in which they created a software program which proports to reveal plagiarism by matching text. The attempts to use the software on an historical text on Abraham Lincoln, an area far outside their responsibilities at NIH, has given their "enemies an excuse to muzzle them."

364. **Fitzgerald, Mark. "An Apology for Plagiarism."** *Editor & Publisher* **126, no. 23 (5 June 1993): 9–10.**
Details reactions of Zack Binkley, editor of *Lansing* (Michigan) *State Journal*, on receipt of a letter of complaint for publishing copyrighted material without permission. Plagiarism was discovered by *State News* editor, Bill Frischling.

365. **Forbes Jr., Malcolm S. "No One Is Safe."** *Forbes* **151, no. 12 (7 June 1993): 26.**
An example of government becoming invasive. Two NIH scientists used work time and a computer program they recently devised to detect plagiarism, to find evidence to support plagiarism charges against an historian, Stephen Oates. Oates had received no funding from NIH. The American Historical Association had already reviewed the information in the accusation and had not pursued the matter. The two scientists were removed from their respective positions, but not before Oates' reputation had been damaged.

366. **Hilts, Philip J. "Inspector Ends a Hunger Strike Against Agency: U.S. Auditor Still Seeks Reopening of Office."** *The New York Times* **142, no. 49, 361 (13 June 1993): 24(L).**
After 33 days, Walter Stewart ended his hunger strike. He was protesting against the NIH reassigning them and sealing his and Ned Feder's files of current investigations. A doctor warned Stewart of possible death from heart failure if he continued his fast. About a dozen whistleblowers who were depending on Stewart and Feder to investigate their allegations of misconduct and sexual harassment volunteered to each

fast one day in continued protest. Promises from Congressman John Dingell, and Senator David Pryor, chairman of the subcommittee overseeing government workers, that the issues would be re-examined aided Stewart in his decision to end the strike.

367. _____. **"Why Whistle-Blowers Can Seem a Little Crazy."** *The New York Times* **142, no. 49,361 (13 June 1993): E6(L).**
    What makes whistle-blowers carry on against great opposition? The author suggests that they have a strong sense of justice and the belief that an organization should live up to the principles it expounds. W. Stewart and N. Feder are given as examples of such spirit. The Glazers, *The Whistleblowers*, 1989, is cited. Photograph of Stewart and Feder on the NIH lawn after their offices were locked.

368. **Maddox, John. "Give the Hunger-Striker a Break."** *Nature* **363, no. 6430 (17 June 1993): 579.**
    Stewart and Feder have made valuable contributions to the scientific community by making others aware of inaccuracies, both accidental and contrived, in published scientific works. Not allowing them to continue to investigate, to add to the knowledge of why such circumstances occur, would be a disservice to the research community. Not much on plagiarism, but a well written tribute to Feder and Stewart. Includes personal anecdotes.

369. **Jones, Robert E. "Not Whistle-Blowers."** *The New York Times* **142, no. 49,366 (18 June 1993): A26(L).**
    [Letters to the Editor, *Corruption in Government-Brought Science Needed Exposure.*]
    The Chairman of the history department which employs Stephen Oates opposes the tone of the June 4 editorial on whistle-blowers. Their stance that Feder and Stewart were removed from duties for revenge rather than their own misuse of government resources against private citizens is a gross misuse of the term "whistle-blower."

370. **Marshall, Eliot. "Fraudbuster Ends Hunger Strike."** *Science* **260, no. 5115 (18 June 1993): 1715.**
    Feeling that they had a strong commitment from within the NIH to review Feder and Stewart's request to continue to investigate the 17 cases of misconduct that were pending and to make public all data surrounding the David Baltimore case, Walter Stewart ended his hunger strike. Supporters for their cause included Barbara Mikulski, Paul Simon, whose questioning of their investigation of the works of Stephen Oates contributed to the reassignment of the two, and David Pryor, chairperson of the Government Affairs subcommittee on civil service. Senator Dingell, for whom they had done much work in the

past, criticized their doing work outside the scope of their department at the government's expense and urged Stewart and Feder to use established channels for lodging complaints about their reassignments.

371. **"Hungry for Justice."** *Economist* **327, no. 7816 (19 June 1993): 88–9.**
An overview of the events leading up to Mr. Walter Stewart's fast. The fast was in response to the closing of his and Dr. Ned Feder's office. The closure came as a result of Stephen Oates, noted historian, questioning their "using federal health-research money to muck about in non-scientific matters." This was one of many allegations of scientific misconduct and fraud they unofficially conducted. Stewart and Feder are particularly concerned that cases in progress continue to be investigated. Details of one of those cases, a sexual harassment case brought by Dr. Maureen Polsby against the NIH and 10 of its scientists and physicians, is outlined.

372. **Wheeler, David L. "Computer Networks Are Said to Offer New Opportunities for Plagiarists."** *Chronicle of Higher Education* **39, no. 43 (30 June 1993): A17, A19.**
While the rise and proliferation of electronic journals available only on computer makes the possibility of plagiarism more tempting with less chance of exposure, electronics may also provide new ways of identifying plagiarists and protecting original works. The "plagiarism machine" of scientists Stewart and Feder found parallel passages in the works of such authors as Amherst's Stephen Oates. Lorrin Garson's "hashing" algorithm provides a way of quickly coding an original document in case investigations require verification of authenticity.

373. **Gould, Stephen Jay. "Poe's Greatest Hit."** *Natural History* **102, no. 7 (July 1993): 10+.**
Unlike most biographers of Edgar Allan Poe, Gould finds Poe's contributions to *The Conchologist's First Book* to be more than assisting in lending his name to a plagiarized work. He and co-author Thomas Wyatt did plagiarize works by British writer Captain Thomas Brown and French anatomist George Cuvier during a time when no international copyright protection existed. Poe did contribute writing organizational skills, translation and creativity to the work. The final product brought a new presentation to biology on mollusks by bringing shell and anatomy together in one work, and gave educational incentive by supplying lecturer Wyatt with a book citizens could purchase at the lectures for a reasonable cost.

374. **Kozak, Ellen M. "The ABCs of Avoiding Plagiarism."** *Writer's Digest* **73, no. 7 (July 1993): 40–1.**

[Sidebar: "What Is Fair Use?"]
Stresses the importance of a writer's integrity, not just his style. Addresses the difference between copyright infringement and plagiarism and gives a few guidelines on acknowledgments.

375. **Warner, Julian. "Writing and Literary Work in Copyright: A Binational and Historical Analysis."** *Journal of the American Society for Information Science* **44, no. 6 (July 1993): 307–21.**
Writing is the constant between documents and computers. Author compares growth of copyright in United Kingdom and U.S., tracking literary works and other forms of intellectual property. References.

376. **Reath, Viki. "A Tail of Plagiarism in Old Nantucket."** *American Journalism Review* **15, no. 6 (July/August 1993): 11.**
Editors Mary Stanton (*Nantucket Inquirer and Mirror*) and Bill Breisky (*Cape Cod Times*) both seemed quite blasé when it was discovered that John Stanton, reporter and husband of Mary, had plagiarized articles for their weeklies. The only people who appear to be concerned about the incidents are the victim, Jeffrey Keegan, the source, Paul Conley, the whistleblower, Teresa DeFranzo and reporter Mark Merchant who left the *Inquirer* and *Mirror* because the paper seemed to be condoning plagiarism.

377. **Fitzgerald, Mark. "Post-Dispatch Columnist Apologizes for Lifting Info."** *Editor & Publisher* **126, no. 27 (3 July 1993): 10.**
Columnist for the St. Louis *Post-Dispatch* Gregory Freeman has written an apology for inadvertently copying sentences from an opinion piece by *Boston Globe* columnist Derrick Z. Jackson and not upholding to a standard expected and deserved by his readers. Readers have responded positively to the admission. Ironically, both Freeman's and Jackson's columns appeared on the same page in the St. Louis newspaper.

378. **Cipra, Barry. "Electronic Time-Stamping: The Notary Public Goes Digital."** *Science* **261, no. 5118 (9 July 1993): 162–3.**
Discusses Haber and Stornetta's digital time stamping concept for securing and authenticating computer data. The time stamp is embedded in the next document with the "hash" stamp of the previous document. A refined process, worked out in conjunction with D. Bayer adds that this stamp be published in a newspaper for archival records. Article has a fairly clear example of "hashing." A more complete example of the process and an exerpt from *The New York Times* archival record is found in a sidebar following the article.

379. **Reid, Calvin. "Novel at Center of 'Roots' Plagiarism Suit Reissued."** *Publishers Weekly* **240, no. 28 (12 July 1993): 13.**

A new edition of Harold Courlander's novel, *The African*, is being printed. The 87-year-old author won a settlement from Alex Haley to compensate for Haley's plagiarizing his works to create *Roots*. Courlander's comment regarding the incident goes to the core of the matter. "Nobody really raised the issue of literary ethics, and Haley continued to receive honorary degrees..." An insight missed by writers of other articles about this case.

380. Taylor, John. "Clip Job." *New York* 26, no. 27 (12 July 1993): 22–5.

A less than flattering account of McGinniss' claim that his work, *The Last Brother*, is meant to be an inspired non-fictional novel of Ted Kennedy during the death of President John Kennedy. He rationalizes the charges of his plagiarizing from *The Death of a President* by well respected reporter, William Manchester, by giving praise to Manchester's work as the only source for much of the information, a few vague references to the work in early chapters, and its listing in the bibliography. No footnotes or endnotes are used. Most of the article contains parallel exerpts for the reader's comparison. Taylor's low opinion of McGinniss' style are quite apparent.

381. Lyall, Sarah. "Enter Manchester, Angrily." *The New York Times*, v. 142, 21 July 1993, sec. C, col. 4, p. 17(L).

William Manchester continues to accuse Joe McGinniss of copyright infringement. McGinniss, author of *The Last Brother,* used material from Manchester's *The Death of a President* in researching his biography of Ted Kennedy. McGinniss' camp claims the information to be facts in the *public domain* and not subject to copyright. Booksellers are pleased with the publicity. It's sure to enhance sales.

382. McGinniss, Joe. "Credit Check." *New York* 26, no. 29 (26 July 1993): 6–8.

[Letters.]

The author expresses outrage at being accused of plagiarizing information he readily admits using from Manchester's book *The Death of a President*. McGinniss defends his use of the information stating that facts included in his soon to be published, *The Last Brother,* are in the public domain. See John Taylor's "Clip Job II" same issue p. 14–15 for more detailed coverage of the concepts involved.

383. Taylor, John. "Clip Job II." *New York* 26, no. 29 (26 July 1993): 14–5.

Taylor expands on the legal possibilities if Manchester sues McGinniss over extensive duplication between *The Death of a President* and *The Last Brother*, both works about the Kennedy family. Areas of possible copyright infringement, professional "misuse" of another's work, and the concept of *fair use* are discussed. The amount of money

McGinniss stands to lose should the work not be published and his claim that the charges are politically motivated as the Kennedy family is not happy with his work are also mentioned. The work is worth reading for the concise information on misuse and copyright infringement even if the case is not of interest.

384. **"Scientific Plagiarism and the Theft of Ideas."** *Science* **261, no. 5121 (30 July 1993): 631.**
[In *Inside AAAS* edited by Karen Hopkin.]
Another conference held on defining plagiarism and procedures for dealing with it. Thankfully, the author gave the reader a concise synopsis from, if one judges the contents, a tedious, repetitive get-together with all defining the problem and offering vague solutions covered by many others in the recent past. Must define the range of plagiarism, need to educate, it is everyone's responsibility, the university should play a vital role...

385. **Corliss, Richard. "Stupid Talk-Show Tricks."** *Time* **142, no. 5 (2 August 1993): 55.**
Who owns material created for a television program, the performer or the show. David Letterman opposes owner NBC for the *Stupid Pet Tricks;* the Larry "Bud" Melman character played by Calvert De Forest opposes CBS. Conversational tone to the article.

386. **Martz, Larry. "Trashing Teddy Kennedy."** *Newsweek* **122, no. 5 (2 August 1993): 50–1.**
[Book review.]
In the controversy between William Manchester (*The Death of a President*) and Joe McGinniss (*The Last Brother*), the author believes that Simon & Schuster fanned the flames of a dispute about whether or not McGinniss plagiarized Manchester's work to sell an otherwise tiresome, dramatized recounting of Ted Kennedy's life. The Kennedy connection with the mafia, the uneven quality of resources, and the observation that the first controversial 127 pages do not closely resemble the rest of the book are discussed.

387. **Podolsky, J. D. "Inside Ted's Head."** *People Weekly* **40 (9 August 1993): 53–4.**
More a condemnation of McGinniss's sensationalism in creating less than realistic dialog in his biography of Ted Kennedy (*The Last Brother*), than a discussion of the plagiarism case. One of the few articles found that also mentions McGinniss's borrowing from Kennedy family biographer Doris Kearns Goodwin's *The Fitzgeralds and the Kennedys* as well as from *The Death of a President* by William Manchester. The author also points out that the Manchester controversy

spurred publishers Simon & Schuster to put McGinniss's book on the bookstore shelves two months ahead of schedule.

388. Walls, Jeannette. "Harvard U. Press Takes Tina to Task." *New York* 26, no. 33 (23 August 1993): 9.
Brief. The similarity in analysis and structure between David Remnick's *Waiting for the Apocalypse in Crown Heights* and Jerome R. Mintz's award winning *Hasidic People: A Place in the New World*, brings up the possibility that Remnick may have gotten a review copy of Mintz's work. Mintz and Harvard University Press "have been trying to get a simple apology or acknowledgment." Editor Tina Brown has refused. There is some question of whether the magazine offered to review Mintz's work.

389. Wickens, Barbara. "Keeping Secrets." *Maclean's* 106 (30 August 1993): 34–5.
Rights of ownership to intellectual property have become big business. Companies generally own rights to any discoveries and products created by employees, but what about the knowledge they take with them to new employment. Cases mentioned include a trade secrets case—General Motors' fight with former employee Jose Ignacio Lopez de Arriotua and Volkswagen AG, and David Letterman and NBC regarding rights to comedy skits.

390. Armstrong, John D., II. "Plagiarism: What Is It, Whom Does It Offend, and How Does One Deal with It?" *American Journal of Roentgenology* 161 (September 1993): 479–84.
Truth is a cornerstone of the academic community. It is the responsibility of all who participate to behave ethically. Part of this ethical behavior is to give recognition to the ideas of others when one is using them. The author uses references within his article to demonstrate correct and incorrect usage of another's ideas and how to reference those things borrowed. These include acknowledging an anonymous contributor from his peer review board, quoting out of context and use of blanket references. Stresses behaving responsibly by examining courses of action and weighing possible outcomes. If plagiarism is discovered it should be dealt with through collaborative effort within the community. (See responses of Haramati, Nathan, Totterman in *AJR 163:3 1994*.)

391. Brush, Stephen B. "Indigenous Knowledge of Biological Resources and Intellectual Property Rights: The Role of Anthropology." *American Anthropologist* 95, no. 3 (September 1993): 653–71.
Explains obstacles in protecting indigenous populations through property rights (1) identifying unique source of the knowledge, (2) segregating group identity and physical boundaries, (3) negotiating with the

official legal authority of the nation as they may not support native interests, and (4) identifying market value. Suggests 3 structures of payment (1) payment made to and administered by a central international agency, (2) traditional patents, copyrights, trade secrets and plant variety protection, and (3) local licensing for plant collection and interviewing. Stresses that using capitalist intellectual property rights to protect native skills should be viewed with caution. Anthropologists have much to contribute to the discussion of balancing conservation with equity for indigenous populations.

392. **"Conference Describes Complexities of Plagiarism."** *RI Newsletter* 1, no. 4 (September 1993): 6.
Summaries of the presentations at the June 21–22 Conference held by the National Institutes of Health and co-sponsored by the American Association for the Advancement of Science and the ORI. Presentations show different aspects in trying to define plagiarism and judge allegations. Ownership of joint efforts, roles of researcher and student, possibilities for tracking using electronic devices are some of the topics covered.

393. **Goodman, Kenneth. "Intellectual Property and Control."** *Academic Medicine* 68, no. 9 (September 1993): 588–91.
Biomedical research in universities has done well throughout history without emphasis on profit and controls. Science builds on itself. Restrictions that interrupt the flow of information are self defeating and contrary to the research universities provide. One of the few articles found that expresses ideas contrary to the current trend of patents on university campuses.

394. **Sorkin, David E. "Practicing Plagiarism."** *Illinois Bar Journal* 81, no. 9 (September 1993): 487–8.
Written simply, this article reminds lawyers that they must take plagiarism seriously when doing their own work. Using forms is appropriate, leaving out citations in source is not.

395. **Franke, Ann. "What Punishment Befits the Plagiarist?"** *Academe* 79, no. 5 (September/October 1993): 64.
The AAUP's statement on plagiarism allows intent as one of the criterion as well as amount taken. Faculty's judgment on penalty should be given the greatest weight as they are in best position to judge on a case by case basis. Franke does not take into account prejudicial factors and rivalry in academia as issues for exacting penalties.

396. **Taubes, Gary. "Fraud Busters: the Rise and Spectacular Fall of Walter Stewart and Ned Feder, SMI (Scientific Misconduct Investigators)."** *Lingua Franca* (September/October 1993): 47.

An excellent synopsis of the investigative careers of Walter Stewart and Ned Feder, the "self appointed ethics cops" from the NIH. Highlights the Baltimore, Darsee, Sprague, and DeLuca cases as well as the handling of the Oates plagiarism charges. Gives examples of Stewart's brash style and their unorthodox tactics in tracking possible misconduct and fraud in the scientific community. Stewart suggests that the actual reason for their dismissal and the need to stop the use of their "plagiarism machine" may be their discovery of "a plagiarism scandal that may involve *their very own superiors at the NIH.*"

397. **Mack, Toni. "Foot in the Door."** *Forbes* **152, no. 6 (13 September 1993): 150.**
Europeans, fearing being surpassed in technology industries, are preparing to fight U.S. industries over intellectual property rights. U.S. industries fear that Europeans will consider U.S. products to be in the *public domain.*

398. **Crawford, M. H. "Plagiarism and Scientific Communication: A Cautionary Note."** *Human Biology* **65, no. 5 (October 1993): 687–8.**
A letter from the editor stating with regret that their journal contains an article allegedly plagiarized. Even with their careful scrutiny, the article slipped by them. He quotes *Webster's* definition, informs readers that authors sign forms stating the work is original, and states that plagiarism undermines the scientific process.

399. **Slaughter, Sheila, and Gary Rhoades. "Changes in Intellectual Property Statutes and Policies at a Public University: Revising the Terms of Professional Labor."** *Higher Education* **26, no. 3 (October 1993): 287–312.**
A study on the commercialization of science conducted at University of Arizona tracks the changes in attitude and policy at the academic and state level. Practices in the 1960s reflected a distinct separation of university from private enterprise, with faculty having "free time" to pursue individual interests. Current trends have the state frequently the initiator of the proposal, with faculty in the role of labor for hire and the administration controlling intellectual property rights.

400. **Anderson, Christopher. "Michigan Gets an Expensive Lesson."** *Science* **262, no. 5130 (1 October 1993): 23.**
The University of Michigan and Marion Perlmutter owe Carolyn Phinney $1,246,000 in damages and interest fees. Perlmutter was found guilty of plagiarizing Phinney's research in a grant request to the NSF. Phinney filed charges under the Whistleblower's Act against Richard Adelman, director of the institute and responsible for the investigation.

401. Fialkoff, Francine. "Inside Track: There's No Excuse for Plagiarism." *Library Journal* **118, no. 17 (15 October 1993): 56.**
Reviewers, particularly librarians, have the opportunity and frequently the expertise to identify instances of plagiarism. The Joe McGinniss biography of Edward M. Kennedy is used as an example.

402. Maes, Marc. "ARS Is Seeing Double in Dispute Over Dance Album." *Billboard* **105, no. 45 (6 November 1993): 55.**
Brief. Belgian ARS accuses Arcade France, with whom they had discussed a similar arrangement, of stealing their idea. The product in question is a collection of dance music. ARS claims Arcade France released a similar produce which cut deeply into their profits. Arcade claims an "unpleasant coincidence."

403. Gates, David. "Not with My Life, You Don't." *Newsweek* **122, no. 19 (8 November 1993): 81.**
British poet Stephen Spender is suing American author David Leavitt for plagiarism and for denying Spender's moral right to not have his work debased in any way. Spender's main objection may be the portrayal of his homosexuality in scenes he considers pornographic. Leavitt does not deny *While England Sleeps* is based on an episode found in *World Within World*. Publication in England is delayed pending court ruling.

404. Himelstein, Linda. "Investors Wanted—for Lawsuits." *Business Week*, **no. 3346 (15 November 1993): 78.**
Patent holders are seeking backers to allow them to afford the extensive costs involved in intellectual property suits against major corporations. Success rates appear to show moderate to good return for the investment.

405. Kranich, Nancy C. "The Selling of Cyberspace: Can Libraries Protect Public Access?" *Library Journal* **118, no. 19 (15 November 1993): 34–7.**
The National Information Infrastructure must support "public space" for use by educational and research institutions, libraries, non-profit organizations and government institutions because the private sector tends to exclude the societal good. Such areas as literacy and job training are overlooked. Libraries as politically neutral institutions must fight to retain this space. Guidelines for accessibility, diversity of providers, community service, interoperability, ease of use, and intellectual property protection on the Information Highway are listed. Includes a sidebar on actions librarians can take.

406. DeLoughry, Thomas J. "Computers and Copyrights." *Chronicle of Higher Education* **40, no. 14 (24 November 1993): A15–16.**

In hearings held by the Working Group on Intellectual Property Rights, a subsection of the White House Information Infrastructure Task Force, representatives from publishing and education supported existing laws and contracts for regulation of electronic sources. Librarians expressed concerns for institutions that could not afford contractual fees.

407. Sussman, Vic. "Policing the Digital World." *U.S. News & World Report* 115, no. 22 (6 December 1993): 68, 70.

As access and increased volumes of information become available on electronic computer networks, there is an increase in will by our social and legal communities to regulate that medium. We must be cautious not to allow over-regulation, overlooking our individual rights of free speech, privacy and protection of intellectual property. Areas of concern are already being addressed within the market itself through licensing agreements, "shareware" and offering the public ways in which to suppress access to personal data and computer files.

408. DeLoughry, Thomas J. "Remaking Scholarly Publishing." *Chronicle of Higher Education* 40, no. 17 (15 December 1993): 15–17.

The increased cost of purchasing scholarly publications and the availability of electronic access have forced universities to re-examine the traditional handling of scholarly publications. Those opposing the current system say publishers take intellectual property produced by university employees and sell it back at considerable markup. Supporters remind of the added value publishers provide in evaluating, editing, publishing and reprinting and the role played by small printing houses and university presses. Topics such as "work for hire" contracts, and some of the difficulties in resource sharing for the more costly foreign titles are also covered.

409. "Intellectual Property Under GATT." *Nature* 366, no. 6456 (16 December 1993): 587–8.

The academic community should be more actively involved in the formulation of the terms of protection of intellectual property in GATT (General Agreement on Tariffs and Trade) as the current system has outlived applicability. Currently, the treaty states that each government may maintain its present system for 4 years, giving time for negotiations to occur among member nations. Current policy supports the need for inventors to reap material reward and monopoly rights on exploitation. The policy also echoes that if the inventor fails to exploit the patent, others will, and that governments may override the inventor's right and replace it with a royalty or licensing agreement.

410. Swinbanks, David. "Survey Battle Leads to Plagiarism Verdict." *Nature* 366, no. 6457 (23 December 1993): 715.

After a $2.1 million court battle, the first verdict of plagiarism for the scientific community has been upheld by the appeal court. Lam Tai Hing, University of Hong Kong, has been found guilty of plagiarizing the questionnaire of Linda Koo. This verdict has also placed a more confining status on use of researchers' questionnaires. Gives chronological summary of the case and includes comments by Richard Peto and Robert Maclennan, expert witnesses in the case.

411. Armstrong, John D., II. "Response." *American Journal of Roentgenology* 163, no. 3 (1994): 727–30.

Armstrong gives a summary of his article by stating "truth in teaching and research is the distinctive underpinning of the academic professional." In response to Drs. Haramati, Armi, and Roy. (See pages 725–727 of this issue for their remarks.) While medical endeavors are collaborative efforts, in this particular work, the manuscript was significantly revised because of the reviewer's comments. Truth demands that others be aware of this. To Dr. Totterman, avoiding plagiarism also supports respecting the ideas and efforts of colleagues. To Dr. Nathan, common knowledge in one area may not be common knowledge to someone in another area. Citation is important. Writers may ask editors for guidelines beyond the journal's usual scope if it seems appropriate for giving credit. An error of page number in a citation should not be construed as plagiarism. Finally, Nathan's own experiences in which others usurped his work emphasizes the need that reviewers be trustworthy. To Dr. Roy again, general references are common in unpublished materials. Acknowledgment is seen by the reviewer even if the writer is unaware of the name of the person.

412. Bloch, R. Howard. *God's Plagiarist*. Chicago and London: The University of Chicago Press, 1994.

The author recounts the exploits of the abbé Jacque-Paul Migne, creator of a publishing empire in France during the mid–1800s. Migne is best known for the *Petrologia Latina* and *Petrologia Greca*, tomes of writings from church patriarchs published to bring the Protestants back to the church. The sheer volume of works published (400 books plus the million plus pages of the *Petrologia*) defies imagination. Migne's methods and justification for publishing without recognition for the original author or royalties to the publishers showed plagiarism on a grand scale. Notes, subject and name indices.

413. Haramati, Nogah, and E. Stephen Amis, Jr. "Plagiarism: An Odious Accusation. Worst If False." *American Journal of Roentgenology* 163, no. 3 (1994): 725–6.

Suggests that Armstrong's article "Plagiarism: What Is It, Whom Does It Offend and How Does One Deal with It?" (*AJR* 1993;161: 479–484) might be too restrictive for the scientific community as many journal publishing guidelines request that only the most relevant, useful references be cited. Referencing practices should not be based on fear of being labeled a plagiarist. (See Armstrong's response on pages 727–730 of the same issue.)

414. **Nathan, M. Herbert. "Variations of Plagiarism."** *American Journal of Roentgenology* **163, no. 3 (1994): 727.**
Describes a personal experience in which a panel member from a grant review board presented the writer's proposal at a national event without giving proper credit. There is definitely a need for Armstrong's article. (See Armstrong's response on pages 727–730 of the same issue.)

415. **Roy, S. "Anonymous Reference: A Contradiction in Terms?"** *American Journal of Roentgenology* **163, no. 3 (1994): 726.**
Armstrong's use of giving credit to an anonymous reviewer, although appealing, opposes the reason for giving credit to the originator. (Armstrong's article "Plagiarism: What Is It, Whom Does It Offend and How Does One Deal with It?" AJR 1993;161: 479–484.) If use of comments from reviewers is indeed plagiarism, he should have taken a different approach. He might have requested the reviewer's name or possibly given co-author status if the contribution was substantial. (See Armstrong's response on pages 727–730 of the same issue.)

416. **Totterman, S. M. "Whose Work Is It Anyway?"** *American Journal of Roentgenology* **163, no. 3 (1994): 726-7.**
Response to J. D. Armstrong's article "Plagiarism: What Is It, Whom Does It Offend, and How Does One Deal with It?" (*AJR* 1993; 161: 479–484.) Considers the crime of taking credit for another's work to promote one's self to be the more serious crime of plagiarism. Gives guidelines of academic responsibility. (See Armstrong's response on pages 727–730 of the same issue.)

417. **Pepall, Lynne M., and Daniel J. Richards. "Innovation, Imitation, and Social Welfare."** *Southern Economic Journal* **60, no. 3 (January 1994): 673-84.**
An economic study of the implications that imitation has on product quality and social welfare and specifically the ratio of imitation to innovative costs. The quality of the product created will vary. In a monopoly, to keep a market, the quality must be high with a high production cost to any who try to imitate, but the quality must not be too high to discourage the market. Found that 40% of all products studied

had not been duplicated. Suggests we need to rethink some of the traditional patent and regulatory policy. Contains economic equations comprehensible to the general reader.

418. **Rogers, Michael. "Librarians Foresee Threat to Copyright."** *Library Journal* **119, no. 1 (January 1994): 36.**
Report on testimony of Robert Oakley (American Association of Law Libraries) to the Working Group on Intellectual Property. Oakley stresses the need to maintain the current protections for *fair use* and owner compensation.

419. **Walls, Jeannette. "Time vs. Times: The 10 Most Vaunted."** *New York* **26, no. 1 (4 January 1994): 7.**
Very brief note in the *Intelligencer* section. Rebecca Sinkler, editor of the *Book Review,* questions similarities between a review of the same list of 10 children's books first appearing in *The New York Times Book Review* and later *Time* magazine. A *Time* spokesperson supported Stefan Kanfer (*Time* reviewer) based on Kanfer's 20 years of reviewing children's books.

420. **Magner, Denise K. "Verdict in a Plagiarism Case."** *Chronicle of Higher Education* **40, no. 18 (5 January 1994): A17.**
In its latest finding against Stephen Oates, the American Historical Association found him guilty of borrowing too much material for his historic biographies of William Faulkner, Nat Turner, and Martin Luther King, Jr. from previous works, but did not find him guilty of plagiarism. Mr. Oates has threatened to sue if he does not get a retraction. Both Oates and Walter Stewart, one of the scientists who brought the case to the AHA, question the redefining of plagiarism by the AHA during the process.

421. **"Sports Columnist Is Suspended."** *Editor & Publisher* **127, no. 3 (15 January 1994): 13.**
Kansas City Star sports columnist Gib Twyman was suspended for 3 weeks after readers accused him of stealing a story from *Sports Illustrated*. He admits to sloppy writing, but claims the idea for the story came from a weekly media lunch held by Chiefs coach Marty Schottenheimer.

422. **Cordes, Colleen. "University Patents Barred."** *Chronicle of Higher Education* **40, no. 20 (19 January 1994): A29.**
New rules set for those participating in the Advanced Technology Program under the Department of Commerce have the universities and colleges ruffled. Under the new plan, universities and colleges would not be able to file for patents on anything developed under the agreements.

They would have the right to negotiate publication interests in these joint ventures. This program is at odds with other government programs, but, as was pointed out by federal officials, the program is to aid private industry, not academia.

423. "Intellectual Property ... Is Theft." *Economist* **330, no. 7847 (22 January 1994): 72–3.**
The new 20 year rule stated under GATT in TRIPS (Trade Related Intellectual Property) has many less developed countries concerned. Under those rules developers of new drugs, software creators, and owners of trademarks have sole use rights for 20 years. Their argument, that protection is needed to encourage research and development. Opposers are concerned that life saving drugs will be too high priced to benefit those in poorer countries. Since the rule is part of GATT, failure to comply may threaten a country's membership in GATT.

424. Gottlieb, Anthony. "Did Sartre Ever Exist?" *The New York Times Book Review,* **23 January 1994, sec. 7, col. 1, pp. 12–13.**
Believes Kate and Edward Fullbrook's book *The Remaking of a Twentieth Century Legend* is trying too hard to find that Sartre used the ideas of his companion Simone De Beauvoir. He suggests the Fullbrooks delve beyond comparison of their novels and into their philosophical arguments.

425. Lyall, Sarah. "Viking and Spender Near Settlement." *The New York Times,* **28 January 1994, sec. C, col. 3, p. 3.**
The dispute between Stephen Spender (*World Within World)* and David Leavitt (*While England Sleeps)* is reaching settlement. The destruction of unsold copies of Leavitt's novel and whether Spender will need to "sign off" on the revisions proposed by Leavitt are the only areas that remain to be solved. The results indicate how much more stringent English law respects the "moral rights" of ownership.

426. _____. "Spender Rediscovered." *The New York Times,* **2 February 1994, sec. C, col. 3, p. 18(L).**
Brief. The plagiarism charges against David Leavitt by Stephen Spender, 85-year-old British poet, are being resolved to the satisfaction of Mr. Spender. A book of his poetry is being re-issued, and his *World Within World* is being republished with an updated foreword outlining the controversy with Leavitt on *While England Sleeps.* Publicity from the incident will aid sales of both works.

427. Hilts, Philip J. "Scientists Lament Inaction on Abuse." *The New York Times,* **6 February 1994, sec. 1, col. 1, p. 23(L).**
The National Academy of Sciences, the Institute of Medicine and the

National Academy of Engineering are disappointed that suggestions made to attack misconduct in science have not been adopted. The community has not drafted or adopted guidelines and standards higher than simple legal definition. Two problems that need addressing are that those who commit a crime can simply move to another institution with their records kept secret, and those judging misconduct may have a conflict of interest. They are holding a meeting to draw attention to the issue, maybe in May.

428. Massie, Robert K. "Safire and Me." *Nation* 258, no. 6 (14 February 1994): 184–5.

Massie steps through the 1958 incident in which material given to Safire was subsequently used in an article which appeared in *Esquire* written by Theodore Irwin. Massie's charges of plagiarism were settled out of court for $1000. He believes Safire, in not disclosing the source of the information, was an accomplice in plagiarism. He offers the incident in support of Bobby Ray Inman's charge that Safire is a plagiarist. Safire disagrees.

429. Rosenthal, A. M. "Five Honest Men." *The New York Times*, 15 February 1994, sec. A, col. 1, p. 21(L).

Praises investigative reporter John Corry for "taking on" the *Village Voice* by denouncing their accusation of plagiarism against Jerzy Kosinski, an avowed anti–Communist, with a detailed investigation of his own. He found their accusation to be "cruelly false." Corey's honesty has made him a target for their wrath. The author also applauds persons of integrity he admires in other professions.

430. "Viking and Spender Settle Dispute." *The New York Times*, 17 February 1994, sec. C, p. 24(L).

David Leavitt will rewrite sections of *While England Sleeps* as specified in the settlement of the lawsuit brought by poet Stephen Spender. Spender sued Leavitt in October, claiming the memoirs too closely resembled his own work *World Within World*. He found the explicit sex offensive. Viking will be reissuing the edited version. Copies of the original are not being recalled.

431. Atlas, James. "Who Owns a Life? Asks a Poet, When His Is Turned Into Fiction." *The New York Times*, 20 February 1994, sec. 4, col. 1, p. E14(N), E14(L).

Eighty-five-year-old British poet Stephen Spender was less concerned that author David Leavitt borrowed his life for the main theme of his current novel *While England Sleeps,* than with the possibility that Leavitt's sexual fantasies might be construed as part of Spender's life. Leavitt intended his work to praise the poet by more explicitly addressing issues of sexual identity and freedom in a time that allows such expression. Leavitt has agreed to rewrite the offending passages. Viking Press has stopped the sale of *While England Sleeps*; it will publish a new edition as soon as author David Leavitt has done rewrites to remove explicit homosexual love scenes.

432. "Leavitt Novel Withdrawn After Spender Suit." *Publishers Weekly* 241, no. 8 (21 February 1994): 10.
Short blurb announcing that David Leavitt will rewrite portions of *While England Sleeps* in response to claims from Sir Stephen Spender that Leavitt took information from his autobiography, *World Within Worlds*. Viking is withdrawing current copies of Leavitt's work.

433. Hamilton, Ian. "Spender's Lives." *The New Yorker* 70, no. 2 (28 February 1994): 72–6+.
An in depth portrait of Stephen Spender. The author had met Spender in the 1960s and again for this article. As before, Spender was both saintly and political, a balancing of the ethereal with the practical, and always entertaining. In the brief reference to the lawsuit Spender has with David Leavitt over passages in *While England Sleeps*, Hamilton includes comments by Natasha, Spender's wife. Hers, some friends suggest, is the driving force behind his pursuing the matter.

434. Lesperance, Robert J. "What Is Intellectual Property?" *Canadian Veterinary Journal* 35, no. 3 (March 1994): 185–7.
Patents, trademarks, copyright and trade secrets are defined. They are part of doing business and those in the veterinary field should be aware of the rights and restrictions. Article appears in a side-by-side format, the left column is English and right column is French. General audience.

435. Tennille, Norton F. "A Rock, a River, a Tree/ A Poetic Controversy." *Harper's* 288 (March 1994): 28–30.
[From a letter written by Norton F. Tennille, Jr. to M. Campbell Cawood regarding Maya Angelou's poem *On the Pulse of Morning*. The poem was given at President Clinton's inauguration in January 1993.]
Tennille believes his poem *Outward Bound* influenced style and content of Professor Angelou's poem. He is not accusing Angelou of plagiarism, but suggests that she may have seen his poem while visiting North Carolina Outward Bound School or offices. In reading the introductory paragraph summarizing earlier parts of the letter, there is a strong sense that political pressure has softened Mr. Tennille's response.

436. **Pallone, Nathaniel J., and James J. Hennessy. "Benevolent Misdiag-
nosis." *Society* 31, no. 3 (March/April 1994): 11–17.**
Mentions in general terms an incident of plagiarism by an associate
professor and the lack of reprisal from peers. Refers to Michael T.
Ghiselin's *Intellectual Compromise*. Article is more useful for those
researching fraud in the sciences who are looking for a critical view
of the acceptance of fraud for the "right reasons."

437. **Bray, Robert. "Reading Between the Texts: Benjamin Thomas's *Abra-
ham Lincoln* and Stephen Oates's *With Malice Toward None*."
Journal of Information Ethics 3, no. 1 (Spring 1994): 8–24.**
Uses parallel copy, referred to as "intertextual relationships," and
Oates's own definition of biography, to show Oates' plagiarized
Thomas', and is a poor example of biography. Notes. (See Oates'
rebuttal on pages 25–41 of the same issue.)

438. **Burlingame, Michael. "'A Sin Against Scholarship'; Some Examples
of Plagiarism in Stephen B. Oates's Biographies of Abraham Lincoln, Martin Luther King, Jr., and William Faulkner." *Journal of
Information Ethics* 3, no. 1 (Spring 1994): 48–57.**
Parallelisms show pattern and content, supporting allegations that
Oates is a plagiarist. The similarities in Lincoln's biography may have
come from identical sources, but that does not hold true for the parallelisms found in his other biographies. At the author's request,
prominent personalities outside the AHA reviewed the biographies.
Those quoted found Oates' work plagiarism and a "disgusting, slimy,
dishonesty at its zenith...," "no longer ... plausible that the similar
phraseology ... can really be coincidental." Includes 7 pages of parallel passages from the three biographies.

439. **Current, Richard N. "Concerning the Charge of Plagiarism Against
Stephen B. Oates." *Journal of Information Ethics* 3, no. 1 (Spring
1994): 78–9.**
The author points out that he has disagreed with Oates on a number
of issues, but supports him in disavowing plagiarism. First, the information was in *public domain*, not the property of Thomas; second, the
biographies are different books. The AHA should devote its time to
investigating serious cases involving theft of ideas, not scattered
matches of words.

440. **Jones, Robert E. "Popular Biography, Plagiarism, and Persecution."
Journal of Information Ethics 3, no. 1 (Spring 1994): 80–2.**
Oates has successfully bridged the gap between scholar and writer for
the general population. Writing in the popular realm uses a different
set of rules. It requires repeating facts about the person's life and a

more friendly writing style without the intrusion of footnotes. Jones praises Oates' works and questions the motives of his accusers.

441. **Kozak, Ellen M. "Towards a Definition of Plagiarism: The Bray/Oates Controversy Revisited."** *Journal of Information Ethics* **3, no. 1 (Spring 1994): 70–5.**
Plagiarism and copyright differ before the law and *fair use* grays the edges. For example, a scholar using part of another's work in their work might be *fair use*, but if not acknowledged properly, might also be plagiarism. As a scholar, Oates should know that plagiarism is more than copying words. The law has changed since Linsey's work in 1952 and since Thomas is not alive to protect his interests, it is proper that fellow scholars should protect the image of historical scholarship.

442. **Oates, Stephen. "'A Horse Chestnut In Not a Chestnut Horse': A Refutation of Bray, Davis, MacGregor, and Wollan."** *Journal of Information Ethics* **3, no. 1 (Spring 1994): 25–41.**
In his rebuttal, Oates suggests that Bray and others have less than honorable reasons for their allegations. He agrees that there are intertextual similarities among biographies of Lincoln as all used the same sources. He cites examples and points out that Thomas and Sandburg were not original either. His style is one of standard practice for one volume biographies for general audiences. Includes an example of how his and Thomas' interpretations differ, and includes scholars who discredit Bray's accusations. (See Bray's article on pages 8–24.)

443. **Swan, John. "Sharing and Stealing: Persistent Ambiguities."** *Journal of Information Ethics* **3, no. 1 (Spring 1994): 42–47.**
That Oates is not a member of AHA is not an argument. His claim that only Lincoln scholars should judge his style is false But his questioning the definition of plagiarism is valid and gives ambiguity to the case. By a Feder/Stewart definition there is clear support for a case, while among colleagues, who may have their own reasons for supporting the scholarship of a peer, there may be no grounds for the accusations.

444. **Trefousse, Hans L. "The Oates Case."** *Journal of Information Ethics* **3, no. 1 (Spring 1994): 76–7.**
Supports Oates as an innovative biographer. He finds the emphasis of the works by Thomas much different than those of Oates, stating that Oates had the benefit of recent findings not available to Thomas. Reiterates that same sources and secondary sources are going to produce some similarity in coverage.

445. **Wollan, Laurin A., Jr. "Plagiarism and the Art of Copying."** *Journal of Information Ethics* **3, no. 1 (Spring 1994): 58–64.**
Plagiarism is not quotation, but is borrowing closely from another. In the case of Stephen Oates, does the copy fall short of plagiarism? Wollen uses a series of questions in his parallelisms to involve the reader in the comparison process. He also questions whether biographies become "bardlike" after many renditions and that some fields support "comradely reciprocity." The author makes only a small reference to electronic copying, and none to his use of computer programming to run his comparisons. The tone is one of discussion, not the "flaming" accusatory voice I was expecting after reading Oates' rebuttal of Wollan's charges.

446. **Yanikoski, Charles S. "When the Trial Is the Punishment: The Ethics of Plagiarism Accusations."** *Journal of Information Ethics* **3, no. 1 (Spring 1994): 83–8.**
The accusation of plagiarism is as damaging as the conviction, and all involved are marked equally whether accuser or accused. Persons reporting plagiarism should first contact the suspected, then the institution and examine personal motivation for bringing charges. Publicity should come only after the adjudication of the complaint. The Oates case shows how not to present charges. We will always have plagiarism and accusers. It is the responsibility of institutions to have clear definitions, policies and guidelines for processing the claims. The author, in his zeal to support his idea, neglects to point out that one of the major complaints by whistleblowers is the lack of punishment for the offender. They are frequently promoted, or at worst, hired by another institution at higher salary.

447. **Zangrando, Robert L. "A Crying Need for Discourse."** *Journal of Information Ethics* **3, no. 1 (Spring 1994): 65–9.**
The AHA should make the terms of the Oates case public and Oates should stop his threats of legal action against those who do not support his stance. To do less damages the image and effectiveness of the scholarly community. References many articles about the Oates case.

448. **Fitzpatrick, Eileen. "Court Rules for Good Times in 'McClintock!' Suit."** *Billboard* **106, no. 20 (14 March 1994): 73, 82.**
Good Times Home Video has retained the rights to distribute the John Wayne film *McClintock!* MPI Home Video had claimed that its licensing rights to music in the film protected its sole rights even though the film is in *public domain.* The courts disagreed.

449. **Baker, Russ W. "Painted Words."** *Village Voice* **39, no. 11 (15 March 1994): 58–9.**

Discusses the controversy between Geoffrey Stokes and Eliot Fremont-Smith, and John Corry's coverage of Jerzy Kosinski's ethics and the authenticity of his works. In a personal conversation with Michael Caruso, Chris Calhoun and Stokes, Kosinski denied connections with the CIA but did not refute that others assisted him editorially.

450. **Morrisy, Jane. "Judge Extends Microsoft's Deadline in Stac Case." *PC Week* 11, no. 11 (21 March 1994): 135.**
Brief. The battle between Microsoft and Stac Electronics continues. Microsoft paid $120 million to Stac to use DoubleStacker. Stac's type of reverse engineering to integrate Stacker with MS-DOS cost them $13.6 million to Microsoft. The companies feel some arrangement can be worked out.

451. **Zurer, Pamela. "Chemistry Panel Weighs Misconduct Cases." *Chemical & Engineering News* 72, no. 12 (21 March 1994): 18.**
Ohio State University chemistry panel has found professor Leo A. Paquette to be guilty of misconduct in his using information gained as an NIH reviewer in one of his own publications. For this he was barred from NIH reviewing for 10 years. The committee found the condensed and paraphrased sections in an NSF proposal to be sloppy work, not plagiarism. Fellow chemists concur. The committee states that recommendations to reduce the size of Paquette's research staff to a more manageable 20 are based on the NIH findings, not the NSF incident.

452. **Bugeja, Michael J. "Poetic Theft." *Writer's Digest* 74, no. 4 (April 1994): 12–15.**
Plagiarism not only robs the poet of his recognition, it also takes space and editorial time that could have been used for original work. The most common type of plagiarism in poetry is changing the title and first line, the indexing points used by index and abstract services. Legal strategies from law professor Dr. Guido Stempel and examples of plagiarized works are given along with a brief summary of the Bowers' case.

453. **Linna, Donna E., and Sami Gülgöz. "Effects of Random Response Generation on Cryptomnesia." *Psychological Reports* 74, no. 2 (April 1994): 387–92.**
Follow-up study on Brown and Murphy (1989) testing the theory that having respondents answer in random order would decrease the amount of plagiarism. The theory proved false. The subject's awareness of when his turn would come had no appreciable affect on the occurrence of cryptomnesia.

454. Leavitt, David. "Did I Plagiarize His Life?" *The New York Times,* **3 April 1994, sec. 6, col. 1, pp. 36–7.**

Leavitt explains that his use of an incident in Stephen Spender's life as portrayed in *World Within World* was the catalyst for his novel *While England Sleeps*. Ideas grow from the ideas of others; it is part of the creative process. The incidents that caused concern covered perhaps 10 pages in his novel. He believes the lack of First Amendment protection in the British legal system and the ambivalent treatment of homosexuality in British culture led to the accusations.

455. "Publisher Withdraws a Novel About India." *The New York Times,* **19 April 1994, sec. C, col. 3, p. 19(L).**

Brief. Because of its similarity in plot and descriptions to *The Rosemary Tree* by Elizabeth Goudge, Ballentine Books has stopped distribution of copies of *Cranes' Morning* by Indian author Indrani Aikath-Gyaltsen. Rights for publication were bought from Penguin India.

456. Lyall, Sarah. "Almost Identical Twins." *The New York Times,* **20 April 1994, sec. C, col. 3, p. 19(L).**

A librarian and a Canadian reader each reported *Cranes' Morning* by Indriani Aikath-Gyaltsen was quite similar to Elizabeth Goudge's *The Rosemary Tree*. U.S. publisher, Ballantine Books has stopped selling and marketing the book. Orion Publishing in London has not decided whether to go ahead with publication or not.

457. "Digital Banditry in China." *Economist* **331, no. 7860 (23 April 1994): 70.**

Theft of intellectual property through piracy has become a hot issue in Sino-American relations. American business hopes that recent efforts by China to crack down on the copyright and patent abuse are not just a ruse to gain admittance to the World Trade Organization. Deng Rong's fury over the blatant copying of her biography of her father, Deng Xiaoping, may also have spurred some action to prosecute violators.

458. Greene, Donna. "Dr. Burton Leiser: When, If Ever, the End Justifies the Means." *The New York Times,* **24 April 1994, sec. 14, col. 1, p. 3(L).**

A brief paragraph in an article on teaching ethics. Most students do not realize that plagiarism is wrong. They need to be told.

459. Hearn, Michael Patrick. "Did I Plagiarize His Life?" *The New York Times Magazine,* **24 April 1994, sec. 6, p. 12(L).**

[Letters.]

Finds Leavitt's role as victim appalling. Leavitt had the right to write anything he wished, but did he betray a moral obligation to Spender's right to privacy?

460. **Lehrman, Sally. "Stanford Falls in Line on Conflict of Interest Rules."** *Nature* **368, no. 6474 (28 April 1994): 787.**
Stanford has changed its rules. Rights for inventions will belong to the university, not the faculty member. The university will retain the right to patent; the copyright remains with the inventor. The new policy also requires faculty to be on campus frequently and to "commit their scholarly expertise, efforts and research primarily to Stanford." Deans are given the authority to decide if conflict of interest matters on a given project are "manageable." One dean commented that the ruling will change little, but might limit gifts and other financial contributions from outside companies to specific faculty. The rules are in anticipation of the NIH and NSF requiring financial oversight.

461. **Conrad, Brad. "Did I Plagiarize His Life?"** *The New York Times Magazine,* **1 May 1994, sec. 6, p. 18(L).**
[Letters.]
Brief. Hopes Leavitt will come to realize that claiming another's experiences to be one's own ideas is truly an invasion of privacy.

462. **Lyall, Sarah. "'J.F.K.' Author Sued."** *The New York Times,* **12 May 1994, sec. C, col. 3, p. 20(L).**
[Book notes.]
Brief. Gene Schoor, author of *Young John Kennedy* sues Nigel Hamilton (*JFK: Reckless Youth*) for using parts of his research without acknowledgment or payment. Requests $20 million in damages. Schoor states his inability to find a lawyer who would accept the case on contingency delayed his bringing the complaint to court for two years.

463. **Gillen, Marilyn A. "Curry's Internet Service Draws MTV Suit."** *Billboard* **106, no. 21 (21 May 1994): 12, 77.**
MTV Network is suing former employee V. J. Adam Curry, claiming his internet site *mtv.com* infringes on trademarks, unfair competition and deceptive trade practices. Curry disputes any confusion, stating the site displays many disclaimers of non-affiliation with the network. Curry believes the suit is in retaliation for his resignation as MTVN had expressed its blessing on the venture, but not in writing and now that the venture is successful, they want the internet address for their own use.

464. **Holtzman, Jeff. "David and Goliath (or) Bill's Bad, Awful Day."** *Electronics Now* **65, no. 6 (June 1994): 27–8.**

Stac has been awarded $120 million in its patent infringement case against Microsoft; Stac Electronics has lost $13.7 million to Microsoft in a misappropriation of trade secrets. The products in question are software compression programs for use with MS-DOS (Microsoft), and Netware and DR-DOS (Stac/Novell) products respectively. The question for product users is how long will Microsoft and Stac continue product support.

465. **Johns, Alessa. "Mary Hamilton, Daniel Defoe, and a Case of Plagiarism in Eighteenth-Century England."** *English Language Notes* **31, no. 4 (June 1994): 25+.**
The author proposes that although Hamilton borrowed extensively from Defoe in style and theme, she used that popular style to convey a social commentary on a woman's place beyond marriage and the supernatural. Article includes a parallel passage from Hamilton's *Munster Village* and Defoe's *Political History of the Devil.*

466. **Julliard, Kell MFA. "Perceptions of Plagiarism in the Use of Other Authors' Language."** *Family Medicine* **26, no. 6 (June 1994): 356–60.**
Survey to determine if perceptions of plagiarism among medical faculty, English faculty, medical students and editors differ with physicians. The questionnaire involved using quotation marks versus just giving reference to the source. Exerpts were taken from medical journal article and linked to test samples for comparison by the subjects. Results indicated physicians perceived reference to be enough, quotation marks were not expected. All other groups held a more restrictive definition of plagiarism. Writers might avoid inadvertent plagiarism if publishers and academics used standard guidelines.

467. **Freedman, Morris. "The Persistence of Plagiarism, the Riddle of Originality."** *The Virginia Quarterly Review* **70, no. 3 (Summer 1994): 504–17.**
Voices concern that plagiarism is too easily accepted today. It is not just theft; it takes a person's originality, his self image. It threatens the basic right to property and personal identity. Cites Mark Rose's *Author's and Owners: The Invention of Copyright, 1993,* on development of the concept and legal parameters of copyright.

468. **Anderson, A. J. "A Lesson in Plagiarism 101."** *Library Journal* **119, no. 10 (1 June 1994): 80+.**
A case study in which an academic librarian is made aware that a student she assisted plagiarized from material she provided. Fear for personal safety versus ethical behavior are the main points of discussion that follow.

469. **"Court Dismisses Suit by Wiesel's Publisher."** *The New York Times,* **8 June 1994, sec. A, col. 1, p. 16(L).**
    Brief. Jacques Attali was accused of stealing 43 passages from interviews with French President Mitterrand conducted by Elie Wiesel. No attribution was given to Wiesel in Attali's book, *Verbatim.* The court ordered Wiesel's publisher to pay legal costs to Editions Fayard, Attali's publisher, but dismissed Fayard's countersuit for $615,000 in damages.

470. **"Court Dismisses Wiesel Suit Against Attali Publisher."** *Wall Street Journal,* **8 June 1994, sec. A, col. 5, p. 13(E).**
    Plagiarism charges brought by Editions Odile Jacob against Librairie Artheme Fayard, alleging Jaques Attali "stole" 43 passages from interviews of Francois Mitterand by Elie Wiesel in his memoir *Verbatim.* Claims were dismissed by the French courts. The plaintiff failed to establish that Fayard publishers had even incomplete knowledge of the discussion between Wiesel and the president. It also rejected Wiesel's publisher's request for damages against expected loss of sales from a book scheduled to be written by Wiesel based on the interviews and dismissed Fayard's countersuit for damages.

471. **Clark, Tim. "Government Tackles Rights Issues."** *Advertising Age* **65, no. 29 (11 June 1994): 24.**
    In an effort to promote the information super highway, the Clinton Administration, in a report released by Ron Brown, urges that copyright laws be revised to include electronic transmissions as well as books, movies, etc. A group of 18 federal agencies will hold conferences to develop guidelines for *fair use* and a curriculum to educate the public about intellectual property laws. Sidebar bullets show recommended policy changes.

472. **Jayaraman, K. S. "Fossil Inquiry Finds Indian Geologist Guilty of Plagiarism."** *Nature* **369, no. 6483 (30 June 1994): 698.**
    Brief. Article would be more accurately indexed as fraud in research. Indian geologist Viswa Jit Gupta is found guilty of fraud—recycling fossils, claiming discoveries on sites he never visited and plagiarism.

473. **Nigg, Herbert N., and Gabriella Radulescu. "Scientific Misconduct in Environmental Science and Toxicology."** *Journal of the American Medical Association* **272, no. 2 (July 1994): 168–70.**
    Gives synopses of 4 cases of misconduct (no names are listed) discovered by peer review and editorial review at the *Bulletin.* The authors were from out of country. The institutions employing the authors did not reprimand, but the *Bulletin* did. No articles containing citations from the authors will be accepted for publication. The list of names was sent to all editors and editorial boards.

474. Jayaraman, K. S. "Intellectual Property Dispute Hits U.S.–India Science Accord." *Nature* 370, no. 6484 (7 July 1994): 9.
      U.S. and Indian relations as research partners seem to be waning again as the 1997 renewal of their agreement approaches. In joining GATT, India must change its intellectual property laws to conform with international standards, but the 5 year compliance window is too lenient for U.S. participants.

475. "Microsoft's Brush with Regulators." *Nature* 370, no. 6486 (21 July 1994): 163.
      The rise of Microsoft has brought with it charges of unfair practices. The author suggests that Microsoft license a core product to competitors and market the "bells and whistles" and the upgrades separately. If this sounds familiar, it is the basis for shareware software.

476. Farber, Michael. "But Don't Call Them Colts." *Sports Illustrated* 81, no. 4 (25 July 1994): 56–9.
      The National Football League, the Indianapolis Colts and NFL Properties have brought charges of trademark infringement against the Canadian Football League's Baltimore Colts. The courts have ruled in favor of the NFL. Speros, owner of the Baltimore team, is honoring the decision. If it is not overturned, the team stands to lose over $2 million in merchandise already carrying the Colts name. Lawyer's fees alone have already cost $250,000 and "the meter is still running."

477. "G. E. Bentley, 92, Princeton Professor." *The New York Times*, 27 July 1994, sec. D, p. 21(L).
      [Obituaries.]
      Brief. The obituary of the Princeton professor who suggested that *The Compleat Angler* by Izaac Walton was copied from an earlier British work *The Arte of Angling*. D. E. Rhodes, a British authority on fishing literature, was quick to defend Walton on the grounds that plagiarism was not a consideration in Britain in the 17th century.

478. Holland, Bill. "RIAA Likes Administration's Position on C'Rights, Berman to Testify." *Billboard* 106, no. 31 (30 July 1994): 123.
      Jay Berman, Chairman/CEO of the Recording Industry Association of America, indicates that RIAA supports the recommendations in the Working Group on Intellectual Property Rights report. The report calls for extending copyright protection to digital copies, denying first-sale doctrine rights to persons such as video store owners to prevent circulation of copied tapes, and encoding all digitally transmitted works to assist in tracking and licensing copies. Holland also mentions a political *faux pas*. Secretary of Commerce Ron Brown,

himself part owner of a radio station, supported the exclusion of broadcasters from paying performance fees. The pending bill does exempt broadcasters.

479. **Durrani, Shandana. "Identical Passages Found in Two Wine Books."** *Wine Spectator* **19, no. 7 (31 July 1994): 14.**
Harper Collins is settling a matter of plagiarism with Henry Holt & Co. When the duplication between Marq de Villiers' *The Heartbreak Grape* and David Darlington's *Angels' Visits* was discovered, de Villiers blamed sloppy note taking as the cause. He inadvertently copied a computer file of notes from Darlington's book, mistaking them for interview notes with Josh Hensen of Calera Wine Co.

480. **Mallon, Thomas. "Dead Ringer."** *Gentlemen's Quarterly* **64 (August 1994): 64+.**
Mallon gives a detailed comparison of content and style in his commentary on the controversy and resulting lawsuit between British poet Stephen Spender and American novelist David Leavitt. Leavitt admitted using Spender's *World Within World* as a basis for his novel *While England Sleeps* without acknowledging the source. The main breach, in Mallon's view, was a lack of common courtesy on Leavitt's part for not respecting and valuing the memories of the aging poet. Includes references to the pieces written by each in *The New York Times*. Mallon stays Mallon in a brief aside when he questions why Leavitt, a nominee for the P.E.N./Faulkener award, should require or be given federal dollars to produce a novel.

481. **Slessor, Catherine. "Outrage."** *Architectural Review* **195, no. 1170 (August 1994): 23.**
Brief. Includes photograph. Author denounces the 3-dimensional wrought-iron gates at a Jersey home as "plagiarism" of the Van Gogh *Sunflowers*.

482. **Case, Tony. "APME Retreats on Strict Ethics Code."** *Editor & Publisher* **127, no. 33 (13 August 1994): 18–19.**
[Abstract written from a reprint of the article in ABI/Inform.]
After much unexpected discussion, the Associated Press Managing Editors have decided to update the existing ethics code instead of using the extended stricter guidelines proposed in 1993. Changes include clearly defining advertising from news, refraining from community activities that could create a conflict of interest, the addition of technological manipulation in guidelines to guard against inaccuracies and bias, and rewording statements in the code that could be considered discriminatory. Supporters believe the changes will boost public confidence; opposers believe it will boost lawsuits.

483. **Ellis, Fay. "Making Scientific Studies More Palatable."** *The New York Times,* **14 August 1994, sec. 13, pp. 1, 13(L).**
Article describes a math program designed to encourage creative thinking and mathematical applications in today's world. Only one sentence mentions that ethics and plagiarism are part of the course content. Not useful for research on plagiarism, but might be helpful in innovative approaches to teaching.

484. **Harris, Lesley Ellen. "Moral Rights Laws Must Be Harmonized."** *Billboard* **106, no. 34 (20 August 1994): 6.**
The importance of moral rights for intellectual property must not be overlooked in U.S. Copyright Law. Many other countries, France and Canada, for example, have such a consideration. This gives persons claiming rights under their laws a greater degree of protection than the same material protected under U.S. law. With the possibilities of electronic manipulation it is even more important that we protect both property and reputation of the originator.

485. **Shepard, Alicia C. "Does Radio News Rip Off Newspapers?"** *American Journalism Review* **16, no. 7 (September 1994): 15–16.**
Two newspapers in Reading, Pennsylvania have gone to court alleging that radio station WIOV was guilty of plagiarism. They are asking at least $50,000 in damages. In an Internet query, the author found that reporters have a range of views on the seriousness of the practice. Reactions run from being flattered to disgusted. Article includes numerous quotes from sources and an example of parallelism from the court case.

486. **Bowers, Neal. "A Loss for Words: Plagiarism and Silence."** *The American Scholar* **64, no. 4 (Fall 1994): 545–55.**
Excellent recounting of Bowers' quest to expose the thief plagiarizing his work. Voices the frustration of having no one interested in coming to his aid, of friends' comments ("You can always write another poem"), of his inability to stop the would be poet from "stalking" his works and his soul searching on the worth of the venture.

487. **Galef, David. "Kidnapping."** *Journal of Information Ethics* **3, no. 2 (Fall 1994): 51–53.**
Covers artists who appropriate the work of others under the guise of art. Includes discussion of Sherrie Levine's copying the work of others and titling "after [the original artist's name]," and of D. M. Thomas' use of Kuznetsov's documentary in *The White Hotel.* Suggests we call wholesale appropriation *kidnapping.*

488. LaFollette, Marcel C. "Avoiding Plagiarism: Some Thought on Use, Attribution and Acknowledgment." *Journal of Information Ethics* **3, no. 2 (Fall 1994): 25–35.**

Variance of citation styles among publishers may make plagiarism easier for those intentionally stealing, and difficult for honest authors to validate. We must not confuse "completeness of citation" with acknowledging the extent of influence. But above all, the fear of plagiarizing must not prevent honest writers from committing word to paper and suppressing ego to honestly give recognition to those who have given the building blocks for the work. Includes brief commentary on the style of notes used by Stephen Oates, an historian under attack for plagiarism.

489. McCutchen, Charles W. "Plagiarism: A Tale of Telltale Words." *Journal of Information Ethics* **3, no. 2 (Fall 1994): 48–50.**

The issue should be stealing another's ideas, not copying words. Copied words should only be a warning flag to check further, not proof of theft. Repeating "catch" words and phrases is one of the ways society examines and accepts new ideas. By closely defining plagiarism we reduce free access to new phrases. If we do not remember the originator, fear of plagiarism might inhibit us from repeating the new phrase and stifle moving of a new idea into our culture.

490. Martin, Brian. "Plagiarism: A Misplaced Emphasis." *Journal of Information Ethics* **3, no. 2 (Fall 1994): 36–47.**

Most works on plagiarism focus on the individual ("competitive plagiarism") and ignore the bureaucratically accepted forms ("institutional plagiarism") such as ghostwriting, "honorary authorship," and using the work of subordinates without acknowledgment. Focusing on the independent protects the elite in the hierarchy. Claims for credit for originality by individuals are the product of capitalistic endeavors. Recognition becomes less important, except as a courtesy, in other economic arrangements. More emphasis should be placed on the institutional variety as that is where intellectual exploitation occurs. References.

491. Price, Alan. "The 1993 ORI/AAAS Conference on Plagiarism and Theft of Ideas." *Journal of Information Ethics* **3, no. 2 (Fall 1994): 54–63.**

Article is an excellent overview of the scholar's perspective of plagiarism. Conference summary. Covers: general concepts of what constitutes plagiarism; handling investigations; the role and accountability of editors; methods of the grant peer review process; tracking and accountability in electronic format; cultural differences in viewing copying. Price's summary at the conference stresses that the responsibility to teach guidelines and personal responsibility, and enforce standards of conduct lies with all involved in scientific endeavors.

492. **St. Onge, K. R. "Plagiarism: For Accusers and the Accused."** *Journal of Information Ethics* **3, no. 2 (Fall 1994): 8–24.**
Scholarly. St. Onge examines the charges of plagiarism against historian Stephen Oates by addressing the controversy using objective scrutiny according to definitions of Linsey and the AHA. He concludes that Bray, the accuser, influenced the AHA resulting in their redefinition of plagiarism and that the case was not proven by any standards.

493. **Wilhoit, Stephen. "Helping Students Avoid Plagiarism."** *College Teaching* **42, no. 4 (Fall 1994): 161–4.**
Instructors have a duty to teach students to identify plagiarism versus collaboration, the differences in acceptable practices among various disciplines, as well as techniques to avoid plagiarism. Instructors must also make sure the punishment fits the crime as most students are not intentional plagiarists.

494. **Russell, Deborah. "Consultant Sues BMG Ventures and TCI: Home Shopping/Music Video Channel at Issue."** *Billboard* **106, no. 36 (3 September 1994): 123.**
Nina Marraccini has filed a $10 million breach-of-contract suit against BMG and TCI. She claims BMG took her idea and promised compensation and a position in the new network. BMG took the idea to TCI failing to give Marraccini credit. The fact that the television network is not going to materialize is not the issue, control of the concept is.

495. **Spender, Stephen. "My Life Is Mine; It Is Not David Leavitt's."** *The New York Times,* **4 September 1994, sec. 7, p. 10(L).**
Excellent article. Spender's rebuttal to Leavitt's suggestion that Spender and Britain were locked in self-censorship. Includes a description of the controversial event found in both *World Within World* and *While England Sleeps*. Spender was pleased that copyright protection prevailed. He showed disdain for Leavitt's lack of knowledge regarding acceptance of literature under British law, and his lack of understanding that sexually explicit material should only be used to further character development.

496. **Risher, Carol A., and Laura Gasaway. "The Great Copyright Debate."** *Library Journal* **119, no. 15 (15 September 1994): 34–7.**
Two opinions expressing agreement that current copyright laws are

adequate to cover the new technology. Risher completely supports the White House Working Group on Intellectual Property report. Gasaway suggests that some thought should be given to new methods of transmission.

497. **Cronin, Peter. "RIAA Thwarts Pirates on Several Fronts."** *Billboard* **106, no. 39 (24 September 1994): 106.**
The Recording Industry Association of America has participated in and brought suit against two music piracy operations, one in California and the other in New York. In addition to over 90,000 counterfeit tapes confiscated, the factory was capable of producing an additional 3.6 million per year. The defendants were convicted in civil and criminal courts. Civil courts are used to deter repeat offenders and help companies recoup losses.

498. **Kwaku. "Dawn Penn Dispute Shows Danger of Reggae 'Voicing'."** *Billboard* **106, no. 39 (24 September 1994): 62.**
Recent Jamaican laws have brought reggae into the intellectual property fray. Artists' adapting songs and "voicing" new lyrics to established rhythm tracks have made reggae musicians and writers more aware of intellectual property protections. Illustrates the threads and difficulties of establishing intellectual property rights to songs and getting permission to use them by tracking the history of Dawn Penn's hit *You Don't Love Me (No, No, No)*.

499. **DeLoughry, Thomas J. "'Fair Use' for Electronic Age: Debate Over Copyright Laws Heats Up."** *Chronicle of Higher Education* **41, no. 5 (28 September 1994): A30.**
The Working Group on Intellectual Property Rights did not specifically address *fair use* for electronic media. They proposed a conference instead. Mr. Lehman, chairman of the group and Assistant Secretary of Commerce, suggested that the conference have some recommendations before the next Congressional year or the Administration would forward its own proposal. Attorney for the Motion Picture Association stated that the marketplace should settle these issues. Representatives from schools, colleges and libraries are concerned about developing tools for classroom use and distance learning, and lending materials in electronic format. (See St. Lifer and Rogers, 15 Oct 1944 for additional information.)

500. **Byrd, Gary D. "Protecting Access to the Intellectual Property of the Health Sciences."** *Bulletin of the Medical Library Assn.* **82, no. 4 (October 1994): 444–5.**
To combat the rising costs of biomedical research publications, researchers should be encouraged to send works to publishers who support

lower costs and widespread access. Universities should grant limited licenses to other publishers to support this venture and develop intellectual property copyright policy in much the same way as they have for patents.

501. **Soukhanov, Anne H. "Word Watch."** *Atlantic Monthly* **274, no. 4 (October 1994): 136.**
The term *freeman* now refers to the amount of plagiarism in a given document. Stewart and Feder coined the term from the Weismann copyright infringement case against her supervisor Leonard M. Freeman. One *freeman* equals complete plagiarizing.

502. **Berry, John N., III. "Keep That Information on the Move."** *Library Journal* **119, no. 16 (1 October 1994): 6.**
Disagrees with Risher and Gasaway (*Library Journal*, September 15, 1994, pages 34–37). Copyright Law does not lend itself to the digital world. Praises John Perry Barlow for his foresight in seeing performance and use as critical. They keep information from stagnating. The premise is not particularly original (it is the foundation of copyright), but his enthusiasm for Barlow's work brings a smile.

503. **Azzopardi, John. "World Within World."** *The New York Times,* **2 October 1994, sec. 7, col. 1, p. 43(L).**
[Letter.]
Uses the response to question Leavitt's concept of homosexuality. Leavitt "may or may not be a plagiarist..."

504. **Dillinham, Thomas. "World Within World."** *The New York Times,* **2 October 1994, sec. 7, col. 2, p. 43(L).**
[Letter.]
The work hardly warrants all the discussion. Spender is protesting far beyond boundaries called for by this plagiarism. It is a shame that defenses must be mounted against works that do not deserve the notoriety; works that would have faded quickly if not for the scandal they generated.

505. **Mitchell, Mark. "World Within World."** *The New York Times,* **2 October 1994, sec. 7, col. 1, p. 43(L).**
[Letter.]
The co-author with Leavitt of an anthology of gay fiction, Mitchell parallels Leavitt's borrowing with Worsley's novel, *Fellow Travellers* (1971). Spender did not object to Worsley's borrowing his work.

506. **Reid, Calvin. "Authors Support Copyright Changes."** *Publishers Weekly* **241, no. 41 (10 October 1994): 12.**
The Authors League supports recommendations of the Working Group

on Intellectual Property Rights, adding recommendations to eliminate devices that promote copyright violation (e.g. page-turning photocopiers), contracts granting rights for "unknown or uninvented media," and limiting library access to access within the physical building.

507. Marshall, Eliot. "A Showdown Over Gene Fragments." *Science* **266, no. 5183 (14 October 1994): 208–10.**

The genetic database created by The Institute for Genomic Research (TIGR) and its for profit partners, Human Genome Sciences Inc. (HGS) and SmithKline Beecham, is proving to be a valuable resource for the research community. TIGR was created to allow research to continue when the NIH chose not to support the project. TIGR is willing to share the information with others if contracts respecting proprietary rights of TIGR and HGS are signed. That they are not putting the results of this multimillion dollar project into the *public domain* is raising concerns among academics and other research institutions. As an alternative, Merck, a primary competitor of SmithKline Beecham, is offering to finance a project to duplicate the EST database for public domain. J. Craig Venter, originator of the concept of the EST database, is pleased that others are recognizing its value but believes the community is overreacting to the restrictions on intellectual property as they are similar to those of other biotechnical companies.

508. Nowak, Rachel. "NIH in Danger of Losing Out on BRCA1 Patent." *Science* **266, no. 5183 (14 October 1994): 209.**

The question of whether the NIH should share in the patent of BRCA1, a cancer related gene, rests in a murky portion of patent law—what constitutes ownership. Participants included the University of Utah, Myriad, Eli Lilly, McGill University, and the National Institute of Environmental Health Sciences. The NIH did contribute, through the University of Utah, a 6 person team and $2 million to the effort. Myriad contributed 22 persons and $10 million and Lilly raised another $4 million. The usual agreement among intramural researchers regarding the commercial aspects of the research results was not signed for this project. The researchers did have the foresight to sign an agreement on "how the academic glory would be divvied up."

509. St. Lifer, Evan, and Michael Rogers. "Libraries Face Altering of Fair Use Portion of Copyright Law." *Library Journal* **119, no. 17 (15 October 1994): 12–13.**

Spotlights the library representatives' reactions after they addressed the Working Group on Intellectual Property. They are concerned that the Group is more interested in meeting deadlines for Clinton's election campaign than seriously addressing the copyright issues on the NII, and Lehman's apparent lack of interest in providing protection for the user. Quotes from ALA President Arthur Curley, and ARL's Duane Webster and Ann Okerson are included.

510. **Baker, Nicholson. "Infohighwaymen." *The New York Times*, 18 October 1994, sec. A, col. 2, p. 25.**
Databases like Magazine Index distributed on the internet by CARL Corporation are using their status as "indexes" to circumvent legal avenues adhered to by the publishing industry when they offer downloading full text to the user. The author was not asked permission, nor would he have given it if asked, to have his articles available electronically. The services are unreliable. Vendors are playing on the fears of magazine editors by suggesting that to remain competitive their products must be available electronically. One solution would be a royalty sharing facility similar to ASCAP.

511. **Millstone, Erik, Eric Brunner, and Ian White. "Plagiarism or Protecting Public Health?" *Nature* 371, no. 6499 (20 October 1994): 647–8.**
An interesting account showing how difficult it can be to publish data that does not support corporate findings. The authors followed accepted procedure for obtaining raw data, did independent analysis, and were blocked from publication by Monsanto, the owners of that data. Monsanto refused to give permission to publish under the guise that they had submitted articles for publication on that same topic. The editor did not have such documents. The topic revolved around whether a growth hormone for increasing milk production was adversely affecting milk quality. Monsanto's charges of plagiarism did not apply as sources were acknowledged.

512. **Grimes, William. "What Rhymes with, Uh, Plagiarism?" *The New York Times,* 25 October 1994, sec. C, col. 1, p. C15+(L).**
A summary of the Neal Bowers' incident in which Bowers successfully tracked down David S. Jones, a.k.a. David Sumner, a teacher who had been plagiarizing his poems and the works of many others from 1990–93. Includes a portion of one of the poems. For the complete account by Bowers, see "A Loss for Words," *American Scholar*, Autumn 1994, p. 545–55.

513. **Heller, Scott. "A Professor's Campaign Against Plagiarism." *Chronicle of Higher Education* 41, no. 9 (26 October 1994): A8.**
A summary of poet Neal Bowers' bout with a plagiarist. Includes information from an interview with Bowers. (See Bowers, *American Scholar*, Aug 1994, and Grimes, *The New York Times,* 25 Oct 1994, for details.)

514. Marshall, Eliot. "Biotech Leaders Give Patent Office a Litany of Complaints." *Science* **266, no. 5185 (28 October 1994): 537.**
Biotech industry leaders are frustrated by a patent process they say is unpredictable, slow, and governed by internal rules not available to the public. Misrock, a patent attorney, believes the requirements for biotech patents frequently borders on areas normally under FDA jurisdiction. PTO commissioner Bruce Lehman, through his efforts to identify and correct areas of their concern, is winning praise from many critics of PTO's past performance.

515. Cranberg, Lawrence. "Plagiarists Steal More Than Just Words." *The New York Times,* **31 October 1994, sec. A, col. 2, p. 18.**
[Letter.]
Response to the Neal Bowers story. Plagiarists also steal the resources from deserving scientists. We must fight this social problem. Perhaps there should be an organization to help investigate plagiarism in those areas. (See Bowers, *American Scholar,* Aug 1994.)

516. Flagg, Gordon. "ALA Testifies on Intellectual Property." *American Libraries* **25, no. 10 (November 1994): 905.**
Over 3 days, librarians representing major library associations in America testified before the White House Information Infrastructure Task Force's Working Group on Intellectual Property Rights. Stress was placed on user's rights and opportunities for research and education. ALA and ARL also supported the creation of yet another commission, a National Commission on New Technological Uses.

517. Welles, Edward O. "Blood Feud." *Inc.* **16, no. 12 (November 1994): 60–9.**
Detailed description of Diametrics' battle with PPG over patent infringement and trade secrets. Although Deetz was clearly the originator, Diametrics finally settled by paying PPG $5.2 million just to keep Diametrics from going bankrupt. Shows the development of David Deetz' idea for IRMA, a portable device used to measure vital gases in blood. IRMA may replace a $30,000 hospital laboratory machine with one the size of a large credit card. Cost of materials is $2; selling price of the product is $5000. The article illustrates the power of using litigation as a business weapon.

518. Millspaugh, Anthony M. "Who Wrote What?" *Writing* **17, no. 3 (November/December 1994): 10–11.**
Defines plagiarism. The correct procedures for researching properly are research; compile notes; combine and cite sources. Article for novice writers and young adults.

519. Franklin, Jonathan A. "Digital Image Reproduction, Distribution and Protection: Legal Remedies and Industrywide Alternatives." *Computer & High Technology Law Journal* **10, no. 2 (1 November 1994): 347–72.**
Franklin clearly describes legal issues of copyright (*fair use*, artistic versus functional, percentage of original, injury to market value) for stock photography and suggests viable ways for handling fees through societies similar to ASCAP and CCC.

520. Putterman, Daniel. "Compromise Sought Over Germplasm Access." *Nature* **372, no. 6501 (3 November 1994): 9.**
New rules are being proposed by the International Plant Genetic Resources Institute. Under the rules, the private sector would not be allowed to file for intellectual property protection unless major modifications were made to the germplasm, and companies would have to negotiate for royalties with the country from which the germplasm originated. M. S. Swarminathan (Madras, India) also proposes a community gene fund financed through a tax on royalties based on gross sales of the commercial products. It was argued that the new rules will, by their restrictive nature, dissuade agricultural advancement.

521. Pace, Eric. "Louis Nizer, Lawyer to the Famous, Dies at 92." *The New York Times,* **11 November 1994, sec. B, col. 1, p. 7.**
A tribute to Louis Nizer. Mr. Nizer gained fame for his role in defending many in the movies against libel and for a victory which led to the end of blacklasting in broadcasting.

522. Bennett, Scott. "The Copyright Challenge." *Library Journal* **119, no. 19 (15 November 1994): 34–7.**
In this digital age, libraries can effectively compete in the marketplace if they promote *fair use* through open access to materials and stress the principles of copyright to users. Commercial vendors must pay royalties and pass on that cost to consumers.

523. Polly, Jean Armour, and Steve Cisler. "Watching the Information Policy Process." *Library Journal* **119, no. 19 (15 November 1994): 26.**
Cisler expresses surprise that only 45 people appeared at the public hearing in Mountain View to discuss the NII policy. Interests of the group included the intellectual property "owned" by companies, and those wanting to preserve current copyright law.

524. Kale, V. S. "Plagiarism." *Current Science* **67, no. 9/10 (25 November 1994): 682.**
Current Science publishes the letter after investigating and finding

substance to Kale's allegations that M. Aslam plagiarized in his 1994 article "Equation of Estimation of Sedimentation Rates: Applications to Sequence Stratigraphy." Kale expresses concern that the unscrupulous taint the reputation of *Indian Science*.

525. Ingrassia, Joanne. "Suit Enmeshes 2 Chiat Clients." *Advertising Age* **65, no. 50 (28 November 1994): 42.**
Body Shop International has filed a trademark infringement suit against Shoppers Drug Mart for an advertisement on a skincare product. Chiat/Day agency handles accounts for both parties. All agree there is no conflict of interest as the accounts are handled by different executives within the company.

526. Arnott, Nancy. "Keeping Company Secrets." *Sales & Marketing Management* **146, no. 14 (December 1994): 57.**
Arnott suggests that the best way to keep trade secrets within your organization is to make the concept of secret a part of company policy and to remind employees of their obligation. It is also helpful to make customers aware that they are working with a company, not just an individual sales person. If the sales person leaves, the company is still there to meet their needs. (Sidebar lists suggested procedures for preventing trade secret thefts.)

527. "ORI Provides Working Definition of Plagiarism." *RI Newsletter* **3, no. 1 (December 1994): 3.**
Plagiarism as applied to ORI cases will include theft or misappropriation of intellectual property and substantial unattributed textual copying of another's work which, when read, might mislead the reader in determining authorship. Disputes among collaborators on former projects and verbatim use of common phrases are not considered plagiarism in their definition.

528. "Researcher Plagiarized Material from Application Under Review." *RI Newsletter* **3, no. 1 (December 1994): 3.**
Dr. Gerald I. August, Ph.D., an Associate Professor at the University of Minnesota Medical School, plagiarized in a grant application to the Public Health Service. He will be barred from membership in committees, peer review groups and boards, and will have to supply source documentation for any future applications or reports for the next 5 years.

529. Holland, Bill. "Congressional Committee Heads Revealed." *Billboard* **106, no. 49 (3 December 1994): 106+.**
Laments the Republican's reassigning of persons to the Judiciary Subcommittees on Patents, Trademarks and Copyrights and on Intellectual

Property and Judicial Administration. Suggests that issues will be put aside to focus on the "Contract with America." Names of possible appointees are given.

530. Van Zuylen, Gary. "Thailand Gets 1st Copyright Law." *Billboard* 106, no. 49 (3 December 1994): 46, 52.

Because Thailand has made progress under its new copyright law, it has been removed from the U.S. priority watch list initiated in 1992. Music piracy had been their biggest offense. Counterfeit tapes account for 30% of foreign sales, down from an estimated 95%. The move is thought to be political, not based on concern for distribution of unauthorized goods.

531. Hogan, Kevin. "Trademarks in Cyberspace." *Forbes* Supplement, no. (5 December 1994): 181.

Brief. Big companies are having to contract for rights to cyberaddresses because speculators preregistered many popular names and now own the rights. Gives addresses for registration on InterNIC.

532. Gillen, Marilyn A. "Discovision Sues Technicolor." *Billboard* 106, no. 51 (17 December 1994): 66.

The case questions whether patent rights have been infringed. The patents in contention are 3 of over 1400 owned by Discovision, originators of an optical disk manufacturing process. Discovision is no longer a manufacturer. Its revenues come from licensing agreements with over 100 companies world-wide involved in recording, manufacturing and playback of compact disks. Royalty fee is currently 3% of pressing fee.

533. Scollon, Ron. "Plagiarism and Ideology: Identity in Intercultural Discourse." *Language in Society* 24, no. 1 (1995): 1–28.

The concept of plagiarism used in academic and economic communities is not based on a true view of communication. Communication involves many levels of exchange. Cultural ideologies of self as animator, author, principal influence this exchange. Taken in the social context, it is not possible for the self to claim authorship of the concrete representation of the idea. Keeping this concept in mind, the author adds that he still feels anger that another plagiarized his work, but realizes that it would be hypocrisy to open a legal discussion when he challenges the concept of plagiarism on ideological grounds.

534. "Intellectual Property in China: Copy to Come." *Economist* 334, no. 7896 (7 January 1995): 51–2.

Tough stance between China and the U.S. on intellectual property theft may be more bluster than substance, much like the threat of rescinding China's most-favored-nation trade status last year. China says they are not being given credit for the strides taken to introduce intellectual property laws during these last 12 years. Both realize that enforcement of those laws is a major difficulty.

535. Koretz, Gene. "China vs. the U.S.: Bejing Blinks." *Business Week*, no. 3409 (10 January 1995): 26.
Brief. America has adopted a tougher stance with China over the dispute on intellectual property rights and piracy because it is losing billions in the trade deficit.

536. Van Gelder, Lawrence. "Plagiarism Suit on Parallel Tales of Arab Wives." *The New York Times,* 10 January 1995, sec. C, col. 3, p. 15.
Friederika Monika Adsani has brought claim that her work, *Cinderella in Arabia*, submitted to agent Peter Miller, was stolen and used as a basis for *Cinderella in Arabia* and *Princess: Sultana's Daughters*. Jean P. Sasson, another of Miller's clients and author of the two works, claims she based her stories on notes and diaries from the Saudi Arabian princess Saltana. A paragraph includes similarities in the plots. Sasson's protectors say the claims are "preposterous," but no notes or diaries have surfaced.

537. Dezzani, Mark. "Michael Jackson Appeals Italian Plagiarism Ruling." *Billboard* 107, no. 2 (14 January 1995): 9, 66.
After 3 years in Italian courts, songwriter/singer Al Bano Carrisi has won his plagiarism case against Michael Jackson. *Will You Be There* was ruled by the judge to be taken from *I Cigni di Balaka* a song written by Al Bano in 1981 and recorded in Los Angeles in 1986. Musicologist Luciano Chailly, appointed to compare the pieces, found enough similarities to convince the judge of the charges. Jackson's lawyers will ask for an annulment based on court procedures and the judge's competency for judging musical issues.

538. Kwaku. "Ghana Protecting C'Rights." *Billboard* 107, no. 5 (4 February 1995): 63, 68.
After 4 years of clamping down on piracy, the musicians and composers in Ghana are benefiting. The Musicians Union of Ghana and the Copyright Office are responsible for the enforcement. The government is still collecting most of the money, but individuals who are able to identify sales are beginning to negotiate royalty deals. False foreign products, especially those from the Far East, are going to be more difficult to uncover.

539. "Intellectual Wars." *Nature* 373, no. 6514 (9 February 1995): 458.
In an effort to curb abuse of intellectual property rights by Chinese

industry, U.S. Trade Representative Kantor threatens a 100% tariff on all exports to the U.S., making the products unaffordable. His argument might carry greater weight if the U.S. manufacturers had shown that they made an effort to offer reasonable terms for local reproduction of software and those offers had been refused.

540. "Is Plagiarism OK?" *Nature* **373, no. 6514 (9 February 1995): 458.**
The University of Hong Kong's plagiarism case of Koo v. Lam has been settled in the courts. The author questions whether it is appropriate for researchers to sue each other for academic disputes and why persons in the same department were funded for parallel investigations. Includes a brief overview of the case.

541. Swinbanks, David. "University Challenges Plagiarism Judgement." *Nature* **373, no. 6514 (9 February 1995): 465.**
University of Hong Kong case of Koo v. Lam continues as Koo and Ho protest the apparent partiality of the university committee. The committee cleared Lam of wrongdoing after the Chinese courts pronounced him guilty. Koo believes the committee was biased in its letters to the experts. They implied she had a vendetta, pleaded to keep questionnaires free for use, hinted of miscarriage of justice and barred her from representation at the hearings. Koo is now looking into possible legal action against the University.

542. Markoff, John. "Intel and Microsoft Added to Apple Lawsuit." *The New York Times,* **10 February 1995, sec. D, col. 3, p. 3.**
Apple sues San Francisco Canyon Company, a company contracted by Apple to develop software which will make some features of Quicktime available for Intel compatible computers. Apple planned to use the greater functionality of the Apple version as a marketing feature. Microsoft was added to the filing when features of the software appeared in Microsoft products and on bulletin boards. Intel has engineers reworking the software. Microsoft is setting up meetings with Apple to resolve the issue.

543. Blumenthal, Ralph. "Thieves in the Idea Marketplace." *The New York Times,* **11 February 1995, sec. A, col. 4, pp. 13–14.**
The ease of copying via computer is outpacing the laws that govern intellectual property protection. It is a lawyer's paradise. The problems are not just with piracy. Actors, dancers, educators, and other interpreters of creative works are confused about how to interpret the law in this medium. Quotes from Beverly Sills, Ernest Boyer, Martin E. Segal, Garrison Keiller, Maxwell L. Anderson, Elizabeth Broun and Joel de Rosnay indicate both concern and optimism. The medium is an excellent way to disseminate information and promote the arts. The

digital outreach projects at Emory and the Museum Educational Site Licensing Project are mentioned.

544. Brahams, Diana. "Conflicting Views on Alleged Plagiarism." *Lancet* 345, no. 8945 (11 February 1995): 379.
Recap of the Koo and Ho v. Lam case at the University of Hong Kong. Although the courts found Lam guilty of copyright infringement for using Koo's questionnaire, the university peer committee sided with Lam. Professional conduct was not improper according to the standards of the community in the 1980s.

545. "Making War on China's Pirates." *Economist* 334, no. 7901 (11 February 1995): 33–4.
Repercussions are threatened by the U.S. against China for intellectual property violations. The tactics appear ritualistic. As Chinese businesses become more prominent, they also want protection for their products, but this liberal wing still does not seem to have a great voice in the negotiations.

546. "The Pirates Who Gave Up." *Economist* 334, no. 7901 (11 February 1995): 34.
Thailand is taking violation of intellectual property rights seriously. This year they are setting up their first intellectual property court. Interest in keeping favorable status with the U.S. may have played a role, but in any case, attention is being paid. China may be more difficult to "crack," as the operations there are larger and better organized.

547. "Right to Punish China." *Economist* 334, no. 7901 (11 February 1995): 15–16.
Unilateral trade sanctions, like those proposed by the U.S. to regulate theft of intellectual property in China, generally make things worse, not better. In this case, China is already outside GATT so that is not a threat, and the economic benefits to its citizens in the short run may outweigh the lack of interest in creating new products. American business may grow tired of waiting for the administration to act. America should make a greater effort to stress the value of free trade and enlist the help of European counterparts to urge China to comply with the rules.

548. "Don't Let China Off the Hook." *Business Week*, no. 3412 (20 February 1995): 110.
U.S. bipartisan support for free trade in the world economy is beginning to erode. China and the U.S. are facing a critical moment in free trade as China decides whether or not to enforce the intellectual property

rights of American business. Now is the perfect time for the U.S. to show that global trading is only open to those who play by the rules.

549. **Neland, Bruce W. "The Future Without a Road Map."** *Time* **145, no. 7 (20 February 1995): 61–2.**
The power struggle for leadership in China has shifted to a group of technocrats and military leaders. The instability is making negotiation for intellectual property protection for U.S. businesses tenuous at best, but Washington is striving to keep trade negotiations open. Hazel O'Leary, Secretary of Energy, will be flying a delegation of U.S. businessmen to Beijing to negotiate contracts worth an estimated $8 billion. The majority of this article deals with profiles of the potential leaders in China, not intellectual property.

550. **Milone, Kim. "Dithering Over Digitization: International Copyright and Licensing Agreements Between Museums, Artists and New Media Publishers."** *Indiana International & Comparative Law Review* **5, no. 2 (Spring 1995): 393–423.**
An excellent overview of the issues involved in licensing art objects for multimedia. Software and CD-ROM/CD-i publishers are finding it easiest to contract with museums worldwide for reproductions of artwork for their new product lines instead of individuals. Museums generally own distribution rights to the works they house. The article discusses international copyright differences and the role museums can play in sculpting licensing agreements that will protect the rights of the artist while preserving the museum's fiduciary duties to the public.

551. **Schnuer, Jenna. "Writers Unite Over E-Rights."** *Folio* **(1 March 1995): 20.**
Freelance writers are turning to professional groups and to each other, looking for ways to best negotiate contracts with publishers for payment when their articles are accessed on-line.

552. **Tabor, Mary B. W. "A Reader Finds That a Current Book Reads Suspiciously Like an Old One."** *The New York Times,* **3 March 1995, sec. C, col. 1, p. 3(L).**
Gives brief accounting of how Cynthia Martin Kiss uncovered the similarity in passages between Alexander Theroux's *The Primary Colors* and the 1954 work of Guy Murchie's *Song of the Sky*. Theroux claims poor note-taking. Six passages appear to have been taken verbatim; three are listed in parallel beside the article. Henry Holt will not be recalling the publications, but will issue any editions with either omission of passages or acknowledgment.

553. "Trade Peace: Deja Vu Again." *Economist* **334, no. 7904 (4 March 1995): 73–4.**
The usual last minute agreement to enforce intellectual property rights has calmed the tariff crisis with China. There are two reasons not to "cheer too loudly." China was more likely to conform to American requests given its interest in being a member of WTO and its dependence on our marketplace for approximately 30% of its export income and our agreements with China have been difficult to enforce.

554. Lehrman, Sally. "University Blocks Efforts to Reveal Researchers' Identity." *Nature* **374, no. 6518 (9 March 1995): 109.**
Disagreement on ownership of documents has University of California at San Diego and Brown & Williamson Tobacco Co. in the courts. The papers, given to the UC library and available to a team of researchers, are said to contain information on the addictive quality of smoking. B & W contends the papers were stolen and contain confidential information and trade secrets. They are also requesting the library records of those accessing the papers and investigating others who received copies of the documents.

555. Markoff, John. "Unraveling Copyright Rules for Cyberspace." *The New York Times,* **9 March 1995, sec. D, col. 4, p. 18.**
Assistant Secretary of Commerce and the Commissioner of Patents and Trademarks, Bruce A. Lehman's response to the initial meetings on protection of electronic/digital intellectual property rights held by Government officials from 11 countries. He stated that although the U.S. copyright law was suited to protection of these rights, nations who are currently net receivers of the technology do not have the same incentives to support that protection. Lehman is optimistic that an agreement can be reached.

556. Gunn, Angela. "Law and Disorder on the Internet." *PC Magazine* **14, no. 5 (14 March 1995): 30.**
Brief. Software designed to screen "spamming" on the Internet may be used for censorship. The Alt.religion.scientology newsgroup finds messages critical to the faith were canceled. The courts stated David LaMaccia innocent of copyright infringement as his BBS, which allowed downloading of $1 million of software, did not profit from the exchange. Unisys and CompuServe modified the royalty scheme for .GIF files after angry internet users complained.

557. Feldman, Gayle. "H. M. to Do 'Revised' Leavitt Novel After Spender Suit." *Publishers Weekly* **242, no. 12 (20 March 1995): 16.**
The plagiarism charges filed by poet Stephen Spender against novelist David Leavitt over some graphic scenes depicted in *While England*

Sleeps have resulted in the rewriting of the offending parts. Viking was cautioned by their legal council that there might still be possibility of further action. The rights for printing the new edition have moved, along with Leavitt's editor, from Viking Penguin to Houghton. Houghton bought the rights to U.S. distribution only.

558. **Boyde, T. R. C. "Questionnaires and Copyright." *Nature* 374, no. 6520 (23 March 1995): 301.**
Response to *Nature,* February 9, 1995 article on Koo v. Lam plagiarism case at the University of Hong Kong. Boyde supports the University of Hong Kong's decision to retain Lam and to base their decision on criterion beyond the civil court case.

559. **Griffiths, John. "Questionnaires and Copyright." *Nature* 374, no. 6520 (23 March 1995): 301.**
[Letter.]
Response to the February 9, 1995 *Nature* article on Koo v. Lam plagiarism case at the University of Hong Kong. Griffiths, counsel for Lam in the University of Hong Kong case, points out contradicting evidence given to the university committee not introduced in the civil proceedings. The evidence supports the committee's allowing Lam to continue his work at the university.

560. **Gungwu, Wang. "Questionnaires and Copyright." *Nature* 374, no. 6520 (23 March 1995): 301.**
Response to the February 9, 1995 *Nature* article on Koo v. Lam plagiarism case at the University of Hong Kong. Wang, vice-chancellor, states he was advised not to pursue in-house investigations while the civil suit was pending. The University had no procedures to cover investigations of this type.

561. **Hertling, James. "Embarrassment in Hong Kong." *Chronicle of Higher Education* 41, no. 28 (24 March 1995): A43–4.**
Higher profile and funds being linked to productivity in the Hong Kong university system may account for current instances of plagiarism among its top faculty and administrators. Cases discussed: Lam Tai-Hing's plagiarism of a research questionnaire; Mr. Chen Yu-Shenk's plagiarism in a textbook; and Kong Shiu-Loon's presenting his translation of a work by Thomas Nagel as his own.

562. **Seymour, Jim. "The Software-Patent Ambush." *PC Magazine* 14, no. 6 (28 March 1995): 95–6.**
Software patents have a place in the market, but the concept needs to be reexamined. The controversy over the use of the algorithm for the .GIF graphics file format is a good example. CompuServe Information

Service (CIS) tried to retroactively claim royalties from developers who used the .GIF process in their software, a process most thought was in *public domain*. CIS was unpleasantly surprised to learn that Unisys Corporation actually owned the patent on the process. Negotiations resulted. CIS paid $125,000 for the rights and the rights to sublicense. Former developers were "grandfathered" in at no charge because of the public outcry on the internet when fees were requested.

563. **"Civic Lesson: MGM Sues Honda Over Ad."** *ABA Journal* **81 (April 1995): 42.**
Brief. MGM files suit against American Honda Motor Co. for copyright infringement and trademark dilution. They claim that an ad for the "low-end-of-the-market Honda" tarnishes the James Bond image. The lawyer for Honda contends that the commercial is a generic helicopter chase scene.

564. **Dabney, James W. "Patent Win Attributed to 3-D Computer Imagery."** *The National Law Journal* **(3 April 1995): C15, 17.**
Summary of a patent infringement case in which the decision was based on computer generated 3D imagery—Mosinee Paper Co. *v.* James River Corporation of Virginia. James River contended that a mechanism used in a towel dispenser was not unique to the industry. The 3D image proved his comparison was inaccurate.

565. **"Barbunkum à la Parisienne."** *Economist* **335, no. 7909 (8 April 1995): 41.**
The author expresses sympathy for Paris-based journal *Jeune Afrique,* condemning Tunis journal *El Hadath* for reprinting without authorization. *The Economist* has suffered similar difficulties with *Jeune Afrique.* Briefly recounts efforts of trying to work with *Jeune.*

566. **Swinbanks, David. "Questionnaire Row Returns to the Courts."** *Nature* **375, no. 6526 (4 May 1995): 8.**
Koo v. Lam continues as Koo and Ho return to the courts for a verdict on the equity of University of Hong Kong's committee decision. The committee cleared Lam of charges of misconduct after the courts had found him guilty.

567. **"*Publishers* Case for Electronic Rights: AAP Circulates New Draft."** *Publishers Weekly* **242, no. 21 (22 May 1995): 9.**
Members of the Association of American Publishers are realizing the control over publication of electronic multimedia is falling outside the traditional publishing world. A drafted resolution gives five reasons why authors' best interests would be served by having publishers represent them in any multimedia rights negotiations based on their written

works. The five reasons are (1) few films result from the many works written, (2) most books do not adapt well to multimedia, (3) publishers can offer more variations in royalty payments, (4) publishers frequently give consultation rights to authors, filmmakers do not, and (5) publishers revert rights to the author if the work is not used, filmmakers do not.

568. **"Texaco Will Pay \$1M to Settle Copyright Suit."** *Publishers Weekly* **242, no. 21 (22 May 1995): 12.**
Copyright Clearance Center is pleased with the outcome of the 10 year infringement suit between Texaco and publishers from the scientific and technical journals (*American Geophysical Union et al. v. Texaco Inc., 1985*). The case involved photocopying publications in their corporate library for use by employees of Texaco. In addition to the \$1 million, the company will also pay licensing fees retroactively and will contract with the CCC for future photocopies. Texaco concedes no wrongdoing and accepts the verdict.

569. **Dalton, Rex. "Ruling Brings Windfall in U.S. Fraud Case."** *Nature* **375, no. 6529 (25 May 1995): 270.**
Pamela A. Berge has won her case against University of Alabama, Birmingham. In a first, the courts decided the verdict on this case of scientific misconduct under the "whistleblower's law." Total payments (over \$2 million) to the NIH and Berge are listed. An overview of the case, including the allegations of misrepresentation of the project to the NIH to secure continued funding, and plagiarism by Karen B. Fowler, the doctoral student involved in the research. Again the question of whether the courts are the best place to resolve misconduct accusations is posed.

570. **Dhar, S. K. "Responses."** *Current Science* **68, no. 10 (25 May 1995): 982.**
[Letter.]
A response to accusations that his professor, R. Vijayaraghavan, plagiarized from Dhar's thesis in a 1983 article "Magnetic Behavior of RRh(3)B(2) Ternary Borides" appearing in *Current Science*, Dhar states that other articles were written in cooperation with fellow researchers but the thesis was his own. *Current Science* solicited and published the responses in hopes of ending the controversy. (See Vajayaraghaven, pages 982–983 for his response to charges.)

571. **Siddhartha, V. "Plagiarism?"** *Current Science* **68, no. 10 (25 May 1995): 982.**
[Letter.]
Siddhartha reports that he suspects plagiarism in the 1983 article and suggests that *Current Science* has an obligation to take action.

Response was solicited by *Current Science* in hopes of putting the matter to rest. (See Vijayaraghaven, pages 982–983 for his response to charges.)

572. Vijayaraghavan, R. "Responses." *Current Science* 68, no. 10 (25 May 1995): 982–3.
[Letter.]
Vijayaraghavan's response regarding plagiarism in his 1983 review to *Current Science*. In it he states that the review article covered results of his and his colleagues' research. He believes that Dhar, as a member of the Solid States Physics group, was given credit for his contributions, and that they continue to work together. The letter also cites papers featured in the review.

573. Taubes, Gary. "Plagiarism Suit Wins: Experts Hope It Won't Set a Trend." *Science* 268, no. 5214 (26 May 1995): 1125.
Pamela Berge has set a precedent among the scientific community by bringing charges under the False Claims Act without first going through the NIH. Berge claimed, and a jury agreed, that information used by researchers at University of Alabama, Birmingham for an NIH grant study had come from her dissertation done a few years earlier at the UAB. After trying unsuccessfully to work within the system at the University, Berge researched the matter herself and, finding grounds for theft of her property, decided to pursue the matter in the courts. Monetary payments included: $1.65 million to the U.S. government from UAB with Berge receiving 30% as a recovery fee. Berge also receives $265,000 in compensatory and punitive damages from the four defendants. Some among the government and scientific communities fear the profit motive will overshadow scientists policing their own.

574. Witherspoon, Abigail. "This Pen for Hire." *Harper's* 290 (June 1995): 49–57.
The diary of a writer working for a business that supplies term papers and essays for a fee. Gives a flavor of the clientele and the cynicism that grows from the work.

575. Lehrman, Sally, and David Dickson. "Promega, Roche Clash Over Use of *TAQ* in Labs." *Nature* 375, no. 6530 (1 June 1995): 348.
Hoffman-Roche and Promega are in dispute because Roche claims Promega infringed on its patent when it broke an agreement not to sell its own *Taq* for use in PCR. Promega has been supplying the enzyme product to researchers. Roche purchased the rights from Cetus in 1992 for $300 million. Although a list of scientists involved was furnished by Roche, they have no intention of involving the

researchers and the ability of researchers to access products for research in the dispute. Their quarrel is with Promega.

576. **Primont, Michael. "Chinese Royalty Reform Is an Int'l Issue."** *Billboard* **107, no. 23 (10 June 1995): 8.**
The Music Copyright Society of China is beginning to have an impact for its 4000 registered composers, but it is the only organization available, has only one office, and lacks the power to enforce sanctions. Although China's place in world trade relies on the existence of intellectual property protection, it is in the international music industry's best interest to start building relationships with members in Chinese society now. Their system relies on relationships, not laws, to get things done.

577. **Kennedy, John W. "AMG Compensates Moody for Plagiarism."** *Christianity Today* **39 (19 June 1995): 42.**
Advancing Ministries of the Gospel has agreed to pay an undisclosed amount to Moody's for copyright infringement. Spiros Zodhiates' *Hebrew-Greek Key Bible Study* borrowed extensively from other similar works, but claims this one is original. Project editor Tim Rake, who saw and reported the copying, is less than satisfied with the efforts put forth to correct the error and has resigned his position. There will be no recalls or public notification for the 1 million copies printed. Only a small pamphlet, available on request, listing the sources will be offered.

578. **Rickard, Leah. "Point-of-Purchase Debate."** *Advertising Age* **66, no. 25 (19 June 1995): 38.**
At a seminar in Milwaukee, Point-of-Purchase Advertising Institute stressed the importance of raising industry standards, especially in the area of intellectual property. Suppliers and clients need to have contracts in place before ideas are discussed because promotional ideas, as well as designs, are legally protected.

579. **Marshall, Eliot. "Authorship: Dispute Slows Paper on "Remarkable" Vaccine."** *Science* **268, no. 5218 (23 June 1995): 1712–15.**
Disputes on authorship are keeping research results on a possible medical breakthrough toward a vaccine for AIDS and meningitis from publication. Sarvanamgala Devi has been battling for three years with NIH colleagues over whose name should appear on the paper. Marshall explains the evolution of the research and subsequent plagiarism and racial and sexual discrimination charges filed by Devi against the NIH. In October 1994, Michael Gottesman of the NIH mediated an arrangement which left Devi free to publish, but she did not realize that freedom until spring 1995. Researchers would just like to see the publication and move forward on the research.

580. Frazier, Kenneth. "Protecting Copyright and Preserving Fair Use in the Electronic Future." *Chronicle of Higher Education* **41, no. 42 (30 June 1995): A40.**

The educational community was not pleased with the recommendations for copyright protection for the National Information Infrastructure made by the Working Group on Intellectual Property and touted as being "on the right track" by the Clinton Administration. If adopted, all control for electronic transmission of information would be controlled by the copyright holder. This would eliminate *fair use* for educational institutions and libraries and severely limit access for those unable to afford the licenses and fees. Frazier suggests that if piracy is the issue, we should concentrate on that aspect and not on exclusive ownership for the copyright holder.

581. Lieberman, Trudy. "Plagiarize, Plagiarize, Plagiarize ... Only Be Sure to Always Call It Research." *Columbia Journalism Review* **34, no. 2 (July 1995): 21–5.**

An excellent starting point for those researching cases of unethical behavior in journalism. A response to questions regarding how the journalism community handles plagiarism, Lieberman, contributing editor for CJR and senior editor for *Consumer Reports*, investigated. The results of the research showed a very uneven handling of cases by editors and in many cases a lack of concern of the ethics involved. Gives brief summaries of recent cases; lists their outcomes as evidence. The gamut of punishment goes from a "don't do that" attitude to resignations and firing. Suggests that journalists should hold themselves to the same standard of honesty as they hold others. References Thomas Mallon's *Stolen Words* and Peter Shaw's "Plagiary" *in American Scholar,* 1982.

582. Reuben, Richard C. "Ruling Cuts Jurors Role in Patent Cases." *ABA Journal* **81 (July 1995): 24–5.**

The U.S. Court of Appeals for Federal Circuits ruled in *Mackman v. Westview Instruments* that patent litigation is a matter for courts, not ordinary jurors. This reflects the debates of whether to use special patent jurors or leave the decisions up to judges. The *Mackman* case will be brought for U.S. Supreme Court review on 7th Amendment grounds, i.e., the right to jury trial. Supporters approve of the possibility of consistency in interpreting patents if this is followed. Opposers remark on increased workloads of judges just as ill equipped to review patents as most jurors. Edward O'Connor sees no significant changes. Courts have always interpreted patent claims and instructed jurors on their meaning.

583. **"Florida, 1528: A Tale with the Same Twist."** *The New York Times,* **12 July 1995, sec. B, col. 3, p. 6.**

Captain John Smith's tale of Pocahontas may be a plagiarized version of the accounting of an earlier Spanish explorer, the Gentleman of Elvas. The subject of Elvas' story, Juan Ortiz, was captured by Timucau Indians of Florida. Ortiz was rescued by the chief's daughter. Elvas' book would have been available in translation to Smith.

584. **Winograd, Shmuel, and Richard Zare. "'Wired' Science or Whither the Printed Page?"** *Science* **269, no. 5224 (4 August 1995): 615.**

It has taken 500 years for policy to evolve from the printed page. Now we confront issues for the electronic medium. Questions of quality control, authorship, intellectual property, and archivability for electronic journal publication need to be addressed.

585. **Rosenberg, Jim. "Hyphen Closes Shop."** *Editor & Publisher* **128, no. 33 (19 August 1995): 29.**

Describes Hyphen Inc.'s going into receivership and the status of its international components. Brief sentence states that HyWay Ltd. of Norwich immediately exercised their option to acquire intellectual property rights to Hyphen's software. Helpful only for those interested in Hyphen. Not helpful for property rights issues.

586. **Gottesman, Michael M. "The Devi Case and More."** *Science* **269, no. 5227 (25 August 1995): 1029–34.**

Under Conduct in Science. Spirited responses to Eliot Marshall's article, "Authorship: Dispute Slows Paper on 'Remarkable' Vaccine." (*Science*, 23 June 1995) and to the Sarvamangala Devi case in general. Includes biting commentary by Devi, Levine, McCutchen, Stewart and Feder, and others. Omissions in various published comments of the case are pointed out as are accusations of bias by the NIH against Devi. Devi accused her mentors of using her research without her consent.

587. **Greene, Donna. "Name That Tune, and Prevent a Rip-Off."** *The New York Times,* **27 August 1995, sec. 13, col. 1, p. 3.**

A Q&A with Judith Greenberg Finell, a forensic musicologist. Explains her work in finding similarities in music and judging whether the similarities are unusual enough to cry "plagiarism." Many come to her before deciding whether or not to sue for copyright violation.

588. **King, Florence. "The Misanthrope's Corner."** *National Review* **47, no. 16 (28 August 1995): 56.**

King summarizes the types, excuses and reasons for apathy about plagiarism. She highlights the stupidity of plagiarists, the predictable responses when they are caught, condemns the practice of writing sequels and supports more stringent punishment for the offenders.

589. **Maddox, John. "Plagiarism Is Worse Than Mere Theft." *Nature* 376, no. 6543 (31 August 1995): 721.**

Praises the efforts of ORI/AAAS Conference of 1993 on plagiarism, stating that though the report was two years in coming, it is well worth reading. Plagiarism is still the most common accusation among scholars, and the most amateurish of thefts. The discrepancy between legal view and academic view of the crime is also in evidence, the legal view being copyright violations. Considers the primary value of the conference to be its stress on the need for procedures to handle accusations. (See the McCutchen letter *Nature,* September 28, 1995, page 282 for a more controversial picture of the conference and the handling of the report.)

590. **Feliciano, Kristina. "Understanding Copyright Law." *American Artist* 59, no. 638 (September 1995): 62–4+.**

Of the five photographs published by California artist Paul Cunningham, only three were actually his own work. The two remaining were from *Carot in Italy* and were in *public domain*. It was an oversight, according to Cunningham. He also stated that copyright should only apply to commercial artists and illustrators. *Rogers v. Koons* in which a sculpture was commissioned to replicate the image in a photograph was also covered. The photographer sued on copyright infringement and won. Monetary gain aside, a true artist's work is one of self expression. It is not a life for the fainthearted.

591. **Grant, Daniel. "Trademark Law: When Style Is Everything." *American Artist* 59, no. 638 (September 1995): 66.**

Artists may choose to contest the work of another through trademark, not copyright infringement. This is effective if one is mimicking another's work. Cases mentioned include Bette Midler and Tom Waits suit against Ford Motor Company in which impersonators of Midler and Waits appeared in Ford commercials, and of Dwight Conley who imitated the work of sculptor Paul Wegner so closely that the public might have mistaken Conley's work for Wegner's. Infringement is based on visual similarity and whether there might be confusion between the original and the imitation.

592. **King, Florence. "Molly Ivins, Plagiarist." *American Enterprise* 6, no. 5 (September 1995): 92.**

Brings the "folksy" writing style of liberal Texas columnist, Molly Ivins under scrutiny. Gives examples where Ivins has borrowed liberally from Florence King's work, giving credit to King in all but the political stances. Ivins plagiarizes King's political views by claiming them as her own.

593. **"Report of the 1993 Plagiarism Conference Published."** *RI Newsletter* **3, no. 4 (September 1995): 3.**
Brief. The Report of the 1993 Conference on Plagiarism and Theft of Ideas sponsored by ORI and AAAS is available on computer disk. Twelve speakers and 150 attendees participated in discussions and panels.

594. **Thompson, Laura C., and Portia G. Williams. "But I Changed Three Words!"** *Clearing House* **69, no. 1 (September/October 1995): 27–9.**
Addresses the difficulties of foreign students grasping the idea of plagiarism. Many cultures stress the importance of memorizing and repeating passages from scholars; some show respect for their professors by using the professor's words. In the ESL groups, Thompson and Williams found the relearning process was extensive. Learning proper citation required student discussion, writing, comparison and writing all they knew on a subject before beginning research.

595. **"Trademark Suit Dismissed."** *Editor & Publisher* **128, no. 35 (2 September 1995): 3.**
The suit filed by *Duluth* (Minn.) *News-Tribune* against the *Mesabi Daily News of Virginia* and the *Hibbing Daily Tribune* has been dismissed. The courts found no basis for confusion of ownership for the *Saturday Daily News & Tribune*.

596. **Altman, Mark. "Stop the Spread of Royalties Buyouts."** *Billboard* **107, no. 36 (9 September 1995): 6.**
"Record companies contributed $12 million to the AFM's Phonograph Record Special Payments Fund and almost $400 million in mechanical royalties to the Harry Fox Agency." It is time for the songwriters, composers and music publishers to also share in the rewards of the home video market.

597. **"Revised EC Contracts Improve Property Rights."** *Nature* **377, no. 6545 (14 September 1995): 92.**
Brief. The European Commission has awarded research groups the legal right to intellectual property on their work and reinforced confidentiality on unpublished scientific results. The updates were introduced by Edith Cresson and Martin Bangemann.

598. **Burns, John F. "Tradition in India vs. a Patent in the U.S."** *The New York Times,* **15 September 1995, sec. D, col. 1, p. 4.**
When W. R. Grace patented the Indian neem tree, the Foundation on Economic Trends sparked a counter-offensive. The controversy is seen

as an example of underdeveloped countries being exploited by richer nations, most specifically, the U.S.A. The Neemix case will be judged on whether it is substantially similar to existing products. The insecticide properties of the neem tree have been used in India for centuries to protect their crops.

599. DeLoughry, Thomas J. "Copyright in Cyberspace." *Chronicle of Higher Education* **42, no. 3 (15 September 1995): A22, A24.**
The report on copyright law for electronic data, released by the Working Group on Intellectual Property Rights and headed by Bruce A. Lehman, Assistant Secretary of Commerce, has been received with mixed expressions. If adopted by Congress, it would eliminate *fair use* for any materials transmitted or stored electronically. It left unanswered, questions for use of materials in classrooms, copying, and liability of system administrators for policing the networks. The panel did recommend that no decision be made until recommendations from librarians and educators regarding limited use be examined. It included the proviso that guidelines would be issued by the administration if there are no recommendations from the group by December 1996.

600. McCutchen, Charles W. "ORI's Unhappy Lot." *Nature* **377, no. 6547 (28 September 1995): 282.**
Informs Maddox (*Nature,* 31 Aug 1995) that the report he read was a carefully edited version of the conference. Parts missing included emotional climate of the conference, and that many participants were enraged that, even with so many rules and procedures in place, cases were still judged on political clout.

601. Flagg, Gordon. "Intellectual Property Group Unveils Report; ALA Has Misgivings." *American Libraries* **26, no. 9 (October 1995): 867.**
Response to modifications suggested by the federal Working Group on Intellectual Property. Flagg identifies points of contention (1) that copyright law is to protect ownership, while ALA stresses the basis is dissemination of ideas, (2) that copyright protection spurs creativity, ALA rejects that premise, (3) that licensing copyright materials on-line is advancing, ALA must continue to see that fair use is not lost in the process, and (4) that the Washington report fails to clarify distance learning access for libraries and schools. The document is *Intellectual Property and the National Information Infrastructure.* Article includes addresses for requesting a copy of the document.

602. Johnson, David. "Vari-Lite vs. High End." *TCI* **29, no. 8 (October 1995): 14–15.**
Moving lights are generic and not subject to patent, but how the lights are controlled and the patterns displayed are patented. Vari-Lite claims

High End has infringed. High End says they will defend their position as they would not knowingly take another's intellectual property. They also suggest that this is a marketing ploy by Vari-Lite to discredit them.

603. **Revah, Suzan. "Dueling Divas."** *American Journalism Review* **17, no. 8 (October 1995): 6.**
Brief. Has photos of Florence King and Molly Ivins. The reaction by the *Star Telegram* to King's discovery that Ivins had plagiarized her work was that Ivins had not done it intentionally and did not warrant disciplinary action. King was not amused.

604. **MacFarquhar, Neil. "Abolishing Class Rank Stirs Anger at a High School."** *The New York Times,* **23 October 1995, sec. B, col. 5, pp. 1, 6.**
Article has one sentence on plagiarism. Those opposed to academic ranking of high school students say abolishing rank would reduce cheating and plagiarism.

605. **Gleason, Mark. "Too Close for Comfort."** *Advertising Age* **66, no. 44 (30 October 1995): 50.**
Creative minds flow in similar channels. Advertising is very lenient with those who borrow another's idea for commercials. They seldom sue for copyright infringement. The latest "rip-off" is a commercial for Southwestern Bell which very closely resembles one aired for AT&T. Ad agencies D'Arcy Masius Benton & Bowles (SW Bell) and Moffatt/Rosenthal (Cellular One [AT&T]) are involved.

606. **Howard, Rebecca Moore. "Plagiarisms, Authorships and the Academic Death Penalty."** *College English* **57, no. 7 (November 1995): 788–806.**
The author proposes modifying the current punitive policy on plagiarism to allow for what she considers the positive aspects of "patchwork" writing. This technique is, to many, an accepted stage in learning to write and should not be put into the same category as buying term papers. She does not state the alternate view that "patchwork" delays the learning process because synthesis of the information does not take place. The policies of collective authorship being brought to the forefront by Internet messaging are for future academicians to define. This author prefers to concentrate on revising policy to adjust to the current practices of pedagogy by allowing the flexibility needed to allow students to go through initial stages of writing without fear of judicious repercussions from their work. A suggested policy is included. Notes.

607. **Sennett, Frank. "Spam vs. Spa'Am."** *Writer's Digest* **75, no. 11 (November 1995): 54–9.**
If writers use negative parody or questionable humor in depicting products, the company might claim copyright infringement. Details the Hormel Company's reaction to the character Spa'am in the latest Muppet Movie produced by Hensen Productions. The companies are currently discussing a resolution to the unsavory pig character. Sennett has spiced this piece with such phrases as "full-boar assault," making the article entertaining as well as informative.

608. **Walls, Jeannette. "Get Me Retrial!"** *Esquire* **124, no. 5 (November 1995): 28.**
Heyward Gould, author and director of *Trial by Jury*, is not planning on suing novelist George Dawes Green, even though thousands of fans have pointed out similarities between movies *Trial by Jury* and *The Juror*. The soon to be released *The Juror* stars Demi Moore.

609. **Woodmansee, Martha, and Peter Jaszi. "The Law of Texts: Copyright in the Academy."** *College English* **57, no. 7 (November 1995): 769–87.**
Discusses how the expanded use of copyright protection affects teachers, scholars and critics. Cited many cases to clarify the constraints and ambiguity of current law on use of materials in the classroom, in research, in biography, and the shrinking number of materials considered to be in *public domain*. Electronic transmissions and digital communications may be stifled by tight regulation of copyright laws. Digital technology requires redefining authorship for "infopreneurs." The authors stress the importance of participating in legislative actions regarding copyright and promoting the natural collaborative nature of writing instead of emphasizing the legal ramifications of plagiarism. Notes.

610. **Stowe, David W. "Just Do It."** *Lingua Franca* **6, no. 10 (November/ December 1995): 32–42.**
Copyright permissions are the bane of authors. Publishers are free to put in any restrictions they like and owners are allowed to charge any fees. The result is nearing censorship whether it be the author's inability to pay excessive fees or owner's refusal to allow inclusion of any information they might consider damaging to their image. Copyright law, although written to promote exchange of ideas, has become a financial fight. Perhaps it is time for scholars and publishers to chance litigation and exercise *fair use*. Uses Cecilia Tichi's efforts to create a work on contemporary music to illustrate difficulties and costs.

611. Johnson, Michael E. "The Uncertain Future of Computer Software Users' Rights in the Aftermath of *MAI Systems*." *Duke Law Journal* 44 (2 November 1995): 327–56.

Argues against the results of *MAI Systems v. Peak Computer, Inc.* The courts erred in considering loading a program into RAM to be a "copy," and by excluding Peak's customers from copyright infringement under 17 U.S.C 117 which allows for legal uses by holders of official copies of a software program. Reminds that the intent of the recommendations of CONTU and the legislation on software copyright is to strike a balance between rights of the originator and rights of the public. Article may be of particular interest to those needing legal citations and arguments.

612. Sipe, Jeffrey R. "Intellectual Property Still Up for Grabs." *Insight* 11, no. 43 (13 November 1995): 30–1.

Each time a new technology comes out, publishers rush to tie in profits and legislators submit bills to modify existing laws. Current discussions involve: filmmakers rights to alter works and how alterations will be disclosed to the public; licensing for performances in commercial establishments so that business owners would only be responsible for music they choose and can control (e.g. not responsible for bands appearing in half-time shows during television football games); and allowing arbitration for licensing disputes by third parties instead of the courts. Another "hot topic" is the author's right to profit from electronic publications.

613. Taubes, Gary. "Scientists Attacked for 'Patenting' Pacific Tribe." *Science* 270, no. 5239 (17 November 1995): 1112.

Medical anthropologist Carol Jenkins was caught off guard. The Rural Advancement Foundation International has flooded the Internet with accusations that she has patented a person. The outrage is the result of filing for patent on the cell from a member of the Hagahai of Papua, New Guinea. His blood cells are found to contain agents which may prove helpful in scientific research to find cures for a number of diseases. Ms. Jenkins works for the Papua New Guinea Institute of Medical Research and in conjunction with the National Institute of Health and has filed for the patent with full knowledge and consent of the Hagahai tribe. All royalties assigned to her will go to the donor's family. Colleagues state that the RAFI is distorting the facts.

614. Remnick, David. "Hamlet in Hollywood." *New Yorker* 71, no. 37 (20 November 1995): 66–83.

Covers discussions with Gail McGrail and Steve Sohmer in their battle for rights to publish research done jointly on Shakespeare's *Hamlet*.

A "not so classic" example of scholars' disputes over intellectual property rights. Sohmer, a Hollywood television writer/Shakespearean scholar, has brought suit against McGrail, faculty member at Boston University/Shakespearean scholar, to keep her from publishing without giving dual credit. The plaintiff claims McGrail was an employee who betrayed commercial secrets; the defense claims she was an independent contractor hired part-time. Sohmer eventually drops the suit. Much of the article explains the scholars' theories on Shakespeare and gives descriptions of the personalities involved in this legal dispute.

615. Hernandez, Debra. "Congress Considers Updating Copyright Laws to Cover Online Information." *Editor & Publisher* 128, no. 47 (25 November 1995): 31, 39.

To address the growing concern over copyright protection for works stored in digital format, the Senate and House have responded with the NII Copyright Protection Act of 1995 (S. 1284 and H.R. 2441). The legislation does not address liability for providers. The Software Publishers Association adds the need for prosecution of offenders; the Digital Future Coalition fears restricted access to the public and educational institutions and the invasion of privacy.

616. Kimball, James. "What's Yours Could Be Mine." *Advertising Age* 66, no. 48 (27 November 1995): 32.

Business on the Internet is finding that it is not easy to protect trademarks and copyright. There are no easy ways to detect violation. An official government report concluded that current copyright laws should be sufficient to cover electronically transmitted intellectual property, but trademark attorneys are not so sure. Mentions the use of Barbie in compromising positions on http://www.desires.com, and McDonalds having to negotiate with a journalist who held the domain name of McDonalds.com as examples of difficulties businesses are encountering. Sidebar mentions IBM and Electronic Publishing Resources' efforts with Copyright Clearance Center to sell Web software that will require users to pay for access to copyrighted documents.

617. Parrish, Debra. "Scientific Misconduct and the Plagiarism Cases." *Journal of College and University Law* 21, no. 3 (Winter 1995): 517–54.

Excellent comparison between plagiarism as defined by NSF and by the ORI. Supports the differences in their bureaucratic approach to plagiarism investigations. Includes case studies and commentary. Although high percentages of their case loads involve accusations of plagiarism in grant applications and publications, most fall outside the category of scientific misconduct as defined by each organization, and are not pursued. Parrish also includes examples of copyright infringement in which plagiarism was not found, plagiarism in which infringement was not upheld and brief examples of patent and intellectual property cases and plagiarism. A must read for those researching scientific misconduct or plagiarism in academia. Case Notes.

618. **Fisher, Lawrence. "Maker of Design Software Accuses Rival of Theft."** *The New York Times,* **7 December 1995, sec. D, col. 4, p. 2.**
Cadence Design Systems, Inc. is suing Avanti, accusing Avanti of stealing their software. The announcement of the lawsuit sent Avanti stocks down $5.75 and Cadence down 62.5 cents. Analysis of source code indicates an original common source for the programming.

619. **Poste, George. "The Case for Genomic Patenting."** *Nature* **378, no. 6557 (7 December 1995): 534–6.**
Excellent explanation on the reasons for patents. Allowing patents on genetic materials, including EST, instead of leaving the discoveries in *public domain* promotes research for the betterment of medicine and human welfare. It is in accord with the intent of patent law. We must be careful not to simplify the matter for popular appeal and not try to use patent law to arbitrate moral and ethical questions. Excellent overview for understanding patents and research.

620. **Garneau, George. "Aggressive Defense."** *Editor & Publisher* **128, no. 49 (9 December 1995): 23.**
Brief. Winner International, maker of the Club, a device which locks steering wheels in automobiles, has successfully defended its intellectual property rights in court 16 times in the last 3 years. Sometimes there were payments as well as injunctions to stop manufacturing.

621. **Tisi, Arthur. "A Little Trust Goes a Long Way on I-Way."** *PC Week* **12, no. 49 (11 December 1995): E12.**
Doing business on the Internet is creating changes in how we interpret intellectual property. By relying on simple honesty as we have with software home use, we have avoided a police state mentality. The author would like to see that sense of trust renewed when laws are created for the internet.

622. **Newcomb, Jonathan. "Stealing on the 'Net."** *USA Today,* **20 December 1995, sec. A, col. 1, p. 11.**
Stresses the need to protect intellectual property on the Internet through updates to current copyright laws. The U.S. claims over $50 billion in copyright revenue generated by our foreign exports. This must be protected. General audience.

623. "Images of Saratoga at Issue in Suit." *The New York Times,* **27 December 1995, sec. B, col. 1, p. 4.**
Artist Jenness Cortez is bewildered by the lawsuit filed by New York Racing Association against her work. The association is accusing her of trademark infringement, claiming that her Cortez Saratoga Collection might be confused with merchandise marketed by their Saratoga Race Course. Ms. Cortez had an amicable agreement with the track for 20 years. Her work displays her name, and she has a right to her freedom of expression. The association is asking for a $5000 per year licensing fee.

Author Index

References are to entry numbers in the Bibliography proper.

Ace, Goodman 50
Adler, Reid G. 88
Agres, Ted 150
Alexander, James D. 145
Allen, Paula Gunn 203
Altman, Mark 596
Amis, E. Stephen, Jr. 413
Anderson, A. J. 468
Anderson, Christopher 316, 341, 400
Armstrong, John D., II 390, 411
Arnott, Nancy 526
Atlas, James 431
Avram, Henriette D. 168
Azzopardi, John 503

Babington, Charles 220
Bailey, Carl 82
Baker, Nicholson 510
Baker, Russ W. 449
Barreiro, Jose 302
Barzun, Jacques 29
Basombrio, Ignacio 213
Beahm, George 303
Begley, Sharon 274
Belich, Vladimar 250
Bennett, Scott 301, 522
Bentley, G. E. 477
Berek, Peter 89
Berger, Jerry 294
Berghel, H. L. 92
Berry, John N., III 176, 502
Betts, Donald D. 295
Blanden, Michael 246
Bloch, R. Howard 412
Blum, Debra E. 135, 139, 162, 180, 189
Blumenthal, Ralph 543
Boffey, Phillip M. 47
Bolan, Richard 226
Borger, Gloria 114
Bower, Gordon H. 347

Bowers, Neal 486
Boyde, T. R. C. 558
Bradley, Clive 214
Brahams, Diana 544
Branscomb, Anne 247
Bray, Robert 355, 437
Broad, William J. 70
Brown, Alan S. 154, 268
Brunner, Eric 511
Brush, Stephen B. 391
Bugeja, Michael J. 452
Burd, Stephen 320
Burlingame, Michael 438
Burns, John F. 598
Butler, Ellis Parker 10
Buzzelli, Donald E. 334
Byrd, Gary D. 500
Byron, Christopher 198

Came, Barry 314
Cane, Melville 33
Carlson, Bob 321
Carmack, Betty J. 84
Carroll, Jerry 243
Carroll, Joyce A. 79
Carson, Clayborne 232
Case, Tony 267, 482
Cerf, Bennett 35
Chaney, Jerry 96
Chapman, Wayne K. 248
Chew, C. 6
Ciardi, John 43
Cipra, Barry 378
Cisler, Steve 523
Clark, Tim 471
Cleveland, Harlan 155
Committee on the Judiciary House of Representatives 215
Conrad, Brad 461
Cooper, Carolyn C. 257, 258
Cordes, Colleen 422
Corliss, Richard 385

Corn, David 212
Cosgrove, Stuart 170
Cranberg, Lawrence 515
Crawford, M. H. 398
Cronin, Peter 497
Culliton, Barbara J. 146, 165
Cunningham, Mark 266
Current, Richard N. 439

Dabney, James W. 564
Dalton, Rex 569
Daniels, Edgar 42
Davis, Bernard D. 344
Dawson, Mitchell 24
DeConcini, Dennis 123
DeLoughry, Thomas J. 109, 148, 406, 408, 499, 599
Dezzani, Mark 537
Dhar, S. K. 570
Dickson, David 575
Dillinham, Thomas 504
Dillon, John 333
Dingell, John D. 360
Dolnick, Edward 306
Doran, George H. 12
Dreyfuss, Rochelle C. 275
Driscoll, Arthur F. 28
Durrani, Shandana 479
Dwyer, Dan 328
Dwyer, Paula 163
Dyson, Esther 111, 172, 201

Easterbrook, Gregg 241
Eaton, Richard 332
Eisenberg, Rebecca S. 309
Eissler, K. R. M. D. 63
Ellis, Fay 483
Ellis, H. F. 41
Elmer-Dewitt, Philip 100
Eng, Paul 221
Ewell, Charles M., Jr. 53

175

Title Index

References are to entry numbers in the Bibliography proper.

Subject Index

References are to entry numbers in the Bibliography proper.

computers *see* computer industry; electronic transmission and storage; Internet; software
Conchologist's First Book 373
Conley, Dwight 591
Conley, Paul 376
Connecticut Yankee in King Arthur's Court 202
contract law versus property law 287
CONTU (Commission on New Technological Uses of Copyrighted Works) 291, 611
Converse, John Marquis 272
cookbooks 57, 95, 479
copyright: definitions of 55, 187, 313, 502, 590; history of 209, 291; inherited 303
copyright, law of 34, 64, 149, 168, 212, 287, 467, 519; in education 153, 338, 609; in electronic transmissions 158, 187, 204, 223, 304, 471, 496, 555, 611, 616, 622; international 217, 230, 249, 288, 530, 550; *see also* NII (National Information Infrastructure); Working Group on Intellectual Property Rights Copyright Acts of 1909 291
Copyright Clearance Center 230, 291, 510, 519, 568, 616
Copyright Protection Act of 1995, response 615
Copyright Revision Act of 1976 125, 212, 291
Corry, John 81, 429, 449
Cortez, Jenness 623
Courlander, Harold 33, 66, 379
Cranes Morning 455, 456
Creedence Clearwater Revival 151
cryptomnesia and inadvertent plagiarism 71, 86, 132, 224, 533; *see also* studies in cryptomnesia
cultural influences on plagiarism 8, 113, 115, 134, 137, 490, 533
Cunningham, Paul 590
Curry, V.J. Adam 463
Cuvier, George 373
cyberaddresses 463, 531

La Dama Duende 183
Damned Thing 17
D'Arcy Masius Benton & Bowles 605
Darlington, David 479
Dartmouth 197, 290
databases *see* electronic transmission and storage
Davis, William M. 58
de Arriotua, Jose Ignacio Lopez 389
Death of a President 380, 381, 382, 383, 386, 387
DeConcini, Dennis 123
DeCosta, Victor 273

Deetz, David 517
Defoe, Daniel 52, 465
De Forest, Calvert 385
Deforges, Regine 127, 176
Demonic Color 305, 307
Deng Rong 457
derivative works 11, 168, 318, 355
developing nations 163, 213, 261, 283, 302, 325, 331, 391, 423, 520, 598
Devi, Sarvanamgala 579, 586
de Villier, Marq 479
Dhar, S.K. 570, 571, 572
Diametrics Medical 517
Diary of Anne Frank 77
Dickens, Charles 40
Dieu et la science 255
digital images 187, 519, 556
digital time stamping 372, 378
Dingell, John 166, 274, 349, 354, 360, 365, 370
Discovision Associates 532
Dishonored Lady 20, 24
distance learning 338, 499
DNA 309, 316; *see also* genes and genomic research
Duchess of York 199
Duluth (Minnesota) News-Tribune v. Mesabi Daily News of Virginia and the Hibbing Daily Tribune 595
Du Maurier, Daphne 23, 30
Dunn, Dawn Pauline 305, 307

economics of intellectual property 160, 163, 188, 236, 283; bankruptcy and receivership 517, 585; bargaining tool 310; impact of imitation on quality 417; impact of litigation on software products development 111, 167, 222; investment in developing countries 283; licensing, patents and copyright as assets 163, 223, 236, 298, 301, 317, 329
economics of plagiarism *see* marketing techniques
education 39, 60, 74, 93, 97, 99, 104, 210, 319, 336, 446, 574, 606; nursing 84; *see also* teaching practices
EDUCOM 109, 228, 277
Eikonoklastes 269
electronic formats *see* electronic transmissions and storage
electronic publishing *see* scholarly publishing
electronic resources *see* scholarly publishing
electronic transmissions and storage 187, 217, 226, 228, 273, 279, 312, 471, 519, 550, 580, 609, 615, 616; author's rights